GEM *of* THE SIERRA

Schemes and Splendor in
Nineteenth-Century Lake Tahoe

GARY NOY

University of Nebraska Press · Lincoln

The University of Nebraska Press is part of a land-grant institution with campuses and programs on the past, present, and future homelands of the Pawnee, Ponca, Otoe-Missouria, Omaha, Dakota, Lakota, Kaw, Cheyenne, and Arapaho Peoples, as well as those of the relocated Ho-Chunk, Sac and Fox, and Iowa Peoples.

Library of Congress Cataloging-in-Publication Data
Names: Noy, Gary, 1951- author.
Title: Gem of the Sierra: schemes and splendor in nineteenth-century Lake Tahoe / Gary Noy.
Other titles: Schemes and splendor in nineteenth-century Lake Tahoe
Description: Lincoln: University of Nebraska Press, [2024] | Includes bibliographical references and index.
Identifiers: LCCN 2023049005
ISBN 9781496237828 (paperback)
ISBN 9781496239310 (epub)
ISBN 9781496239327 (pdf)
Subjects: LCSH: Tahoe, Lake (Calif. and Nev.)—History—19th century—Sources. | Tahoe, Lake (Calif. and Nev.)—Description and travel. | Travelers—Tahoe, Lake (Calif. and Nev.)—History—19th century—Sources. | BISAC: HISTORY / United States / State & Local / West (AK, CA, CO, HI, ID, MT, NV, UT, WY) | HISTORY / United States / 19th Century
Classification: LCC F868.T2 N68 2024 | DDC 979.4/3809034—dc23/eng/20240215
LC record available at https://lccn.loc.gov/2023049005

Set in Miller Text by A. Shahan.

In memory
of my remarkable friend and colleague
Rick Heide,
a gentleman, a scholar, an extraordinary wordsmith,
and the world's greatest NBA fan

Contents

Illustrations

Following page 83

Preface

In the early 1870s a British journalist named J. G. Player-Frowd visited California for a few months. His journey commenced with some trepidation. After all, he explained, prior to the completion of the transcontinental railroad, California was often "regarded as teeming with gold and abounding in iniquity; a paradise for paupers, and a refuge for the scum of the earth." And, he added, "To a certain extent this was true." However, J. G. Player-Frowd soon dispelled this notion as "misrepresented." He loved California, especially Lake Tahoe. Player-Frowd predicted that the fortunate tourist would enjoy a respite from "the monotony and conventionalities of European travel, [and] will find an immense relief and sense of freedom."

His objective was to explore the expanding travel opportunities to the Golden State following the completion of the transcontinental railroad in 1869. In 1872 Player-Frowd published his observations in a book entitled *Six Months in California*. As he noted in his introduction, his visit to California was so pleasurable that he was inspired to write a travel guide "as an inducement to those uncertain where to go, to enjoy the trip from ocean to ocean, and the wondrously beautiful country they will find at the extreme western end of the line."

J. G. Player-Frowd's initial glimpse of Lake Tahoe was indelibly imprinted in his memory book:

> An opening in the trees, a turn in the road, and Lake Tahoe is before me. Not a ripple on its surface. Surrounded on every side by snow-clad hills, whose sides are covered with pine forests, all of which are reflected as in a mirror, it looks like a painted lake. There is a sense of mystery in its unfathomable depths, a feeling of awe at this volume of water suspended six thousand feet in the air, . . . fed by the everlasting snows, and full of great fish, bred

heaven only knows how, I look upon Lake Tahoe as one of the most striking objects in Californian scenery.

But following this reflection, the British visitor offered a passage that encapsulated the dichotomous visions of Lake Tahoe in the nineteenth century. Player-Frowd rhapsodized at some length about a proposed project to deliver Lake Tahoe water to San Francisco via massive infrastructure development involving tunnels, canals, railroads, mining interests, and an intense application of political will.

Lake Tahoe, which J. G. Player-Frowd fervently hoped would remain a breathtaking setting for "the perfect enjoyment of purely natural scenery," also had sweeping utilitarian value, he concluded. The lake's water was crucial to regional economic development. Player-Frowd argued, "Thousands of mining claims high up in the mountains cannot be worked for want of water. The canal will pay almost along every mile of its course; and the surplus water, after being used for mining, will irrigate the gardens and ranches that supply the wants of the miners."

J. G. Player-Frowd recapped his Lake Tahoe visit by remarking that "I left [the lake] . . . with regret. One could spend a month there most delightfully. The most picturesque scenery; excursions in all directions; shooting, from grizzly bear to the mountain quail; lake fishing and river fishing; [and] mining, if that may be called an amusement."

Player-Frowd was not alone in this assessment. For generations before and since, Lake Tahoe has always been an object of love and desire, simultaneously celebrated for its beauty and coveted for its bounty. Generations of visitors and residents have viewed the lake with both astonishment and avarice. This anthology, *Gem of the Sierra: Schemes and Splendor in Nineteenth-Century Lake Tahoe*, examines these contrasting visions from precontact to the dawn of the twentieth century.

Our story begins with the creation of the lake itself.

Although for many years it was the consensus that Lake Tahoe formed in a volcanic caldera, more recent geological studies have reckoned that the lake developed in a landscape sculpted by the clash of fault zones that began some twenty-four million years ago. Over geologic eons, two faults evolved as the main actors. One produced the Carson Range, the mountain ridges to the east of Lake Tahoe, and the other developed into the Sierra Nevada, located on the western perimeter of the lake.

In between developed a large and deep valley, the feature known as the lake basin or lake valley.

Mount Pluto, a now-extinct volcano on the northern boundary of the lake basin centered in today's Northstar Resort, erupted some two million years ago. The volcano's lava and mudflows dammed the basin's natural outlet, today's Truckee River, forming a huge obstruction. Gradually, precipitation, snow melt, and streams filled the basin, creating a lake several hundred feet higher and deeper than the current lake. Through erosion, a new outlet for the Truckee River was carved.

A series of ice ages followed the faulting and volcanic period, lasting at least one million years. The last ice age lasted one thousand centuries, until about fifteen thousand years ago. Glaciers filled the canyons, particularly on the western slope, and scoured out *U*-shaped formations. When the glaciers receded, they left behind magnificent bays (such as Emerald Bay), gleaming glacier polish, and crystalline lakes and streams. The Lake Tahoe we know today emerged.

According to the United States Forest Service, Lake Tahoe is the third-deepest lake in North America and the tenth-deepest in the world. To date, the greatest measured depth of the lake is 1,645 feet, and the average depth is 1,000 feet. The lake is twenty-two miles long and twelve miles wide and features seventy-two miles of shoreline. Nestled near the western margin of the lake are two smaller tributary lakes—Cascade Lake and Fallen Leaf Lake. Nearly 155,000 acres of Forest Service lands surround the Lake Tahoe Basin. Lake Tahoe is at 6,224 feet elevation and is under the legal jurisdiction of both California and Nevada. The California-Nevada state boundary line bisects the lake.

Gem of the Sierra: Schemes and Splendor in Nineteenth-Century Lake Tahoe focuses on the human history of Lake Tahoe. For many, if not most, the history and literature of Lake Tahoe is simply an endless love letter to its extraordinary splendor. This is best exemplified by Mark Twain's famous description in his 1872 classic *Roughing It*:

> At last the Lake burst upon us—a noble sheet of blue water lifted six thousand three hundred feet above the level of the sea, and walled in by a rim of snow-clad mountain peaks that towered aloft full three thousand feet higher still! It was a vast oval, and one would have to use up eighty or a hundred good miles in traveling around

it. As it lay there with the shadows of the mountains brilliantly photographed upon its still surface I thought it must surely be the fairest picture the whole earth affords.

But, as with most historical chronicles, the story is much more complicated. Lake Tahoe in the nineteenth century was marked by insult and mistreatment of the indigenous population; commercial exploitation of the lake's timber, water, and fisheries; a paroxysm of resorts, from luxurious and trendy to cut-rate and scruffy; environmental calamities; and venal political backbiting.

Lake Tahoe's human history is estimated to have begun approximately ten thousand years ago. The land was the domain of several Native tribes, but the dominant nation was the Wá·šiw people. The Wá·šiw are better known as the Washoe. Their name for Lake Tahoe is dáʔaw, from which "Tahoe" is generally believed to have been derived. Lake Tahoe is the Washoe homeland, or, as eloquently stated by the Washoe Tribe of Nevada and California, "The center of the Wá·šiw world is dáʔaw [Lake Tahoe], both geographically and spiritually."

For thousands of years (and continuing today), the Washoe people carefully used and thrived on the abundant natural resources available at the lake. Primarily during the summer and fall months, they fished for the large Lahontan cutthroat trout and harvested freshwater clams. Game was abundant. Pine nuts and acorns were collected. Plants for food, medicine, and a wide variety of other practical uses were gathered. When the snows came, the Washoe people traveled to lower elevations to escape the harsh Sierra Nevada winters. That cycle of promise and renewal has repeated for centuries.

All that changed with the California gold rush of the 1850s and the ensuing silver rush in Nevada that lasted throughout the remainder of the nineteenth century. Within a few years, the Washoe Native country was inundated by the human tsunami of Euro-American miners, timber interests, commercial fishers, hydraulic engineers, political opportunists, tourism moguls, and the curious of many foreign nations. These new arrivals placed enormous demands on Lake Tahoe's once plentiful natural reserves. Fisheries were dramatically reduced. Mountain ridges and valleys were stripped of their timber and the native plants upon which the Washoe depended. The amazing transparent waters of the lake were occasionally choked by sawdust. Introduced livestock pushed out the resident herbivores. The indigenous inhabitants were displaced by the onslaught. These changes severely disrupted the Washoe's centuries-old environmental and societal practices. Although the Washoe Nation remains a vibrant and respected community, the Washoe people never fully recovered from the events of the nineteenth century. The imprint of the Euro-Americans on the Lake Tahoe region was profound, especially in timber production, mining, market fishing, and tourism.

The Lake Tahoe Basin was a rich resource for timber. At the advent of Euro-American dominance, large stands of virgin forest were ripe for harvest. In the eyes of timber barons, it was an inexhaustible supply. The establishment of gold and silver mines and the development and construction of the transcontinental railroad accelerated the removal of the forests. Underground mining was dependent upon timber to shore up its mine shafts. In 1860, inspired by honeycombs, German engineer Philip Deidesheimer invented square-set timbering, a mine-framing system that used interlocking rectangular timbers to support the surrounding unstable rocks, or "heavy ground." This new and very successful technique, perfected in the Comstock Lode's Ophir Mine in Virginia City, Nevada, immediately intensified the need for lumber in the mines.

A flourishing, ruthlessly effective, and environmentally ruinous lumber industry soon mushroomed. It was not long before lumbering became a significant force in the regional economy. As early as 1858, Nevada County in California, which borders Lake Tahoe, had forty-two lumber mills that produced over thirty-nine million feet of lumber in that calendar year alone. A 1924 Stanford University study determined that the number of California lumber mills from 1855 to 1860 increased from 80 to 320 but indicated that number was imprecise and probably low. The report also stated that the vast majority of the mills were concentrated in the western counties of the northern and central Sierra Nevada. Lake Tahoe is located in the central Sierra Nevada.

The nineteenth-century lumber industry also followed purposeful practices that ranged from slipshod to permanently destructive. Most loggers were not consciously attempting to despoil the forests; they were simply doing a job, but the timber industry itself was cold-blooded. Trees were cut three feet above ground level for the sake of convenience—leaving landscapes peppered with hazardous stumps. Sawmills generated massive amounts of sawdust, which were unceremoniously dumped into streams and rivers, killing fish and compromising water quality. Logging operations disturbed spawning runs and destroyed spawning grounds. In 1888 John Muir noted that on his trip up the Truckee River to Lake Tahoe that the river canyon was littered with "fallen burnt logs or the tops of trees felled for lumber." During the peak years, seventy million board feet of timber was harvested annually in the Lake Tahoe region alone. This is enough wood to build a wooden walkway—constructed of four-inch-thick planks and thirty feet wide—around the globe.

A predictable food supply was essential to Lake Tahoe region miners, loggers, fishers, and residents. Meat, grains, and vegetables supplied much of this need. But, particularly in the earlier years of Euro-American settlement at Lake Tahoe, wildlife was hunted for market. However, it was commercial fishing in the lake, particularly for the large Lahontan cutthroat trout, that came to be a prominent feature. Commercial fishing began with the opening of the Comstock mines in 1859. In the 1870s, about twenty-five commercial fishing operations plied the lake waters. Fishing for consumer sales locally and for markets such as San Francisco, Chicago, and New York became a major economic activity. Fishing was also a leading tourist amenity and heavily promoted. A statistic from October 1880 demonstrates the extent of the fishing enterprises. In that month alone, seventy thousand pounds of trout were taken from Lake Tahoe. Market fishing in the Lake Tahoe and Truckee River drainage, added to the effects of mining and logging, brought a sharp reduction in fish populations. Commercial fishing in the Lake Tahoe Basin was banned by the California State Legislature in 1917.

By the 1860s and afterward, campers packed food, tents, even canoes, on their backs or on animals, and trekked to their favorite spot. Others headed for the resorts that were springing up. Once road or railroad connections were established or improved, vacationers headed for the hills. Lake Tahoe was a favorite destination, especially after the transcontinental railroad was completed, and numerous lodgings and recreation venues were offered very quickly. Though varying in quality and levels of opulence, the resorts were wildly popular. Boating, fishing, picnics, boat tours, hunting, and horseback riding were available. And for those so inclined, more "shady" pursuits, such as gambling, dancing, and drinking, were offered. All could be had at such institutions as the Grand Central Hotel in Tahoe City, for a price. In its early advertising, this grand lakeside resort, the finest at Lake Tahoe, which operated from

1869 to 1895, promised guests "Health, Beauty, Grandeur of Scenery. Pure Air, and Rational Recreation." The cost? In 1893, for a package including round-trip rail fare from San Francisco to Lake Tahoe, plus seven days room and board, the rate was $27. With inflation, $27 in 1893 would be the equivalent of $923 in 2023. The rates for seven days of just room and board was $12–$16, or $410–$547 in 2023 money. Most Lake Tahoe accommodation rates were expensive by nineteenth century standards, but some lodgings cost less. Even as late as the 1890s, Charles H. Parrish's Bijou House in South Lake Tahoe offered meals for 50¢ ($18 in 2023) and rooms for 30¢ ($11 in 2023).

But Lake Tahoe in the nineteenth century was more than just a stunning natural wonder, a popular vacation mecca, and a commercial hub—it became a commanding emblem of national longing and resolve. Lake Tahoe was particularly attractive to those who viewed all things American as bigger, better, and more beautiful than what had come before. In a land dominated by ostentatious expectations and Manifest Destiny, these passionate advocates viewed the magnificent alpine lake as a transcendent symbol of American ideals, a land exemplifying the promise and preeminence of an exceptional social experiment. This was an era in which taming and wresting treasure from the wilderness was a considered a test of national will and duty. A well-known axiom in the historiography of the American West is the theory that everything relates to the land—namely, who controls it and what one can get from it. The control might be political, military, cultural, or economic, and the benefits could be wealth, territorial dominance, spiritual resonance, or social respectability. Nineteenth-century Lake Tahoe offered these threads in abundance and led to admiration and devotion, but also bickering, scheming, tension, and abuse. *Gem of the Sierra: Schemes and Splendor in Nineteenth-Century Lake Tahoe* considers all these reveries and realities.

The title of this book stems from the common nineteenth-century usage of "Gem of the Sierra" as a nickname for Lake Tahoe in literature and advertising.

The principal source material for *Gem of the Sierra: Schemes and Splendor in Nineteenth-Century Lake Tahoe* is the plentiful collections of nineteenth-century letters, diaries, books, journals, guidebooks, photographs, and newspaper articles recounting the escapades, captivating personalities, and impassioned sense of ownership of the remarkably varied Lake Tahoe population. Some of the documents used in this book have not been published for decades. As is the case with nineteenth-century documents, often they abound with the prejudices of the participants and authors and are burdened with misspellings, loutishness, misogyny, racism, callousness, and brutality. When used, these selections are presented unedited, as any other approach would be dishonest.

In this anthology, accounts of Lake Tahoe in the nineteenth century are presented. We read legends of the Washoe people, exploration journals, quasi-religious musings, economic proposals, tourist complaints, guidebook promotions, and even children's stories. The readings run the gamut from the serious and reverential to the silly. There are scientific reports, heartfelt reminiscences, bluster, melancholy contemplations, exhilarating adventures, fairy tales, tall tales, travel journals, and backstabbing. These are tales of worship, worry, and weirdness. These are the meditations of people struggling to fathom the present trajectory of *their* Lake Tahoe and predict the future of a geographical marvel.

So, let's begin our historical journey. Our first destination is the Lake Tahoe world of the Washoe people, a giant bird called the Ong, and some evil water-beings.

Acknowledgments

My deepest appreciation and greatest respect go to my friends at the University of Nebraska Press—Bison Books, especially W. Clark White-horn and Taylor Gilreath. *Gem of the Sierra* is my third book with the University of Nebraska Press, and they have always made the publishing experience a pleasure.

My heartfelt gratitude goes to the following institutions for their excellent and extremely professional assistance: California State Library, Sacramento; the Huntington Museum, Library, and Botanical Gardens, San Marino, California; the Bancroft Library, University of California, Berkeley; University of Nevada, Reno; University of California, Berkeley, Anthropology Department; the J. Paul Getty Museum, Los Angeles; and the California Historical Society.

Finally, extra-special thanks go to my late and beloved parents, Howard and Velma Noy, who introduced me to Lake Tahoe as a young child. I owe my lifelong love affair with the Gem of the Sierra to them.

In multiple instances throughout the book, text is used with permission from:

Cengage Learning, from Downs, *The Two Worlds of the Washo: An Indian Tribe of California and Nevada*, 1965; permission conveyed through Copyright Clearance Center, Inc.

Donald J. Pisani, "'Shouldn't California Have the Grandest Aqueduct in the World?': Alexis Von Schmidt's Lake Tahoe Scheme."

University of California Press, from Verna R. Johnston, *Sierra Nevada: The Naturalist's Companion*, 1997; permission conveyed through Copyright Clearance Center, Inc.

University of California publications, American Archaeology and Ethnology, The Bancroft Library, University of California, Berkeley.

University of Nevada Press, from Michael Hittman, *Great Basin Indians: An Encyclopedic History*, 2014; permission conveyed through Copyright Clearance Center, Inc.

GEM *of* THE SIERRA

ONE

Roots and Reconnaissance

Precontact to 1860

Imagine Lake Tahoe a few moments before humans arrived. It was a realm dominated by the forces of nature, both benign and brutal: Gentle zephyrs and blustery storms. Crystalline wind-roughened waters shimmering like diamonds. Raging whitecaps. Snowy tempests and lazy summer sunshine. A panorama embraced by mountain ridges draped in virgin forests. Garlands of wildflowers. Kaleidoscopic sunsets. Giant trout cruising in plain sight one hundred feet below the surface. Deer and grizzlies roaming the shoreline. A breathtaking, idyllic environment engaged in the daily dance of life and death. All this would change with a single human footprint.

Lake Tahoe's human history began ten thousand years ago. For centuries, the land was the province of several native tribes, but the central nation came to be the Wá·šiw people, better known as the Washoe (sometimes spelled "Washo"). While their territory stretched over hundreds of square miles along the Eastern Sierra from Honey Lake in the North (near Susanville in northeastern California today, about 120 miles from Lake Tahoe) to Topaz Lake in the South (about forty-five miles from Lake Tahoe), eastward to the Virginia Range (roughly forty miles from Lake Tahoe) and westward into the Sierra Nevada foothills, Lake Tahoe was the center of Washoe social, economic, and spiritual life.

The Washoe people were resource harvesters (often characterized as "hunter-gatherers") who routinely managed native flora and fauna to enhance their quality and quantity. The Wá·šiw people commonly utilized burning, weeding, pruning, and selective gathering as subsistence strategies. The Washoe also developed a rich and sophisticated worldview that melded their resource manipulation with cultural traditions and beliefs that profoundly respected the landscape and expressed unshakable gratitude for its physical and psychic value. The earth, their existence, and their essence were inextricably linked.

Euro-Americans filtered into the Lake Tahoe Basin beginning in the 1840s. In February 1844, the first known Euro-American to observe Lake Tahoe was John C. Frémont While on an expedition for the United States Bureau of Topographical Engineers, Frémont viewed the lake from a nearby ridge. Frémont attached the generic name *mountain lake* to the beautiful blue body of water and suggested the lake be named Lake Bonpland after French botanist Aimé Jacques Alexandre Bonpland. Three months later, in May 1844, six members of the Stephens-Townsend-Murphy emigrant party became the first Euro-Americans known to set foot on the shores of the mountain lake.

With the advent of the California gold rush in 1848, roads to the beckoning gold fields developed near Lake Tahoe, but they primarily bypassed the lake to provide easier passage through the mountains. In 1851 Martin Smith, the first recognized permanent white settler, established a trading post near the south shore of the lake. In 1853, the lake was dubbed Lake Bigler in honor of John Bigler, the third governor of California. The naming was controversial, with some supporting the designation (touting Bigler's heroic efforts on a Sierra Nevada rescue mission), while others were critical (emphasizing Bigler's questionable character and a dubious misrepresentation of the governor's mission). Many simply referred to the lake as Tahoe, ostensibly the anglicized version of the Washoe name for the lake dáʔaw, pronounced "da'ow ga."

As the California gold rush progressed, additional roads that linked Gold Country directly to Lake Tahoe were constructed. These roads represented a growing transportation web to the Lake Tahoe Basin. These roads—Johnson's Cut-Off, the Carson Emigrant Ridge Road, the Georgetown—Lake Bigler Trail, the Placer County Emigrant Road, and Luther Pass Road, to name a handful—would, in future years, transition into today's Highway 28, Highway 50, Highway 89, Highway 267, and Old Highway 40.

In 1854 there were reports of skirmishes between the Washoe and the newly arrived Euro-Americans over access and fishing rights at the lake. In 1859 the first commercial fishing venture was established. The operation known as The Fishery was launched near the mouth of the Upper Truckee River.

In 1855 the first of several contentious state boundary surveys was spearheaded by George Henry Goddard, a prominent San Francisco surveyor and architect, and Seneca H. Marlette, surveyor-general of California. Clashes between California and Nevada over state and territorial boundary lines seemed inevitable and, unsurprisingly, they occurred.

Two momentous events occurred in Lake Tahoe history in 1859. The first was the onset of limited logging for local consumption. This was a small-scale endeavor at first, but logging assumed huge proportions only a few years hence. The second event was explosion of public consciousness of a silver strike in what came to be called the Comstock Lode near Virginia City, Nevada. This led to a startling reversal of migrant patterns in the region. Whereas previously immigration was from east to west—to California—now the pattern was west to east—from California to Nevada. Lake Tahoe became a major hub linking California's Mother Lode region and Nevada's Comstock Lode. As a result, many more people became aware of Lake Tahoe, and the lake was increasingly enticing for visitors and merchants alike.

≈≈≈

Tahoe was a revered Washo place.

—Verna Johnston *Sierra Nevada: The Naturalist's Companion,* 1998

In 1998 Verna Johnston, naturalist, author, and photographer, published a book entitled Sierra Nevada: The Naturalist's Companion. *The book examined many aspects of Sierra Nevada history, natural history, and culture, including a section on the Washoe people pre-Euro-American contact.*

Born in 1918, Verna Johnston attended the University of Illinois and received a graduate degree in zoology. Johnston taught biology and environmental science at San Joaquin Delta Community College in Stockton, California, from 1945 until her retirement in 1982. For seventeen years, Johnston studied photography with the famous photographer Ansel Adams. Verna Johnston published more than one hundred articles in professional journals and popular publications.

Following her retirement from San Joaquin Delta College, she moved to California's Calaveras County, residing near Calaveras Big Trees State Park. In November 1998 Life *magazine featured her in an article entitled "Verna: An 80-year-old Naturalist's Passion for a Western Mountain Range."*

Verna Johnston was honored by the National Wildlife Federation and the National Science Foundation and was an active and valued member of many environmental organizations, including the Committee for the Preservation of the Tule Elk, the Mono Lake Committee, the Calaveras Big Trees Association, the Sierra Club, National Audubon Society, and the Wilderness Society. Verna Johnston was a key figure in the establishment of the Point Reyes National Seashore.

Verna Johnston died in 2014 at the age of ninety-five.

In this selection from Sierra Nevada: The Naturalist's Companion, *Verna Johnston detailed the importance of Lake Tahoe to the pre-Euro-American contact Washoe people. Lake Tahoe "gleamed like an enormous gem," Johnston wrote, and the lake provided sacred soil, life-giving nourishment, indescribable beauty, and a connection to the eternal.*

For their tools of bone, wood, or stone, the Indians used whatever was at hand. They made bows out of juniper or occasionally desert mahogany, arrows of willow. Obsidian arrowheads were wrapped on with sinew, which was sealed with a sticky exudation from sagebrush. Looped willow stems furnished traps for small animals; plant fibers made nets for fishing. They wove willow baskets for every purpose: collecting food, cooking, storing food, winnowing, seed beating, and, after the insides were waterproofed with a coating of pitch, as water containers. With big game such as deer, antelope, and mountain sheep to furnish occasional breaks in their diet, the Indians lived chiefly on pine nuts, small game, insects, and seeds.

Washo hunting and gathering habits were almost identical with those of the Paiute most of the year. The Washo country was perhaps the most verdant of the eastern valleys. East Sierran streams generally disappear rather quickly into lakes and sinks of the low desert. The Carson and Walker, the larger rivers in Washo territory, flowed during the entire year. There were green belts along the rivers and around the sinks. Waterfowl fed in the sinks; sage grouse, ground squirrels, gophers, and field mice abounded. Compared with the bone-dry country to the east, Washo land was a haven. But in summer the valleys grew hot and dry very early, and Washo life moved upmountain to the blue lake they called Tahoe, meaning "big water" or "high water." Lying at 6,239 feet in a basin between the main crest of the Sierra and the Carson spur range to the east, Tahoe was a revered Washo place.

The huge rock along the eastern shore was the site of a sacred cave; the creeks flowing into the lake, certain stands of trees, and rock outcroppings were tied to the sacred myth of the creation of the Washo world. The lake itself gleamed like an enormous gem set among illimitable tall conifers, sugar pines dangling long cones full of small sweet seeds, Jeffrey pines, white and red firs, incense cedars. The waters seemed alive as they changed color during the day from emerald to cobalt blue to deep purple. Never freezing over completely even in the coldest winters, they held a supply of fish vital to the Washo diet.

As soon as the snow melted from foothill trails in the spring, the young people of the tribe began the trek up the steep east-side passes. Arriving on the still-snow-covered shores of Lake Tahoe, they lived in caves, gathering spring plants for vegetables and fishing for mountain whitefish (*Prosopium williamsoni*), which they brought back to the rest of the tribe in starvation years. As summer approached, the lowland families left winter camp and one by one moved up to the lake. By early June the entire east-side Washo population was encamped on Tahoe's shores.

They arrived in time for the spawning runs of the large lake fish. The Lahontan cutthroat trout (*Oncorhynchus clarki henshawi*) and Tahoe sucker (*Catostomus tahoensis*), in particular, swam out of the deep lake waters into the side streams by the thousands, sometimes so thick that their bodies filled the streams from bank to bank. Men, women, and children armed with baskets waded into the streams, scooped up the swarming fish, and tossed them onto the shore. There, others split and boned them, producing two fillets. Female fish were stripped of their roe, which was eaten raw or spread out to dry, and everyone feasted on broiled fish, the first fresh protein since autumn for most of them. At the height of the run, fishing went on through the night, torchlights reflecting off the shiny backs of the fish. During the two weeks or so of the spawning runs, the Washo ate and dried enormous numbers of fish. Had they known how to smoke them, as the Indians of the northern coasts did, they could have lived nearly the year round on the resources of Lake Tahoe's streams. As it was, the dried fish spoiled if taken into their foothill and desert valleys, and so were edible only as long as the tribe remained in the cool mountains.

This they did for most of the summer. When the spawning runs diminished, families left their lakeside camps and headed into the higher mountain meadows. The meadows offered a wide variety of bulb and root plants, greens, and berries, which the women, armed with a digging stick and a burden basket, sought and gathered. Granite boulders pock-marked with mortars still show where they sat pulverizing dried fish roe and grinding seeds and berries.

In the higher meadows grew an early summer native sunflower whose seeds could be ground into flour. From damp spots came the new shoots, roots, and seeds of the common cattail. Before the cattail grew fluffy its seeds could be wrapped in leaves and cooked; they made a brown paste that was eaten like candy and with equal zest. Another confection was the sugary exudation for which the sugar pine is named. Hard white crystals of "sugar" form on the upper side of wounds in the tree's wood. They contain resin and have cathartic properties, but are as sweet as cane sugar. Adults and children alike picked these "sap balls" from the bark and chewed them.

Wild strawberries and gooseberries were eaten fresh as they appeared at successively higher elevations in July and August, the strawberries sometimes mashed into a thick drink. Wild onions and wild rhubarb grew in profusion. Small game was available—pocket gophers in the meadows, chipmunks and golden-mantled ground squirrels in the open pine and fir forests. The men and boys fished wherever the lakes and streams held prospects. In the upper reaches of the Carson and Truckee Rivers, minnows by the hundreds were caught in shallow pools with winnowing baskets and baked in an earthen oven. Water and food were plentiful, shelter and firewood readily obtainable, temperatures comfortable. Excursions to the subalpine meadows and rockslides above yielded an occasional deer or plump marmot to vary the menu.

As summer waned, many Washo dropped back down the eastern slope to the foothills and valleys, where grasses were ripening and the seed harvest was at hand. Seeds of wild mustard, pigweed (*Chenopodium*), rabbitbrush (*Chrysothamnus nauseosus*), saltbush (*Atriplex*), and certain grasses were especially prized because they kept so well; every ounce of surplus summer food that would store was a bonus against the nonproductive winter.

A few Washo families often climbed the crest above Lake Tahoe and descended to the western foothills to collect ripening acorns. Occasionally, if early snows made a return hazardous, they wintered on the western side alone or moved into Miwok villages. But most of them were back in the eastern foothills for the vital autumn pinyon-nut harvest.

The discovery of gold in the Sierras western foothills in 1849 brought the first serious trespass of cross-country emigrants on Washo and Paiute lands.

≈≈≈

Darkness crept over the lake, and into the
darkness the Ong vanished.

—Nonette McGlashan "The Legend of Tahoe,"
Sunset, August 1905

The Washoe people are a Native American community whose homeland is in the region surrounding and including Lake Tahoe. Primarily a flora-and-fauna-harvesting nation, the Washoe had a population of perhaps 1,500 prior to contact with Euro-American settlers. While dramatically altered by the mid-nineteenth-century arrival of Euro-Americans, the Washoe culture endures. Its society is dynamic and enlightening. For example, the Washoe's traditional environmental practices offer a valuable blueprint for sustainability. Today, the Washoe people remain an active and essential component of the Lake Tahoe community.

The Washoe people have a rich and evocative body of legends and stories that stretch back centuries. Gifted from generation to generation both orally and in written form, these tales encompass the entire human pageant from birth to death and even into the spirit world. The Washoe legends and stories consider countless aspects of life, such as childbirth, respect for the family, marriage, death, geography, animal behavior, climate, flora, and many more. Day-to-day activities, such as home construction, food gathering, and meal preparation, are subjects of Washoe lore as well. These are stories with a point, stories that instruct, stories that impart valuable lessons, stories that are warnings, and stories that connect the present with the ancestral past.

In 1976 the tribal historian Jo Ann Nevers explored the remarkable chronicle of Washoe life in her book Wa She Shu: A Washo Tribal History. *This fascinating volume examines history from the Washoe perspective, examining the people's homeland, facets of their everyday existence, traditions, the cultural and physical impacts of Euro-American conquest* of the land, loss of Washoe hegemony, and the decades-long battles with the United States government over tribal sovereignty. As Nevers noted, "Washo children learned a great deal about their people, their land, and their culture by listening to legends. The old people of the tribe told the stories, which they had heard from their parents and grandparents. . . . As the stories passed from generation to generation, young Washo learned the same lessons their parents had." Jo Ann Nevers was a Northern Washoe, born at the Stewart Indian School in Carson City. A graduate of the University of Nevada, Reno, with a degree in anthropology, Nevers was considered the unofficial historian of the Washoe Tribe of Nevada and California. Nevers died in 2020 at the age of eighty-four.

Sometimes the legends of the Washoe People were cautionary tales. An example is the story of the Ong. The Ong (often spelled "Ang") was a huge bird that lived in a gigantic nest in the middle of Lake Tahoe. As Jo Ann Nevers stated in Wa She Shu, "The Washoe greatly feared this monster, who was so powerful that the wind from his wings could bend the trees when he flew near shore." This monstrous creature terrorized the Washoe people, snatching and devouring those who dared to ignore the Ong's warnings.

In the nineteenth and early twentieth centuries, it was fairly ordinary for Euro-American writers of popular literature to reimagine Native American society in romantic terms. This exercise was often characterized by the authors as a heartfelt expression of respect for Indigenous values. However, it could also be regarded as a straightforward case of what today is known as cultural appropriation.

Regardless of the motivation, Lake Tahoe was not exempt.

In 1905, Nonette McGlashan published a short essay entitled "The Legend of Tahoe" that appeared in Sunset magazine's August issue. The story used the Washoe legend of the Ong as its skeleton.

The age-old Washoe version of the Ong story is quite spare, but McGlashan fleshed it out, occasionally scattering a few of the standard literary references to Native Americans quite common for the era. For example, her tale has allusions to "Indian maidens," "the Great Spirit," and "a mighty band of warriors"—all familiar tropes to readers of nineteenth-century popular prose. "The Legend of Tahoe" also mentioned one of the earliest and longest-lasting legends of Lake Tahoe—that drowned bodies never resurface.

Nonette McGlashan was the daughter of Charles McGlashan, a lawyer, *journalist, chronicler of the Donner party, member of the California State Assembly and, in his later years, champion of the Truckee Method of anti-Chinese suppression that used starvation, boycotts, and denial of services as its modus operandi.*

Nonette McGlashan was born in Truckee in 1878, the oldest of eight children. One sister, Ximena, was a famous entomologist, known far and wide as the Butterfly Queen.

In addition to writing, Nonette McGlashan was a prominent sculptor. One of her works, a sculpted group study called Vanity, *was displayed at the 1915 Panama-Pacific International Exposition in San Francisco. A May 26, 1915,* Sacramento Union *review of* Vanity *gushed, "[McGlashan] is classed a genius and her work is grouped among the foremost of California artists."*

Nonette McGlashan's adaptation of the Washoe legend of the Ong begins with a description of the enormous and treacherous bird.

I wish I could tell you the tale in the broken words and the strange gestures of the old Indian woman, for it will doubtless lose is weird pathos, even if I try ever so hard to tell it exact.

The Ong was a big bird, bigger than the houses of the white men. Its body was like the eagle's, and its wings were longer than the tallest pines. Its face was that of an Indian, but covered with hard scales, and its feet were webbed. Its nest was deep down in the bottom of the lake, out in the center, and out of the nest rushed all of the waters which fill the lake. There are no rivers to feed the lake, only the waters from the Ong's nest. All the waters flow back near the bottom of the lake, in great under-currents, and after passing through the meshes of the nest are sent forth again. Every plant and bird and animal that gets into these under-currents, and sometimes even the great trout are swept into the net-like nest and are there held fast to furnish food for the Ong.

He ate everything, he liked everything, but best of all he liked the taste of human flesh. No one ever heard or saw anything of such poor mortals as were drowned in these waters, for their bodies were carried to the Ong's nest and no morsel ever escaped him. Sometimes he would fly about the shores in quest of some child, or woman or hunter, yet he was a great coward, and was never known to attack anyone in camp, or when two or more were together. No arrow could pierce his feathers, nor could the strongest spear do more than glance from the scales on his face and legs, yet his coward's heart made him afraid, for his toes had no claws, and his mouth no beak.

Late one fall the Washoe were making their final hunt before going to the valleys and leaving the lake locked in its winter snows. The chief's daughter was sixteen years old, and before leaving the lake he must select the greatest hero in the tribe for her husband, for such had been the custom of Washoe chiefs ever since the tribe came out of the Northland. Fairer than ever Indian maiden had been was this daughter, and every unmarried brave and warrior in the tribe wished that he had performed deeds of greater prowess, that he might be certain of winning the prize. That last night at the lake, around the big council fire, each was to recount to the Chief the noblest achievement of his life, and when all were heard, the Chief would choose, and the women join the circle and the wedding take place. For many years the warriors had looked forward to this event and the tribe had become famed because of acts of reckless daring performed by those who hoped to wed the Chief's daughter.

It was the morning of the final day, and much game and great stores of dried trout were packed ready for the journey. All were preparing for the wedding festivities, and the fact that no one knew who would be the bridegroom, among all that mighty band of warriors, lent intense excitement to the event. All wore joyous and happy, except the maiden and the handsome young brave to whom she had given her heart. In spite of custom or tradition, her love had long since gone out to one whose feet had been too young to press the war-path when last the tribe gave battle to their hereditary foes, the Piutes. He never had done deed of valor, nor could he even claim the right to sit with the warriors around the council fire. All day long he had been sitting alone on the jutting cliffs which overhang the water, far away from the laughter and shouts of the camp, eagerly, prayerfully watching the great lake. Surely the Great Spirit would hear his prayer and give him the moment he longed for, yet he had been here for days and weeks in unavailing prayer and waiting.

The afternoon was well-nigh spent, and the heart of the young brave had grown cold as stone. In his bitter despair he sprang to his feet to defy and curse the Great Spirit to whom he had trusted, but ere he could utter the words his very soul stood still for joy. Slowly rising from the center of the lake, he saw the dreaded Ong. Circling high in the heavens like a great black thunder-cloud, the monster swept now here, now there in search of prey. The young brave stood erect and waited. When the Ong was nearest, he moved about slightly to attract its notice. He had not long to wait. With a mighty swoop the bird dashed to earth, and as he arose, the young brave was seen by all to be clasped fast in its talons. A great cry of horror arose from the camp, but it was the sweetest note the young brave had ever heard. The bird flew straight up into the sky until lake and forest and mountain seemed small and dim. When it reached a great height it would drop its prey into the lake and let the current draw it to the nest. Such was its custom, and for this the young Indian had prepared by unwinding from his waist a long buckskin cord, and tying himself firmly to the Ong's legs. The clumsy feet could not grasp him so tightly as to prevent his movements. At last the great toes opened wide, but the Indian did not fall. Again they closed and opened, and the enraged bird thrust down his head to see why his victim refused to fall. In a mighty rage the Ong tried to grasp the man in his mouth, but the strong web between the bird's toes sheltered him. Again and again the bird tried to use his horrid teeth, and each time his huge body would fall through the air in such twistings and contortions that those who watched below stared in bewilderment. But what the watchers could not see was that every time the huge mouth opened to snap at him, he young brave hurled a handful of poisoned arrow heads into the mouth, and down the big throat, their sharp points cutting deep into the unprotected flesh. The bird tried to dislodge him by rubbing his feet together, but the thong held firm. Now it plunged headlong into the lake, but its feet were tied so that it could not swim, and though it lashed the waters into foam with its great wings, and though the man was nearly drowned and wholly exhausted, the poison caused the frightened bird such agony that it suddenly arose and tried to escape by flying toward the center of the lake. The contest had lasted long, and the darkness crept over the lake, and into the darkness the Ong vanished.

The women had been long in their huts ere the council fire was kindled, and the warriors gravely seated themselves in its circle. No such trifling event as the loss of a young brave could be allowed to interfere with so important an event, and from most of their minds he had vanished. It was not so very unusual for the Ong to claim a victim, and besides, the youth had been many times warned by his elders that he should not go hunting alone as had been his habit of late.

But while the warriors were working themselves up to a frenzy of eloquence over their bygone deeds of daring, an Indian maiden was paddling a canoe swiftly and silently toward the middle of the lake. Nona, the Chief's daughter, understood no more than the rest why her lover had not been dropped into the lake, nor why the Ong had acted so queerly, but she knew that she could die with her lover. She took her own frail canoe because it was so light and easy to row, though it was made for her when a girl, and would scarcely support her weight now. It mattered nothing to her if the water splashed over the sides; it mattered nothing how she reached her lover. She kept saying his name over softly to herself, "Tahoe! My darling Tahoe!"

When the council had finished, the old women went to her hut to bid her come and hear the decision her father was about to render. Their consternation caused by her disappearance lasted until the rosy dawn tinged the Washoe peaks and disclosed to the astounded tribe the body of the Ong floating on the waters above its nest, and beside it an empty canoe. In the foreground, and gently approaching the shore was the strangest craft that ever floated on water! It was one of the Ong's great wings, and the sail was the tip of the other wing! Standing upon it clasped in each other's arms, was the young brave Tahoe and the daughter of the chief. In the shouts of the tribe, shouts in which warriors and women and children mingled their voices with that of the chief, Tahoe was proclaimed the hero of heroes! The decision was rendered, but the Ong's nest still remains, and to this day the drowned never rise In Lake Tahoe.

≈≈≈

A species of evil water-beings was called mɛtsuŋ'ɛ´.

—Robert H. Lowie, "Ethnographic Notes on the Washo," *University of California Publications in American Archaeology and Ethnology*, 1939

The Ong is not the only Washoe mythological creature living in the mysterious blue waters of Lake Tahoe. There is also the mɛtsuŋ'ɛ´, or Water Babies.

The Water Babies are shadowy presences that primarily cluster near Cave Rock and can be either evil or good, depending upon the circumstances and the level of respect paid them. The small beings live underwater and, at night, cry like babies. They do not like the Washoe, and, if not treated with honor, they will harm the Washoe people.

One Washoe story relates that to cross or fish Lake Tahoe, a Washoe person should perform a ritual to appease the Water Babies. They must prepare a leakproof basket and fill it with bread and pine nuts. The basket would then be sealed and sunk in the lake for the use of the Water Babies. The stealthy lake dwellers would then protect the travelers or fishers. However, if a basket was not left, the Water Babies would become angry, sink the boat, and drown the passengers.

Water Babies also feature in Washoe creation myths. One tells of Tamálili? or "Little Weasel" (some sources spell the name "Damalali" or "Damollale") stealing the hair of a Water Baby. Enraged, the creature causes the water level of Lake Tahoe to rise almost to the rim of the surrounding mountain ridges. Only when Little Weasel returns the Water Baby's hair does the water recede, leaving Lake Tahoe and other nearby lakes and streams looking as they do today.

In 1939 Robert H. Lowie wrote an article for the journal American Archaeology and Ethnology entitled "Ethnographic Notes on the Washo" that, in part, examined the story of the Water Babies. In 1926 Lowie spent several weeks in Minden, Nevada (east of the south shore of Lake Tahoe), and Coleville, Mono County, California (about fifty miles southeast of Lake Tahoe), collecting and recording the stories of Washoe people as told to him primarily by three members of the Washoe Nation—Dave Cheney, Jack Pitts, and Bill Cornbread. These versions were published close to the nineteenth century and are considered reliably transcribed examples of stories told by the Washoe people in the previous century.

Born Robert Heinrich Löwe in Vienna, Austria, in 1883, Lowie immigrated to the United States in 1893. In 1908 Robert Lowie received a doctorate in anthropology from Columbia University. After a stint as a curator at New York's American Museum of Natural History, Lowie became a professor of anthropology at the University of California, Berkeley, in 1917. He spent the next thirty-three years at Cal, retiring in 1950.

Lowie was an acknowledged expert on North American Indigenous people and, in the words of Julian H. Steward, a pioneer in cultural ecology, Lowie was "one of the key figures in the history of anthropology." Robert H. Lowie died in 1957 at the age of seventy.

In 1959 the newly constructed museum of anthropology on the University of California, Berkeley, campus was named the Robert H. Lowie Museum of Anthropology in his honor. It would retain that designation until 1991 when it was renamed the Phoebe A. Hearst Museum of Anthropology.

In this passage from Lowie's "Ethnographic Notes on the Washo," the anthropologist describes the mɛtsuŋ'ɛ, which he characterizes as "a species of evil water-beings" and shares stories of Water Babies, particularly the story of Tamálili and the Water Baby, as related to him in 1926.

A species of evil water-beings was called mɛtsuŋ'ɛ´. The Washo were afraid to meet them. Once, when walking in the sand around Lake Tahoe, Dave [Cheney, a Washoe residing in Minden, Nevada, at the time of the article publication] saw the tracks of one. These beings would travel about a little, always along the shore, at night, then go back into the Lake again. They made the sound of babies at night; the Indians would hear them. They live in a house under the water, possibly twenty feet below the surface. Men and women both live there. They do not like Indians; the Washo avoid them and never dream of them. A Washo would be terrified, paralyzed "a little bit," bleed from the nose, and fall sick if he saw one of these beings. Judging from their tracks, their feet are only the length of a little baby's.

[Robert H. Lowie quotes Dave Cheney:]

Once, a Washo was fishing in the Lake with a line and reel, when the line got caught at the bottom. He thought it was a snake, but it was a mɛtsuŋ'ɛ´ pulling the line down. He was pretty strong. After a while he let go, and the line got slack. There was a tuft of hair on the point of the hook. The Indian was paralyzed and fell down unconscious in his boat for possibly an hour. There was no wind. At last he woke up terrified and made for home. He cut off the hook and line with the hair, and threw them back into the water. He told his wife and children about his experience. For a week after that the fish would not bite. All the Washo were afraid. About half a mile from shore there is a spring; that is where these water-beings probably come from. Their hair reaches down to the knee.

[The story of "The Two Weasel Brothers" as told to Robert Lowie by a Washoe storyteller]

There were two weasel brothers; the smaller one, Tama'lili, was a funny fellow; he wouldn't mind (just like a hoodlum). He said to Spider, "You can't catch me. I'm going to jump over this stump, you can't jump over it." Spider said, "I can run after anyone, I'll follow you around." The Weasel jumped. Spider, instead of jumping, ran under the stump and got pretty close to him. Weasel said, "Do you think you can run across the water? I can go on top of the water." He ran across. Spider also went quickly across and nearly caught up. Weasel was tired out and Spider killed him.

Tama'lili's elder brother had sent him for something. When he did not come back, the elder brother looked around, but found no track. He followed him all over, but could not find any. He asked Sun: "Have you seen my brother? I couldn't find him. Have you seen him? I have lost him. Tell me, you must see him." Sun said, "I haven't seen him, I don't know where he is." He asked again and again. At last Sun said, "I didn't want to tell directly. I think your brother has no sense. He was fooling with a bad boy. Something bad chased him, killed him, and dragged him into his house [hole]. I saw him a little while ago." Then the elder Weasel went into the hole and made smoke. Spider got sick from it, he was suffocated. Weasel dragged his younger brother out and stepped over him. Then the little one got up alive again.

Both walked away. The elder said, "You'll have to look out, you always fool with anybody, you must be careful. Don't do that any more. Go ahead, I think there are deer in that brush; scare them, we'll kill them." The younger went running and met Beaver. He walked toward him and shook his house. Beaver asked, "What is that ?" He saw him. Weasel said, "My brother has sent me up here to get something to eat tonight; we are camping out there somewhere." "I have nothing to give you to eat." He asked two or three times. "I haven't got it, I tell you." Then Weasel got angry, broke up the beaver house, and ran away. Plenty of beavers came out and ran after him. They grabbed him and bit him to death, then dragged him into their house.

The elder brother waited for a long time. He got tired and went hunting for him. He again asked Sun, who would not tell him at first. At last he said, "That man got him, killed him, dragged him into his house." The elder Weasel went in and dragged out Tama'lili.

He stepped over him. He got up. They walked off. He told him again, "You haven't any sense. I told you to be careful and not to fool when you meet somebody. I'm tired of you."

He sent him off again: "Go over to that tree where there are deer tracks. Go round that big brush, and drive deer to me, so we can kill them and have something to eat tonight." Young Weasel went into the thick brush, found a bear cub, caught him, and brought him to his brother. He rubbed the cub's back, and said "We have a nice puppy." He held him toward his body. "Let him go, Grizzly might come." After a while he let him go. The Weasels walked away.

He sent him off again. "Look at that tree. I'll stand under it, you come round, and if you scare up deer we'll kill them and camp here somewhere." He found no deer, only Woodchuck . . . making smoke against the other woodchucks and trying to kill them. He got two or three. Young Weasel came along and fooled Woodchuck, who had a long stick with which he was poking into the hole. Woodchuck was looking in, kneeling, when Weasel with a little stick struck him in the buttocks. Woodchuck thought he was being burnt. He again poked in his stick, and Weasel again did as before. "Who did that? It must be someone coming along to fool me." He tried again, looking between his legs, and caught sight of young Weasel, who laughed at him, saying, "Well, my brother has sent me to get a great big woodchuck to eat tonight. You have killed one, you have got it, my brother wants a big one." He refused; then Weasel seized it and fled. Two or three woodchucks ran after him, killed him, and dragged him into a hole.

Then the elder Weasel looked everywhere for the younger. He could not find him and again asked Sun, "Have you seen my brother?" At first Sun would not tell him, but after being asked several times he said, "Your brother fooled Woodchuck, he tried to steal from him, then two or three of them ran after him, killed him, and dragged him into their hole." He went to the hole, made a smoke and killed Woodchuck, pulled out his brother and stepped over him. Then he came to life again.

Both of them walked away and went to a hillside. They saw a deer lying on the upper side of a tree. "Look out, that big deer is what we are looking for." The elder brother sneaked up, saying, "Do you stay here, and don't move until I've shot him." The younger one would not obey, but kept sneaking alongside of his brother. "Stay here, don't move, don't follow me, I am going to sneak up and kill him. If you come alongside of me and shoot when I shoot, he won't die, he'll run away." Still the younger would not listen. The elder Weasel shot, and so did his brother. Then the deer did not die, but ran down, far away. They followed and tracked him, but could not catch him.

The younger Weasel saw a water baby and fooled him. The Water Baby said, "Look out, don't fool with me. If you do and kill me, the water will flow over you, following you down, and will drown you." But the Weasel killed him, scalped him—he had long hair and brought the scalp to his brother. The elder Weasel said, "Why, what are you doing! Don't you stop fooling? The water is going to drown us. Throw the hair back immediately!" The water followed the young Weasel and nearly overtook him, but when he threw the hair back the water receded.

≈≈≈

A man who dreamed of rabbits or antelope was more than simply lucky, he was a possessor of a special power.
—James F. Downs, *The Two Worlds of the Washo*, 1966

The Washoe people have existed in two worlds—a practical, physical world and a world of spirits, dreams, and other supernatural phenomena that influence and direct their everyday actions. Personal and tribal power flow from the conjunction of these potent forces.

In this excerpt from The Two Worlds of the Washo, *anthropologist James F. Downs examines how supernatural assistance influenced all aspects of precontact Washoe life, including treatment of illness, identification and training of shamans, attitudes toward hunting, and child-rearing practices.*

James Francis Downs was an anthropologist with a remarkably varied personal history. Born in 1923, Downs served in the U.S. Navy during World War II and the Korean War, raised horses, worked as a newspaper reporter, toiled as a farmer, and owned and operated a public relations consulting firm—all before enrolling at the University of California, Berkeley, at age thirty. Within five years, he earned two graduate degrees (including a PhD) in anthropology at Cal while also working full-time as a consultant. His doctoral studies included field research of the Washoe people. Additionally, Downs studied the Navajo Nation and the Tibetan culture. He taught at many universities, including the University of Washington, University of Arizona, University of Wyoming, and the University of Hawaii at Hilo. In addition to The Two Worlds of the Washo, *Dr. Downs also wrote* Washo Religion *(1961) and widely respected articles, monographs, and textbooks on Navajo culture, physical anthropology, and cultural ecology. James F. Downs died in 1999 at the age of seventy-six.*

A successful hunter was more than skilled and careful, he was aided by a special power. A man who dreamed of rabbits or antelope was more than simply lucky, he was a possessor of a special power. The nature of this power is not clearly defined in all cases. We can see how power works most clearly if we learn how a man becomes a "doctor," or shaman, among the Washo. The shaman was expected to carry his share of the burden of living, but his special powers set him apart from his fellows and contributed to his livelihood because his services were valuable and demanded payment. The shaman's special power was the ability to diagnose and cure illness.

Illness might come from three sources. A ghost, angry because some piece of his property was being used by the living, might make the user sick. A sorcerer might cause illness by using magic to "shoot" a foreign body into his victim. Or a person might become ill because he had violated some taboo such as mistreating pine nuts or pinon trees. To affect a cure, a shaman was called to perform a ceremony over the patient. The cure was felt to be brought about not by the shaman's skill but by his "power" which was felt to be apart from the person of the shaman himself. The shaman served as a medium through which the power could be used to the benefit of the sick person. A treatment required that the shaman work for four nights. In addition to the shaman, the patient's family and a number of friends gathered. On each of the nights the shaman prayed to his power to assist him, smoked tobacco, frequently a sacred or semi-sacred act among Indians; and sang special songs which were his alone. Accompanying his singing with a rattle made of dry cocoons, he passed into a trance and while in this state located the site of the illness and identified the cause. . . . For his services a shaman was paid in food and valuable objects. The process of becoming a doctor illustrates the nature of power as the Washo conceived it.

The power to become a shaman was not sought by the Washo, it came unsought and often unwelcomed. The first signs of receiving power were often a series of dreams. In these dreams an animal, a bear, an owl, a "ghost" or some other being would appear. The vision would offer him power and assistance in life. The Washo feared power; it was dangerous for one who had it and the greater and more clearly defined the power, the more dangerous it was. The trancelike state which was part of the curing ceremony seemed to many Washo to be akin to death, a loss of spirit. Because of this, a young man might ignore the offers of spiritual power. But a spirit being, or *wegaleyo*, frequently refused to be ignored. It would begin to inflict a series of ailments upon its chosen vehicle. Although it was not considered good social form to brag of having power or to openly seek it, some men did secretly hope for power. Men of this type today invariably complain of a long series of illnesses, seizures, and ailments. To the outsider such a person might appear to be simply a hypochondriac, but the Washo recognized this as a veiled claim to power. Under pressure from the *wegaleyo*, a man would usually succumb and accept his power. Once he had made this secret decision, his dreams would become instruction sessions. The *wegaleyo* would tell him where he could find a special spring or pool. This was "his water" to be used in ceremonies or for ritual bathing or to decontaminate sacred articles collected by the shaman in his career. The spirit also taught his pupil a special song which he would remember word for word when he awoke. In later years a shaman might learn many such songs from his spirit. He would also receive instructions as to what equipment to collect. This would always include a rattle and eagle feathers. Individuals might also possess special stones, shell jewelry, or animal skins. These objects were usually obtained under unusual or miraculous circumstances. . . .

Shamans were always considered to be potential sorcerers. Their power was neither good nor bad in itself and could be used for whatever ends the shaman sought. . . .

If a shaman lost his sacred paraphernalia or it was destroyed, he would most certainly become seriously ill. Because of these dangers, many men tried to avoid power if it was thrust upon them and would employ a shaman to help them rid themselves of the persistent spirit.

If this was successful they could resume the normal Washo life. If not, they had little choice but to quiet the spirit and accept its gift. . . .

We have spoken of shaman as being males, but women could also become shaman and many did. Their experiences and training did not differ from those of men. Power was not exclusively a gift of the spirit beings to humans. In a general way, everything was viewed as having some power. Merely to live required some supernatural assistance. Successful survival was a sign of power. . . . This general power was extended to all living things, animals, and plants and . . . was the basis of many of the behavior patterns associated with hunting, fishing, and gathering. . . .

The twirling dust devils so common in the summer in this region were thought to be ghosts, and a sudden puff of warm air on a still summer night was most certainly a shade. The belief in ghosts and personal power was an important factor in Washo child raising practices. Parents avoided striking or spanking or striking a child for fear of angering some dead relative. In this instance the ghost seemed to have some friendly concern for the living, but the manner of showing it was to cause the death of the child as a punishment to the parents. The fear of sorcery led the Washo to encourage their younger children to remain within their own family group. Associating with strangers, particularly old strangers, could be dangerous. This belief is obviously related to the development of deep ties of dependence on one's close relatives and the strengthening of the all important Washo family unit. The two major concepts of Washo religion are: ghosts, to be feared, avoided, and appeased; and power, to be used to accomplish the business of living. . . .

[W]e see ritual reflecting a Washo view of the supernatural woven through nearly every act of the day. Hunting ritual, dreams of rabbits and fish and antelope, special power to obtain food, respectful treatment of the remains of animals, the minor ceremonies of childbirth and childhood were all viewed as essential parts of the activities with which they were associated.

≈≈≈

Washoe ceremonial gatherings were called *gumsabay*.

—Michael Hittman, "Washoe," from *Great Basin
Indians: An Encyclopedic History*, 2013

The Washoe people have an astounding ritual and ceremonial life that stretches back centuries.

By countless years, many of these rites predate initial Euro-American contact around Lake Tahoe in the 1840s. Many continue to the present day. These observances have been an essential component of the Washoe people's identity and belief systems. Rituals and ceremonies mark turning points, such as puberty, marriage, and death. They also provide spiritual fuel to confront and conquer challenges in life.

In 2013 Michael Hittman, professor of Anthropology at Long Island University, considered several of these Washoe rituals and ceremonies in an entry for his book Great Basin Indians: An Encyclopedic History. *In this excerpt, Hittman discusses treatment of illness, coming-of-age ceremonies, and death rituals.*

Michael Hittman has been studying Native American cultures for decades, focusing on the Great Basin Indigenous population. In 1965, while a graduate student at the University of New Mexico, Hittman was part of a National Science Foundation program collecting ethnographic data among the Northern Paiutes. Over the next seven years, he independently continued his research with the Northern Paiutes. His investigations culminated in his 1973 doctoral dissertation, "Ghost Dances, Disillusionment, and Opiate Addiction: An Ethnohistory of Smith and Mason Valley Paiutes," an examination of the 1870 and 1890 Ghost Dance Movements and a subsequent rise in opiate addiction in the Northern Paiute Nation. In addition to Great Basin Indians: An Encyclopedic History *(2013), Hittman's other books include* Corbett Mack: The Life of a Northern Paiute *(1996) and* Wovoka and the Ghost Dance *(1997).*

Washoe leaders were called *detumu,* "the one in front." So-called rabbit bosses were individuals (men) whose combined knowledge both of the habits of lagomorphs and of people skills resulted in their invitations to coordinate annual communal hunts in the fall, the logistics of which required positioning three-hundred-foot sagebrush nets woven by women across Great Basin desert valley floors, into which frightened jackrabbits were stampeded, ensnared, and killed by groups of men, women, and children.

As was also true among all Great Basin Indians, certain Washoe individuals possessed *degelyu* or supernatural "power." . . . *Degelyu* either arrived unexpectedly through dreams, was inherited along family lines, or was deliberately sought in special places. . . . Those aspiring to become healers, however, were additionally required to apprentice under well-known practitioners before embarking upon what could be a risky profession. . . .

Moreover, a Washoe shaman owned his or her medicine kit, which reportedly typically included cocoon rattles, eagle feathers bound with buckskin, miniature baskets, stone mortars, bird-bone whistles, tobacco pouches, tubular stone pipes, red and white mineral pigments, decorative headdresses, and other personal amulets. The Washoe held theories of illness that were similar to other Great Basin Indians: the notion of "object intrusion," for example, that is, sorcerers shooting material objects into unsuspecting victims' bodies, thereby requiring they be sucked out of patients' bodies in their homes by healers during all-night cures that involved singing as well as dancing. . . .

Washoe ceremonial gatherings were called *gumsabay* and not only included the annual fall Pine Nut Festival, but also included a unique "First Fruit Harvest" associated with the ripening of other food resources. Although girls' puberty rites were found throughout the Great Basin, the Washoe were unique because of its elaboration and their California Indian influences. Briefly described, at the first sign of menarche, an adolescent girl was lectured by an older woman about her future duties as a woman. What then followed were four days of isolation that included the imposition of food and other restrictions—no salt, meat, fish, or fat allowed, for example. Along with the requirement that they fast, girls had to wash repeatedly, not scratch themselves with their fingers or comb their hair (for one month in fact), and were supposed to be daubed with red ocher. Moreover, pubescent girls were required to gather firewood and to literally run up hills and light four sacred fires. Along with this, they were otherwise kept busy with tasks assigned to them by older women during those four days, that is, the obligation of working hard and hurrying about, lest they be lazy in life.

Finally, on the fourth day, a fire was lit on a hill, signaling the end of her relative isolation. Not only was there a four-day feast following her first period, but three more of these subsequently occurred: the second feast fifteen days later, the third on the fourth day following her second menstruation, and the fourth feast some fifteen days later. At the first of these ceremonial gatherings, the girl performed a "jumping dance," which was described as a series of hopping steps from side to side that were believed to encourage the flow of menstrual blood throughout her entire reproductive life, hence by implication assuring the menarche a life of fertility. . . . Older women also sang puberty songs during these occasions, . . . and the ubiquitous circle dance was performed. . . . Gifts were exchanged after the girl's puberty rite, and both the painted (elderberry) wooden staff each young woman had been given to support herself throughout those initial four days and her clothing were ritually disposed of, after which there was a ceremonial bath, which included water being poured over the girl's heads, and she was subsequently washed clean with ashes (or ocher) at midnight and given a new dress to wear. Although these young women's hair was trimmed twice at the second and fourth feasts, pending a haircut after the last of those four puberty rites, they were thus declared eligible for marriage. . . .

Washoe pubescent boys, by contrast, were required to do relatively little more to qualify for manhood status and marriage than crawl under the horns [and toward the animal's eyes] of the first deer they had successfully hunted. . . . Knocking over its horns was considered dangerous, and in fact believed to forebode a lifetime of bad luck as a hunter. . . .

Other Washoe traditional teachings were that the soul at death initially traveled southward before finally elevating skyward. Designated speakers at funerals would admonish the recently deceased, "Don't come back!"—much as their counterparts did throughout the Great Basin. Sharing yet another cultural area-wide belief among Great Basin Indians, the Washoe viewed heavy rains (or windstorms) following an individual's death as representing powerful supernatural figures' determination to eliminate the deceased's footprints from this earth.

≈≈≈

We had a beautiful view of a mountain lake at our feet, about
fifteen miles in length, and so entirely surrounded by mountains.
—John C. Frémont, *Report of the Exploring Expedition*
to the Rocky Mountains in the year 1842, and to Oregon
and California in the years 1843-'44, published 1845

John Charles Frémont was arguably the most recognized explorer of the
nineteenth-century American West. He could also be a self-promoting

and self-glorifying showboat. Frémont achieved wealth and fame, but he died in enduring poverty—a victim of bad judgment and imprudent investments.

Frémont was born in Savannah, Georgia, on January 21, 1813. Early in life, his family moved to Charleston, South Carolina, where Frémont grew to manhood. John C. Frémont attended college—briefly—but was expelled for "incorrigible negligence." Soon afterward, he shipped out on the war sloop Natchez as a mathematics instructor. By 1836 Frémont had returned to the United States, where he would serve as a railroad and Indian lands surveyor in the Carolinas and Tennessee. In 1838 Frémont was commissioned a second lieutenant of the U.S. Corps of Topographical Engineers. His first assignment was to assist in a reconnaissance of the Minnesota and Dakota territories.

In 1841 John C. Frémont's life would change dramatically. In that year he married Jessie Benton, daughter of Thomas Hart Benton, the prominent senator from Missouri and ardent champion of Manifest Destiny. With Jessie's marketing skills and Senator Benton's influence, Frémont quickly gained notice within government circles.

In 1842 the first of Frémont's two most successful expeditions to the West was organized. Its purpose was to investigate South Pass and chart the best route to Oregon, an increasingly desirable locale in the 1840s. With the assistance of guide Kit Carson and the publication of a report, written with Jessie, Frémont became well-known. His second exploration in 1843–1844 made him famous.

During the second expedition, Frémont's party crossed the Great Plains to the Rockies, explored the Great Salt Lake, traveled to Washington and then south into eastern California, crossed the Sierra Nevada at Carson Pass, trekked to Sutter's Fort, turned south into the San Joaquin Valley, then veered eastward along the Old Spanish Trail and Arkansas River to return to Saint Louis. His journal of the second expedition was even more wildly popular than the first and cemented Frémont's reputation as the "Great Pathfinder."

The accounts of these two expeditions were combined as Report of the Exploring Expedition to the Rocky Mountains in the Year 1842, and to Oregon and North California in the Years 1843–'44. The journals were reprinted many times over in both official and unofficial versions, some complete, some abridged, with a few editions printed in England and Germany.

The reports were similar in structure. Each account contains daily descriptions of events and scientific data. Frémont's duties were remarkably diverse, including collection of geographical information, military intelligence, road surveys, zoological and botanical observation, rock collecting, soil and water analysis, and recommendations for settlement and land policy.

But what fascinated the public was Frémont's tales of daring-do and the encounters with awe-inspiring natural beauty by his exploratory corps during its travels. Mixing fact and fancy, Frémont's stories of food scarcity, Indian threats, harrowing cliff-hanging exploits, seemingly insurmountable obstacles, and severe weather are partly scientific monograph and partly rip-roaring adventure. It is little wonder that the journals were so popular.

John C. Frémont's role after the second expedition became less explorer and more soldier-politician. Following a third expedition through the Rockies, Frémont was influential in the Bear Flag Revolt in 1846 California. Soon afterward, on a military expedition in northeast California and southern Oregon, three of Frémont's men were killed by Klamath warriors. In retaliation, he commanded his troops to massacre dozens of Native people near Klamath Lake. He was active in the Mexican War, where he ordered the execution of several unarmed Californio civilians. Following a dispute with Brigadier General Stephen Kearny over control of California, Frémont was ordered to Washington DC, where he was court-martialed for disobedience and mutiny. He was to be dismissed from the army, but President James K. Polk canceled the order. Frémont resigned his commission, in protest of what he viewed as abuse and aspersions.

Frémont organized a fourth expedition in 1848. It was largely a failure, remembered mostly for the deaths of one-third of his men in a blizzard. Settling in gold rush California, Frémont fruitfully invested in land and mining. Soon after California achieved statehood in 1850, Frémont was elected United States senator from the newly minted Golden State. He served only a short time. In 1853 Frémont outfitted a fifth expedition to cross the Rockies in midwinter. It was not successful; in fact, most considered the expedition to be a disaster. Frémont did not publish accounts of either his fourth or fifth expeditions.

In 1856 John C. Frémont was the first presidential candidate of the fledgling Republican Party. He lost to the Democrat James Buchanan.

Soon after the election, Frémont's life began to deteriorate, as his gold mining and real estate interests fizzled. Reinstated to the army during the Civil War, his service record was unremarkable. Following the war, he bankrolled some poorly conceived railroad projects and lost his fortune. From 1878 to 1883, Frémont was governor of Arizona Territory. His legacy in the post was "to have done nothing worse than neglect his duties," in the words of historian Hubert Howe Bancroft.

By the time of his death in 1890 at age seventy-seven, John C. Frémont was celebrated—and broke. Shortly before his passing, Congress had promoted him to the rank of major general (largely as an act of charity) and increased his pension. John Charles Frémont left an evocative record of exploits that helped define the American West but also a legacy of conspiracy, tainted triumphs, unmistakable failures, cruelty, and controversy.

In this selection from his second expedition, Frémont describes crossing the Sierra Nevada in the harsh winter of 1844, just south of present-day Carson Pass—named after his scout, Kit Carson. The excerpt also includes Frémont's reference to his "discovery" of "a mountain lake"—what came to be called Lake Tahoe.

February 13th.—We continued to labor on the road; and in the course of the day had the satisfaction to see the people working down the face of the opposite hill, about three miles distant. During the morning we had the pleasure of a visit from Mr. Fitzpatrick, with the information that all was going on well. A party of Indians had passed on snow-shoes, who said they were going to the western side of the mountain after fish. This was an indication that the salmon were coming up the streams; and we could hardly restrain our impatience as we thought of them, and worked with increased vigor.

The meat train did not arrive this evening, and I gave Godey leave to kill our little dog, (Klamath,) which he prepared in Indian fashion; scorching off the hair, and washing the skin with soap and snow, and then cutting it up into pieces, which were laid on the snow. Shortly afterwards, the sleigh arrived with a supply of horse-meat; and we had to-night an extraordinary dinner—pea-soup, mule, and dog.

February 14th.—The dividing ridge of the Sierra is in sight from this encampment. Accompanied by Mr. Preuss, I ascended to-day the highest peak to the right; from which we had a beautiful view of a mountain lake at our feet, about fifteen miles in length, and so entirely surrounded by mountains that we could not discover an outlet. We had taken with us a glass; but though we enjoyed an extended view, the valley was half hidden in mist, as when we had seen it before. Snow could be distinguished on the higher parts of the coast mountains; eastward, as far as the eye could extend, it ranged over a terrible mass of broken snowy mountains, fading off blue in the distance. The rock composing the summit consists of a very coarse, dark, volcanic conglomerate; the lower parts appeared to be of a slaty structure. The highest trees were a few scattering cedars and aspens. From the immediate foot of the peak, we were two hours reaching the summit, and one hour and a quarter in descending. The day had been very bright, still, and clear, and spring seems to be advancing rapidly. While the sun is in the sky, the snow melts rapidly, and gushing springs cover the face of the mountain in all the exposed places; but their surface freezes instantly with the disappearance of the sun.

≈≈≈

Bigler Lake is a noble sheet of water.

—George H. Goddard, *Report of a Survey of a Portion of the Eastern Boundary of California and of a Reconnaissance of the Old Carson and Johnson Immigrant Roads over the Sierra Nevada*, 1855

When the California gold rush commenced, it was akin to a social earthquake—the Gold Country was shaken beyond recognition, and California and Nevada were never the same again. Knowledge of the landscape was woefully inadequate. For instance, there was a sizeable contingent of 49ers who assumed that the Sierra Nevada possessed the same physical attributes as the Pacific Coastline—namely, that the mountains were blanketed with palm trees, not pine trees. As the gold rush proceeded, the nascent government made concerted efforts to enhance the geographical record to aid in decision-making about roads, economic opportunities, and utilization of available natural resources.

One thorny issue was the location of the boundary between California and the then Utah Territory (later Nevada Territory). In 1855 a survey team was dispatched to survey the eastern boundary and reconnoiter the primary immigrant roads over the Sierra Nevada. The report that ensued was entitled Report of a Survey of a Portion of the Eastern

Boundary of California and of a Reconnaissance of the Old Carson and Johnson Immigrant Roads over the Sierra Nevada. *Coming just before the human tidal wave of the Comstock Lode silver rush, the report offers valuable insights into the condition of the Lake Tahoe Basin prior to the commotion soon to occur.*

The survey report refers to the lake as Bigler Lake, an accepted but not most-popular name due to controversies surrounding its namesake, Governor John Bigler. Goddard's report often has gaps that were filled by subsequent investigations. For example, the survey team vaguely estimated Lake Tahoe's length at somewhere between fifteen to twenty miles (it is twenty-two miles long) and, perhaps most glaringly, it could not find an outlet for the lake. As the survey journal entry for September 19, 1855, states, "The lake is entirely closed in with mountains, and it is impossible to detect the opening by which the Truckee River flows from it. Indeed, no one I have spoken to on the subject has been able to give me any exact information in relation to it, and some even have expressed a doubt as to whether the lake has an outlet at all!" Later expeditions would find the very noticeable river outlet at today's Tahoe City.

The survey team was headed by George Henry Goddard Sr., a leading architect, civil engineer, and surveyor headquartered in boomtown Sacramento. Born in England, Goddard came to California in 1849 and tried his hand at gold mining near Mariposa. As did most, he failed, but survived by producing landscape paintings for other argonauts. Goddard then briefly operated a drugstore in the mining camp of Columbia but was fully employed as a professional surveyor by 1853. He was selected to spearhead several mapping expeditions for the new State of California. One of these was the 1855 reconnaissance of the route over Carson Pass and the survey of the eastern boundary of California excerpted here.

George H. Goddard was known for his meticulous method, recording observations and measurements with state-of-the-art altitude and azimuth transits and chronometers. In 1864 a California Geological Survey party, headed by William Brewer, named a mountain in the north section of today's Kings Canyon National Park after George H. Goddard. Mount Goddard has an elevation of 13,564 feet, and the first recorded ascent was in 1879.

Goddard was also renowned as a collector. During his career as a surveyor and civil engineer, Goddard accumulated a vast array of historical documents and books, hundreds of paintings, and many breathtaking mineral specimens. This library and objets d'art were so impressive that Jane Stanford, wife of railroad magnate Leland Stanford, wanted to obtain them and construct a dedicated building for the collection, called the Goddard Museum, on the grounds of Stanford University. Sadly, this was never to occur as Goddard's treasures were destroyed by the San Francisco Earthquake and Fire of April 1906. Eight months later, George Henry Goddard died at the age of eighty-nine.

REPORT. Sacramento, Dec. 15th, 1855.

To the Hon. S. H. MARLETTE, Surveyor-General: Sir: I have the honor to submit the following Report of the Survey, intrusted to my charge, and carried out, as near as circumstances permitted, in conformity to the following instructions received from you: SURVEYOR-GENERAL'S OFFICE, Sacramento, Aug. 3, 1855. Sir: As you are now provided with the necessary men, animals and instruments, you will proceed without delay to Placerville, en route for Carson Valley. At the former place you will determine the latitude and longitude, and the rate of your chronometers, by astronomical observations, and by comparing your chronometers and local time with those of San Francisco, which you can readily do, by means of the Telegraph lines which have been kindly placed at your service for this purpose. From Placerville to Carson Valley, via Cold Spring Ranch and Carson Pass, you will take such barometrical observations as will enable you to construct a profile of the route. You will also take, so far as practicable, a somewhat accurate sketch of the country traversed, and collect such other data as in your opinion will be of service in comparing the merits of this with other routes, for the Immigrant Wagon Road, in respect to both practicability and economy of construction. At or near Carson Valley you will determine, astronomically, with some precision, the position of the eastern boundary of the State; and I would suggest that such portion of the State line as shall fall in Carson Valley, or so much of it as you may deem necessary, be measured and defined with tolerable accuracy, in other that it may be used as a primary base for the determination, trigonometrically, of the position of such points as it may be found necessary to determine for the purpose of connecting our surveys and explorations, and for fixing the eastern terminus of the road. Somewhat durable and conspicuous monuments should be erected at the termini of the primary base, and perhaps at the extremities of some of the secondary bases, from which shall be taken the bearings of the prominent and well defined peaks of other objects of the Sierra Nevada, and other mountains, and of the adjoining country, of which you may obtain a view. The men and animals provided you, have been furnished by Judge Hyde, of Utah Territory, who will provide all the assistance and provisions requisite, after you leave Placerville until you return to the same place. On what route you had better return I have not decided, but this is of no consequence, as I intend meeting you in Carson Valley, but should I not do so, you will consult with the Hon. Sherman Day, with whom you will probably meet in that vicinity, and return by such route as is in his judgment will most facilitate the selection of the most practicable and economical route for the Immigrant Road. You will, of course, take the same observations coming as going, so far as practicable. Inform me of your progress as often as you shall find it convenient to do so, and oblige,

Very respectfully, your obedient servant, S. H. Marlette, Surveyor-General

September 14. [1855].—The whole of the hills in this neighborhood are composed entirely of white granite, the breccia has quite disappeared. We halted for a couple of hours at Smith's where I took observations and sketched in our route. We now followed the Johnson Road, and crossing a small stream just past Smith's, we continued along a low ridge of granitic sand and pebbles, slightly elevated above the flats, and lying parallel with the base of the mountain. The whole country is so heavily timbered that we saw nothing of the lake and very little of the mountains; a large stream runs alongside of this ridge for several miles, at the base of the mountains, while the Truckee flows along on the northern side, winding through a large marshy flat which continues down to the lake. At about four miles from Smith's we arrived at the end of this singular ridge and crossed a large creek which falls into the Truckee, the road then winds along over spurs of the mountains to the east, crossing several smaller creeks, all of which empty into the Truckee. At length we reached the point to leave the road for the lake. We had been obliged thus to wind round the lake to avoid the swampy ground which forms its southern shore. Bigler Lake is a noble sheet of water, from fifteen to twenty miles in length by six to seven in width; we arrived at its shore at dusk, and camped at the point of timber which forms the eastern boundary of the swamps on the southern end of the lake.

September 15.—I went along the beach of the lake to the mouth of the Truckee River; this beach is a strip of firm, solid ground inclosing the swampy flats. I selected a favorable site for our astronomical station, one from which Round Top and several of the other points on that ridge, as well as all the mountains surrounding the lake, could be seen. It was near the mouth of the river and sufficiently far from the timber to prevent its intercepting our view. I had a block cut and prepared for the instrument; in the forenoon I took a set of time observations, but the afternoon closed in cloudy and windy; sent Ferrel and Hancock down to Carson Valley for more provisions.

September 16.—Had a raft made and floated the block half a mile along the lake shore to the place chosen yesterday. The tent was set up and the instrument put into adjustment; took an observation of Polaris at the eastern elongation, and set the instrument on an approximate meridian. The party sent to Carson Valley for supplies returned to-day, bringing with them very little, and that so bad that it is hardly eatable; the flour is about half smut. They complain that they are entirely out of provisions in the valley.

September 17.—Took observations for time. There are so many clouds on the hills that we cannot make out any of our flags, not even with the large telescope. The lofty peak of Job's Group visible from this camp turned out afterwards not to be the eastern peak on which my flag was erected. I set out and measured a base line of seventyeight chains on the flat, and had a flag put up on the granite knob some three miles to the south which overlooks this portion of the valley. Mr. Merkley went to Carson Valley to-day, as he is desirous of returning to California in search of his son, and thus I am all the time short of hands. The afternoon closed in with heavy rain and wind, and the men went off into the forest and built themselves a brush shanty; I remained at the tent but did not get any observations.

September 18.—The mountains are white with snow, so there will be little chance of seeing any of our distant flags. Spent the morning in computing some of the recent observations. In the afternoon crossed the

Truckee on our raft, and went to the point of timber on the western side of the flats, from which I took bearings to our tent and the flag on the granite knob as well as to all the points round the lake. In the evening I took transit observations on an approximate meridian; obtained also an emersion of the first satellite of Jupiter, which gives as the longitude of the camp, 119° 56′ 30″, while by rate it should be Lon. 119° 58′ 15″.

September 19.—After taking a set of time observations I crossed the Truckee on our raft, and, accompanied by Dustin, went to my station on the granite knob, from which I took a complete set of bearings. This knob is an exceedingly rough white granite hill, or rather mass of rocks, standing in the center of the flats, connected, however, to the main ridge of the Sierra on the west, by a low, smooth and even ridge, that runs out in a north-easterly direction from the mountain, on the south of a low gap in the Sierra, which is certainly the lowest pass in these parts. I have not heard it spoken of under any name and believe it is unexplored; it leads over to the Slippery Ford branch of the South Fork, and unquestionably would be the pass most suitable for a railroad should the hight of this valley not be insurmountable; the pass cannot be 500 feet above the flats of Bigler Lake Valley. I would have liked much to have explored it. A fine view of the lake is obtained from this station. The lake is entirely closed in with mountains, and it is impossible to detect the opening by which the Truckee River flows from it. Indeed, no one I have spoken to on the subject has been able to give me any exact information in relation to it, and some even have expressed a doubt as to whether the lake has an outlet at all! The mountains on the north-western shore gives some indication that there might be a passage that way.

≈≈≈

There is no lake in California, which for beauty and variety of scenery, is to be compared to Bigler Lake.

—GHG, "Lake Bigler," *Hutchings' Illustrated California Magazine*, September 1857

In September 1857 Hutchings' Illustrated California Magazine *published an article entitled "Lake Bigler." Although attributed to GHG, publisher James Mason Hutchings would later note that the author was George H. Goddard, the surveyor who led the mapping expedition that produced the*

1855 Report of a Survey of a Portion of the Eastern Boundary of Califor-
nia and of a Reconnaissance of the Old Carson and Johnson Immigrant
Roads over the Sierra Nevada for the Office of the California Surveyor-
General. In the 1857 magazine article, GHG, or Goddard, revisited Lake
Tahoe, provided updated details, and expanded on some of the human
history his 1855 report did not adequately address. GHG concludes that
through his "poor attempt of the pencil" he hopes "to induce a desire to
visit one of California's noblest lakes." GHG will soon get his wish, but
visitors will arrive not for the "beauty and variety of the scenery," but
for dreams of riches. Within a few months, thousands would descend
upon Lake Tahoe as the Comstock Lode silver rush detonates.

This beautiful lake is situated in a valley of the Sierra Nevada at the
eastern base of the central ridge, a few miles north of the main road of
travel to Carson Valley. It lies at an elevation of some 5,800 feet above
the level of the sea, all about 1,500 above Carson Valley, from which it
is divided by a mountain ridge three to four miles across.

The southern shores of this lake were explored during the state wagon-
road survey of 1855, all its extreme southern latitude determined at
38° 57'. The 120th meridian of west longitude divides the lake pretty
equally, giving its western shore to California and its eastern to Utah.
Its northern extremity is only known by report, which is still so con-
tradictory that the length of the lake cannot be set down with anything
like accuracy. It can hardly exceed, however, twenty miles in length by
about six in breadth; notwithstanding, it has been called forty, and
even sixty miles long.

The surrounding mountains rise from one to three, and, perhaps,
in some cases, four thousand feet above the surface of the lake. They
are principally composed of friable white granite, so water-worn that,
although they are rough, and often covered with rocks and boulders,
yet they show no cliffs or precipices. Their bases, of granite sand, rise in
majestic curves from the plain of the valley to their steeper flanks. Many
of the smaller hills are but high heaps of boulders, the stony skeletons
decaying *in situ*, half buried in their granite *debris*.

The shores of the lake, at least of its southern coast, are entirely formed
of granite sand; not a pebble is there to mar its perfect smoothness.

A dense pine-forest extends from the water's edge to the summits
of the surrounding mountains, except in some points where a peak

of more than ordinary elevation rears its bald head above the waving forest. An extensive satampy [swampy] flat lies on its southern shore, through which the Upper Truckee slowly meanders, gathering up, in its tortuous course, all the streams which flow from the south or south-east. The deep blue of the waters indicates a considerable depth to the lake. The water is perfectly fresh. The lake well stocked with salmon trout. It is resorted to at certain seasons by the neighboring Indians, for fishing.

Although lying so near the main road of travel, little has been known of this lake until quite a recent period. There is no doubt this is the lake of which the Indians informed Colonel Fremont, when encamped at Pyramid Lake, at the mouth of the Salmon-Trout or Truckee river, and which he thus relates, under date of January 15, 1844: "They made on the ground a drawing of the river, which they represented as issuing from another lake in the mountains, three or four days distant, in a direction a little west of south; beyond which they drew a mountain, and farther still two rivers, on one of which they told us that people like ourselves travelled." How clear does this description read to us, now that we know the localities!

Afterwards, when crossing the mountains near Carson Pass, Colonel Fremont caught sight of this lake, but, deceived by the great altitude of the mountains to its east, and the apparent gap in the western ridge at Johnson Pass, he laid it down as being on the California side of the mountains, at the head of the south fork of the American River. In the map attached to Colonel Fremont's report, it is there called *Mountain Lake*, but in the general map of the explorations by Charles Preuss it is named *Lake Bonpland*. In Wilkes's map, and others published about the period of the gold discovery, it bears the former name. When Colonel Johnson laid out his road across the mountains, the lake was passed unnoticed, except under the general term of Lake Valley. General Winn's Indian expedition, or the emigrant relief train, first named it Lake Bigler, after our late governor. Under this name it was first depicted in its transmountain position in Eddy's state map, and thus the name has become established.

There is no lake in California which, for beauty and variety of scenery, is to be compared to Bigler Lake; but it is not its beauty of situation alone that will attract us there. A geological interest is fastening upon it, for there we see what so many other of the great valleys of the Sierra once were. The little stream of the Upper Truckee, though but of yesterday, has yet carried down its sandy deposits through ages, sufficient to form the five miles of valley flats, from the foot of the Johnson Pass to the present margin of the lake, and still the work progresses. The shallows at the mouth of the river are stretching across toward the first point on the eastern slope of the lake, and at the same time the water level of the lake is evidently subsiding. . . .

The point at which the Upper Truckee discharges into the lake is indicated by the smoke of our camp fires. The first depression in the mountains to our right is the Daggett Pass to Carson Valley; beyond the next group of mountains lies the old pass of the Johnson Wagon Road to Eagle Valley. Nearly opposite, under a rocky point on the east shore of the lake, is the celebrated Indian cave, with its legendary romance. On the north rises the lofty mountain of Wassan peak. From the western side, the Truckee river finds its outlet, but the exact position seems to be still a myth. The high peaks to the northwest, in the distance, are near the Truckee Pass.

But our poor attempt of the pencil can give but a faint idea of the beauty of the spot; we can only hope to recall to those whose eye has already beheld the scene, what must ever be one of memory's most pleasing pictures; while in those who have not yet seen it we hope to induce a desire to visit one of California's noblest lakes.

≈≈≈

The very romantic and singular position of the
lake will yet make it famous the world over.

—"Description of Lake Bigler," *Tulare County Record*, July 23, 1859

Beginning in 1859, the Comstock Lode silver rush inundated the Lake Tahoe region.

Roads to the Lake Tahoe Basin provided main arteries to the Comstock Lode boomtowns of Virginia City and Gold Hill. Cognizance of the lake exploded, and business soared. Settlements, trading posts, taverns, and way stations experienced a meteoric rise. New settlements materialized everywhere. Supplying food and supplies to the wayfaring strangers yielded immediate and immense profits. More people meant more and better roads, expanding entry to the Comstock and boosting economic expectations.

There was also a demand to learn more about Lake Tahoe or Lake Bigler or whatever the lake might be called on any given day. Newspapers and journals were filled with sketches and advertisements for the exquisite blue lake high in the Sierra Nevada. An example is presented here. On July 23, 1859, the Tulare County Record *newspaper reprinted a short article recently published in the* Genoa (NV) Enterprise *extolling the splendor and commercial possibilities of Lake Tahoe. It was a representative sample of the full-blown promotion of Lake Tahoe common at the start of the Comstock Lode rush. The word* beautiful *is used four times in the brief item.*

The Tulare County Record *was published for only a few months in the middle of 1859. It relied heavily on reprinted articles from other publications, a standard practice of the era.*

DESCRIPTION OF LAKE BIGLER.—The southeastern extremity of the lake, where we camped for the night, is bounded by the most beautiful shore we ever beheld, describing a beautiful curve of the most astonishing regularity, the length of which is about six miles. The lake, as near as we can judge, is about fifty miles long by an average width of fifteen miles. Though situated as it is, near the summit of the Sierras, at an elevation of about six thousand feet above the level of the sea, the peaks of the mountains, with which it is almost entirely surrounded, seem only as hills. The very romantic and singular position of the lake will yet make it famous the world over, and doubtless in after years it will furnish themes for the romancer; its fame will be sung by a poet, and its beauty described by the pen of Goldsmith. Capt. Simpson's artist, Beck, executed two or three sketches of the lake, which certainly do him credit. The water of the lake is perfectly transparent and apparently pure.

Although the surrounding peaks are yet white with snow, from which the inlets to the lake derive their waters, the water in the lake is of a very desirable temperature for bathing; and though this beautiful and interesting body of water is situated only about sixty miles from Placerville, by an excellent stage road, and is beyond all doubt naturally one of the most interesting and agreeable resorts for pleasure and amusement on the borders of the Pacific, yet there are no boats of any description on, or any improvements about the lake. It abounds in a variety of fish, principally consisting of salmon and speckled trout. The Truckee river, leaving the lake from the north end, is its only outlet.

The mountains surrounding the lake come in many places precipitately to the water's edge, while at other points, particularly at the southern end, the country spreads out into a beautiful valley several miles in extent, affording ample pasturage for a large number of stock.

[Originally published in] *Genoa [NV] Enterprise.*

TWO

Development and Disquiet

1860–1869

The spotlight shone brightly on Lake Tahoe in the 1860s. The history of Lake Tahoe from 1860 to 1869 marked the moment when the Euro-Americans unmistakably realized that the Gem of the Sierra could be both an emotional sanctuary and an exploitable resource.

The catalyst of the Comstock Lode silver strike placed Lake Tahoe smack-dab in the middle of the main routes to the lode's nucleus of Virginia City. Awareness of the lake skyrocketed, and business boomed. Settlements, trading posts, taverns, and way stations sprung up seemingly overnight. Newborn communities ringed Lake Tahoe, popping up in Lake Valley, McKinney's, Tahoe City, Lake Forest, Agate Bay, Tahoe Vista, Kings Beach, Glenbrook, and Edgewood. The earliest resorts opened their doors by 1860, and by mid-decade, nearly fifteen hotels were constructed. With the completion of the transcontinental railroad in 1869, access to Lake Tahoe through the Truckee Station, twelve miles to the north, improved dramatically. It fostered a tourist surge, and soon additional lakeside resorts flourished.

Ranchers, livery stables, truck farmers, dairies, and commercial fishers reaped immediate profits. Lucrative hay production yielded hundreds of tons annually.

Additional roads to Lake Tahoe were carved through the forests and granite knobs, cresting the mountain ridges, significantly expanding access to the Comstock, and enhancing commercial prospects. The increase in traffic was startling. Over a three-month period in 1866, 6,667 pedestrians, 3,164 stage passengers, 5,000 pack animals, 2,564 teams, and 4,649 cattle would navigate the Lake Bigler (or Tahoe) Wagon Road skirting Lake Tahoe's south shore. In 1860–1861, a segment of the Pony Express, operated by William Russell, Alexander Majors, and William B. Waddell, hugged the lake. Friday's Station was established as a Pony Express stop near Kingsbury Grade at what is today known as Stateline, Nevada.

But as none of these roads encircled the lake and even the popular thoroughfares were often in disrepair, steamship travel was preeminent. Hopeful silver seekers, timber, and fish were frequent passengers on the steamers. The vessels, ranging from merely functional to comfortable, transported visitors to docks and resorts at Carnelian Bay (sometimes spelled "Cornelian"), Brockway, Glenbrook, Tallac Point, and Emerald Bay.

Utilizing the extraordinary translucent lake water for public benefit was also debated. In 1865 civil engineer and surveyor Alexis Von Schmidt detonated the first controversy over Lake Tahoe water when he proposed to supply San Francisco by diverting lake water down the Truckee River Canyon via a series of tunnels and canals through the ridges above the North Fork American River. Needless to say, some disagreed, often vehemently, with the huge and expensive venture. It was a hullabaloo that would continue for many years. Other voices, usually lonely ones at the time, warned of adverse consequences of overdevelopment and resource depletion at Lake Tahoe.

Among the cautionary concerns were those that rightfully lamented the rapid loss of Washoe dominion and ancestral lands. The territory of the Washoe people was overrun by miners, ranchers, merchants, settlers, and other interests with the approval and encouragement of all levels of government. This *encroachment* (the legal term of art used by the federal government to describe the seizing of tribal lands) was completed within a few years. By December 1862 the Washoe had lost all their lands. Despite their loss, the Washoe people resolved to remain on their homeland. Many refused to relocate and survived by forming communities on the outskirts of Euro-American settlements. Washoe maintained personal association with their native country by working in the timber and dairy industries or for resort owners. The men worked as hiking and fishing guides. Washoe women toiled as domestic labor or crafted baskets for the tourist trade. Washoe leaders petitioned government officials for redress of their losses and the destruction of their territory, but these entreaties were mostly ignored.

In addition to the economic boom, Lake Tahoe was rapidly becoming an artistic mecca. Painters, writers, and even the pioneers of the new medium of photography flocked to chronicle and celebrate the Gem of the Sierra. Although the lake was bursting into public consciousness, for many, Lake Tahoe remained largely a mysterious, unknown, perhaps unknowable, landscape. With pen, paintbrush, and film, artists helped fill some gaps, albeit occasionally with inaccurate, exaggerated, or fanciful descriptions and images.

For the burgeoning tourist population, the primary allure of Lake Tahoe was as a splendid setting to refresh their spirit, to commune with nature as they understood it, and, if people could afford it, simply to relax. It is a vision of the lake that has continued unabated to the present day.

However, a pressing question for growing numbers was simply what to call the lake. Should it be Lake Bigler, or Lake Tahoe, or perhaps something else? One alternative name was introduced by Yuba County assemblyman David L. Haun in Assembly Bill 437 in the 1861 California State Assembly. Haun's suggestion? The lake should be christened Tula Tulia. It did not pass.

≈≈≈

I . . . have seldom witnessed any scene in Europe or elsewhere to compare with it in extent and grandeur.
—J. Ross Browne, "A Peep at Washoe," *Harper's New Monthly Magazine*, December 1860

As the 1860s dawned, Lake Tahoe was in transition. While the California gold rush of the 1850s had only marginally affected the Lake Tahoe Basin, the Comstock Lode silver rush was immediately impactful, not only in Lake Tahoe but throughout the surrounding territory, usually referred to as Washoe. Commencing in earnest in 1859, the silver rush was in full flight as the new decade began. Thousands descended on the Lake Valley and the Washoe region, with most following the route from Placerville to the south shore of the lake. The economy of the Basin boomed, dozens of communities blossomed, and merchants happily catered to the needs and desires of the arriving throng.

But getting there was often frenzied. Pack trains jammed the roads. Lodgings and way stations teemed with the hopeful and the hotheaded. Expensive meals of questionable quality were dished up, sometimes with only minutes to bolt them down. Tempers flared. Dreamers dreamed. Grifters schemed. The road to Washoe was chaotic.

In 1860, author J. Ross Browne recounted the hectic scene in an article entitled "A Peep at Washoe" for Harper's New Monthly Magazine. *Inspired by the Silver Rush, Browne chronicled the follies, serendipities, anxieties, good cheer, and desperations of those seeking a better life in the Washoe. While couched in humor, Browne's eyewitness narrative is evocative, full of detail and remarkably authentic.*

J. Ross Browne was memorable in his own right. Born in Ireland in 1812, Browne emigrated to the United States in 1833, when his father, Thomas, a zealous Irish nationalist, was imprisoned by the British but released upon agreeing to leave Ireland for good. By the early 1840s J. Ross Browne was living in Kentucky but possessed a peripatetic soul. He worked on a riverboat, sailed on a whaling ship bound for Zanzibar, and wrote and illustrated books and articles, including a well-received 1846 volume entitled Etchings of a Whaling Cruise.

In 1849 Browne contracted gold fever and joined the California gold rush. In California, J. Ross Browne was seemingly everywhere. He held various government offices, including agent for the Treasury Department; surveyor, or the chief administrative officer, for Custom Houses and Mints; investigator of Indian and Land Office disputes; and official reporter of the debates of the California State Constitutional Convention in 1850. While best known for his popular nonfiction, Browne also authored, in 1867, the Report of J. Ross Browne on the Mineral Resources of the States and Territories West of the Rocky Mountains, *an important scientific monograph for the U.S. Department of the Treasury.*

Scholars suggest that Browne's lighthearted writing style influenced other American West literary lights, such as Mark Twain, Bret Harte, and Dan De Quille. In 1872 some of Browne's illustrations were used in Mark Twain's Roughing It.

J. Ross Browne died in 1875 at the age of fifty-four.

In this passage from "A Peep at Washoe," J. Ross Browne describes his arrival at the Lake Tahoe Basin, featuring a wobbly descent of a slick mountain slope, an encounter with "four large brown wolves," and a miserable night at the Lake House, a "hotel" of sorts. At the Lake House, Browne spends the night with two or three hundred other intrepid sojourners, stomachs filled with meager vittles and bad whiskey, and barely tolerates the hotel's edgy proprietor, who did more "scolding,

swearing, gouging, and general hotel work, in the brief space of half an
hour, than any man I ever saw."

I walked on rapidly in the hope of making Woodford's—the station
on the eastern slope of the mountain—before night, and by degrees
got ahead of the main body of footmen, who had left Strawberry that
morning. In a narrow gorge, a short distance from the commencement
of the descent into Lake Valley, I happened to look up a little to the
right, where, to my astonishment, I perceived four large brown wolves
sitting on their haunches not over twenty feet from me! They seemed
entirely unconcerned at my presence, except in so far as they may have
indulged in some speculation as to the amount of flesh contained on
my body. As I was entirely unarmed, I thought it would be but common
politeness to speak to them, so I gave them a yell in the Indian language.
At this they retired a short distance, but presently came back again as
if to inquire the exact meaning of my salutation. I now thought it best
not to be too intimate, for I saw that they were getting rather familiar
on a short acquaintance; and picking up a stick of wood, I made a rush
and a yell at them which must have been formidable in the extreme.
This time they retreated more rapidly, and seemed undecided about
returning. At this crisis in affairs a pack train came along, the driver of
which had a pistol. Upon pointing out the wolves to him he fired, but
missed them. They then retreated up the side of the mountain, and I
saw nothing more of them.

The descent of the "grade" was the next rough feature in our day's
journey. From the point overlooking Lake Valley the view is exceedingly fine. Lake Bigler a sheet of water forty or fifty miles in length by
ten or fifteen wide lies embosomed in the mountains in full view from
this elevation; but there was a drizzling sleet which obscured it on
this occasion. I had a fine sight of it on my return, however, and have
seldom witnessed any scene in Europe or elsewhere to compare with
it in extent and grandeur.

The trail on the grade was slippery with sleet, and walking upon it
was out of the question. Running, jumping, and sliding were the only
modes of locomotion at all practicable. I tried one of the short cuts,
and found it an expeditious way of getting to the bottom. Some trifling
obstruction deprived me of the use of my feet at the very start, after
which I traveled down in a series of gyrations at once picturesque and

complicated. When I reached the bottom I was entirely unable to comprehend how it had all happened; but there I was, pack and baggage, all safely delivered in the snow—bones sound, and free of expense.

At the Lake House a tolerably good-sized shanty at the foot of the grade we found a large party assembled, taking their ease as they best could in such a place, without much to eat and but little to drink, except old-fashioned tarentula-juice, "warranted to kill at forty paces."

The host of the Lake was in a constant state of nervous excitement, and did more scolding, swearing, gouging, and general hotel work, in the brief space of half an hour, than any man I ever saw. He seemed to be quite worn-out with his run of customers from a hundred to three hundred of a night, and nowhere to stow 'em all cussin' at him for not keepin' provisions: and how could he, when they ate him clean out every day, and some of 'em never paid him, and never will?

I was not sorry to get clear of the Lake House, its filth, audits, troubles.

≈≈≈

This lake . . . must soon become the Summer resort of the
wearied man of business and the seeker after pleasure.

—"A Day on Lake Bigler," *Sacramento Daily Union*, September 9, 1862

The rapid population growth of the Lake Tahoe Basin following the inception of the Comstock Lode silver rush did not escape the notice of the business minded. The commercial prospects offered by Lake Tahoe in the 1860s seemed limitless to entrepreneurs, whether for the exploitation of natural resources, such as timber and fish, or for draining the purses of the hopeful miners and other visitors passing through on their way to the Washoe silver strike.

But for some shrewd investors and proprietors, Lake Tahoe was increasingly viewed as a potential gold mine for tourism. A few small-scale campgrounds and boarding houses, with aspirations to become resorts, had been established. But visionaries projected many more would soon materialize.

In the September 9, 1862, edition of the Sacramento Daily Union, *an article entitled "A Day on Lake Bigler" appeared. Written by a correspondent for the* Union, *identified only as EH, the article was a harbinger of many to follow.*

EH was in the vanguard of promoting Lake Tahoe as a vacation spot and refuge from the "busy, bustling world" for the upper classes. Rejecting any attempt at "poetical descriptions and displays of fine writing," EH was practical in his advocacy. He touted a laundry list of Lake Tahoe's attributes: "pure air, pure water, cool nights, freedom from noxious insects or reptiles, fine trees, fine cascades, clear, gurgling brooks, running over white sand and pebbles, picturesque rocks, good fish and easily caught, fine sailing, fine rowing." EH added, "This lake, being in a direct line between Sacramento and Carson, the Capitals of California and Nevada, and easily made accessible by good roads, must soon become the Summer resort of the wearied man of business and the seeker after pleasure."

EH made Lake Tahoe sound like paradise—and profitable. The argument was made repeatedly in subsequent years by innkeepers, resort owners, restaurateurs, real estate speculators, founders of religious retreats, artistes, merchants, and the occasional con artist.

A Day on Lake Bigler

[Correspondence of the *Union*.]

The only aim in writing out this sketch, from notes taken on the spot, is to convey to the distant reader a few plain matter-of-fact views in regard to a locality which, at no distant period, seems likely to attain a world-wide notoriety. Poetical descriptions and displays of fine writing, must be left to men of other tastes and other qualifications.

The exact elevation of this sheet of water, above the ocean, is not well settled, there being considerable difference in the measurements taken by engineers. It may be safely assumed, however, to be at least 5,000 feet, and is probably two or three hundred feet more. An inland sea, much larger, I believe, than the Sea of Galilee, at the elevation of one mile above tide water, is something remarkable in itself, and is hardly to be found anywhere else upon this planet. The basin of Lake Bigler is about 40 miles long by 15 to 20 wide, and is surrounded by a granite rim rising up one to three thousand feet above the level of the water. The lake itself covers little more than half the valley, the remainder being occupied by grassy meadows and heavy forests of pine and fir timber. The only break in this granite rim of the basin, is at the point where the pent up waters first found an outlet, and have worn down, during a series of years, a narrow channel in the solid rock, forming a deep chasm through which the Truckee river now flows. All around the sides of the valley the evidence is quite conclusive that, at some former period, the waters have been many hundreds of feet higher than now. The Western ridge, or chain of mountains, rises up to its full elevation (about 8,000 feet) within five or six miles of the lake, and then slopes off gradually to the Sacramento valley, in a distance of sixty miles. The Eastern chain, or rim of the basin, is quite narrow as compared to that on the West, and its altitude is much less. It rises a thousand feet or more above Lake Valley and slopes down rapidly to the series of valleys on the East. l am told by Mr. [Butler] Ives, a Government Surveyor, that Carson and Eagle valley are about 1,200 feet below Lake Bigler, and that Washoe is 200 feet above Eagle, (or 1,000 feet below Bigler). There is said to be a point between Washoe and Lake Valley where a tunnel of little more than two miles would bring all the waters of the Truckee on to the Eastern slope, where it could all be led to proper sites for milling purposes, in the vicinity of the silver mines, and where its power could be used in falling a thousand feet or more.

The great amount of water condensed by these high ridges is, to me, a matter of profound astonishment. The rain gauges kept last Winter on the Western slope, at elevations of 1,500 to 3,000 feet, all go to show that as we ascend the sides of the mountain the fall of rain or snow is rapidly augmented. In all that portion of the mountain which is 5,000 feet or more above the ocean, there must have been an aggregate fall of six to ten feet of water during the past season. Although this is far above the average, the amount must always be very great. The floods, so disastrous to California and Nevada, last season, were mainly produced by heavy falls of snow succeeded by rain storms which melted and carried off the previous deposits of snow, at elevations below 5,000 feet. Even now, (Sept. 1st,) I can look out from my window, here at Carson, upon huge banks of snow, not more than three or four miles distant, which are sending down their bright gushing streams upon the thirsty valleys. Were it not for these great reservoirs of pure water, crystalized and held fast upon the mountain tops during the Winter and Spring, and then, when the heats of Summer come and the rain has ceased to fall, are again gradually changed to a fluid state, and suffered to flow down in limpid streams to the parched and thirsty valleys; were it not for these beautiful provisions in the Divine economy, this whole region must have been a desert,

Treeless, lifeless, manless.

But I must not get poetical—I have promised to talk about Lake Bigler, a theme that is anything but poetical, at least so far as the name is concerned.

The first impression upon the mind, when emerging from the tall pine forest on the western shore of the lake, and looking out upon its placid waters, is that you have, at last, become truly isolated from the busy, bustling world, which has been left far behind. You have a full view of the opposite shore, embracing a circle extending thirty or forty miles, and yet no sign of human effort or human habitation is to be seen. At your foot there are three or four small boats in the little haven, and a solitary cabin, just back among the undisturbed trees. These small tokens are all which can be seen of the advanced guard of civilization. The main army is, I suppose, like John Brown's soul, "marching on" not far behind, and may soon come up and take possession. You have before you an expanse of water, three hundred or more square miles in extent, as clear, pure and transparent as it is possible for water to be. No muddy stream falls into Lake Bigler. All the gushing rivulets and cascades come from the granite mountains, and are consequently clear and pure at all times. In short, there is nothing in the whole basin to render the water turbid, and therefore it must always be transparent. This lake, being in a direct line between Sacramento and Carson, the Capitals of California and Nevada, and easily made accessible by good roads, must soon become the Summer resort of the wearied man of business and the seeker after pleasure. The locality seems to have all the elements which serve to make up a good watering place—pure air, pure water, cool nights, freedom from noxious insects or reptiles, fine trees, fine cascades, clear, gurgling brooks, running over white sand and pebbles, picturesque rocks, good fish and easily caught, fine sailing, fine rowing. All that is now wanted is a few good hotels and boarding houses, which will no doubt come along in proper time. . . .

After a sound slumber of a few hours, I rose up next morning, found a good breakfast on the table, a pleasant hostess to pour out the Coffee; recognized in one of the boarders an old acquaintance, . . . was shown round a fine vegetable garden where everything looked prosperous, and then started over the ridge to Carson, a wiser if not a better man for having spent a day on Lake Bigler.

E.H., Carson City, September 5th. [1862]

≈≈≈

At present the timber and lumber capabilities of the
borders of Lake Tahoe seem to be illimitable.
—"Foreign Gossip," *Sacramento Daily Union*, August 13, 1863

*The juxtaposition of Lake Tahoe as a road hub leading to the Comstock
Lode, a booming economy, and the need for lumber for structures, mine
timbering, railroad construction, and flume building made Lake Tahoe
Basin timber resources even more attractive during the 1860s.*

*Of course, lumber production in the broad Sierra Nevada territory
enveloping Lake Tahoe was operational prior to the silver rush. Demands
of the California gold rush had led to rapid development of timbering in
the region. In 1858, a year before the Comstock Lode silver rush began in
earnest, there were already more than forty lumber mills functional in
Nevada County, California, which borders Lake Tahoe. In the five-year
period prior to 1860, more than two hundred new lumber mills were
opened in California, the vast majority of which were in the Central
Sierra Nevada—where Lake Tahoe is. The Comstock Lode silver rush
was an additional impetus to timber production, and the Lake Tahoe
Basin was targeted for large-scale lumber ventures.*

*With the Lake Tahoe forests now subject to increased harvesting, the
questions became, how much lumber was available, and how long could
the resource last before depletion?*

*The desired answer sought by many of the era is best exemplified by
a widely referenced statement printed in the August 13, 1863, issue of the*
Sacramento Daily Union, *under the odd headline of "Foreign Gossip."
The* Union *evidently felt that Washoe City, Nevada Territory, a mere
thirty-five miles northeast of Lake Tahoe, was "foreign" when it reprinted
a brief article from the* Washoe Times, *a short-lived Washoe City newspaper. Washoe City (referred to historically as Old Washoe City), founded
in 1860, was primarily a lumber camp that also featured ore mills.
In the mid-1860s, it had a population of about six thousand and was*

the Washoe County seat. *The community faded with the completion of the Virginia and Truckee Railroad in 1869 and the transferring of the county seat to Reno in 1871. Today, Old Washoe City is a ghost town.*

In the reprinted article, the editor of the Washoe Times *described a recent visit to Lake Tahoe and rhapsodized over the "illimitable" timber resources and the "brilliant agricultural future" offered by the lake basin. The article concluded that the availability of timber appeared endless, and besides, the editor argued, if the forests are finally depleted, the harvested lands can be then used as "good ground" for growing cereal grains.*

The editor of the *Washoe Times* has lately made an excursion to this beautiful sheet of water and thus speaks of it: Lake Tahoe lies between the eastern and western summits of the Sierra Nevada—for, strange as it may seem, the Sierra Nevada really has two summits, a good many miles apart. It lies right in the line of the eastern boundary of California; and, somewhere in the southern half of it, is the angle whence that boundary, departing from a due north and south line, on the meridian of 120 degrees, breaks off in a southeast diagonal to the Colorado river at Mohave. The engineers, who are now surveying that boundary line, have cruelly robbed the lake of some ten miles of length with which imaginative tourists had previously invested it. Instead of its being from thirty to thirty-five miles long, it is now, under the "procrustean determination of science," but twenty-two. Whether the change of name from Bigler to Tahoe has caused it to shrink within its limits, is a question for politicians and not for philosophers. It has so many bays and promontories, on both its eastern and western sides, that to determine its average width is a matter of some difficulty. It may be ten miles and it may be less. The water of the lake is as pure as purity itself. People, with good eyes, tell us that they can distinctly see objects in it at the depth of two hundred feet. Its extreme depth has never yet been ascertained. It has been sounded by a line, nearly half a mile in length, without finding the bottom. They tell us that the biggest and best kind of trout bite voraciously at the hook two hundred feet beneath the surface.

As a general rule, the shores of the lake are the bases of bold, bluff mountains, whose tops are crowned with eternal snow, making what sailors call an "iron-bound shore;" but there are some deliciously agreeable exceptions to this general rule. The ground on which we stood when we made these observations is one of these exceptions. It is one of those tongues of low land, which, some thousands of years ago, was submerged by the waters of the lake, but, by the drainage of the lake, has become dry land, and has managed to clothe itself with a dense garment of colossal pines. A great part of this tract, which, aside from its present wealth of timber, promises a brilliant agricultural future, has been lately taken up by enterprising gentlemen of Washoe City, to whom we wish the best of luck. This land is covered with colossal specimens of yellow, sugar, pitch and fir pines, which, when connected with civilization on the east and west, will afford colossal fortunes for their owners. And it is not too great a tax on our prescience to prophesy that, in after years, when the arborescent honors of the day shall have been expelled, as good ground for the cereals will be found here as in any portion of California or Washoe. At present the timber and lumber capabilities of the borders of Lake Tahoe seem to be illimitable.

≈≈≈

It is conceded by all that for beauty and grandeur
the views . . . cannot be excelled.
—"A Few Notes about Lake Tahoe," San Francisco
Daily Alta California, July 1, 1865

By the mid-1860s, Lake Tahoe was in a transitional phase. Still focused on the demands of the nearby and booming Comstock Lode, the lake primarily featured a service economy supplying goods and services to the hopeful and the transient still flooding the Lake Tahoe Basin. Statistics bear this out. For example, in three months in 1866, a total of 7,000 pedestrians, 3,200 stagecoach passengers, 5,000 pack animals, 2,500 freight teams, and 4,700 cattle passed through Lake Tahoe's south shore communities.

But tourism was becoming increasingly important. Travelers, while impatient to reach the beckoning mineral wealth of the Washoe, needed a place to stay, some hearty nourishment, and a few drams of whiskey during their short visit to Lake Tahoe. Some, enchanted by the scenery, decided to linger. Prescient merchants and proprietors catered to this growing market. Lodgings that heralded the dawn of more luxurious resort properties to follow developed, particularly on the main route that passed through Lake Valley, around Cave Rock, by Glenbrook, until spilling over the ridge and slaloming down to Carson City.

These new accommodations were popular and offered a wide variety of activities, including boating, fishing, picnics, boat tours, hunting, horseback riding, fine dining, dancing, and gambling. And fueling this mid-decade surge were myriad depictions of the Lake Tahoe Basin offered by recent visitors and newspaper correspondents on assignment that enticed the interested to visit the lake. Some of these accounts were rudimentary, but many offered useful particulars wrapped in typically Victorian purple prose. An example is presented here.

On July 1, 1865, a correspondent to the San Francisco Daily Alta California, identified only as Stereoscope, recounted a visit to Lake Tahoe in an article entitled "A Few Notes about Lake Tahoe." The reporter provided capsule reviews of prominent locations such as Zephyr Cove, Cave Rock, and Emerald Bay. The rates for differing levels of lodging and comfort are itemized. The most intriguing sightseeing locales are noted. Highlighted is what awaits the wanderer in what Stereoscope labeled the "Silverland" of Virginia City and the Washoe.

The article was written two months after the end of the Civil War. Tensions still ran high, and memories were fresh. For instance, Stereoscope portrayed Cave Rock showcasing a "view [that] meets the eye that cannot be surpassed by any on this coast" with "the waves dashing musically at our feet." He then bitterly interjects: At "the summit stands a lofty flag-pole, from which floated proudly our glorious flag, until some dastardly wretch, to whom it was a reproach for his treason, vented his spite by cutting the ropes and destroying the flag."

Even in the Lake Tahoe wonderland, the outside world intruded.

A Few Notes about Lake Tahoe

From an Occasional Correspondent of the *Alta California*

Zephyr Cove Hotel, Lake Tahoe, June 25, 1865. Its Location, Etc.

Editors *Alta*:—This magnificent lake is situated between the eastern and western summits of the Sierra Nevada Mountains, at an altitude of 6,167 feet. It has a mean breadth of ten miles, by 25 in length, running north and south. The new road from Carson City runs along the Eastern shore of the lake for a distance of about fifteen miles. Coming from Carson, we first strike the lake at the residence of Captain

Pray, who has a beautiful ranch, residence and saw mill on its shore. Continuing along the shore for a mile or so, we arrive at the Logan House, situated on a bluff, near the shore, and from where we have a picturesque view of the lake. The hotel has some conveniences for sailing on the lake in the shape of good boats and a good pier, which affords a fine chance to enjoy some of the celebrated trout, cooked by one who takes a pride in so doing. From this place to Zephyr Cove the road, along the shore of the lake, runs through the grandest scenery and most varied portion of the lake. . . .

Cave Rock

. . . Nothing can be more beautiful than the view from this position. The road comes to the edge of the lake; it is well watered, smooth, and has running water every half mile. We next come to the Cave Rock, where there is a fine, smooth and broad road leading around its base, at some distance above the water, while above us rises a perpendicular mass of rock to the height of two hundred feet, and on the summit stands a lofty flag-pole, from which floated proudly our glorious flag, until some dastardly wretch, to whom it was a reproach for his treason, vented his spite by cutting the ropes and destroying the flag. Here one can obtain a fine view of the lake, being able to see almost the whole of that noble sheet of water. The summits on the western shore loom up grandly, and the waves dashing musically at our feet. You clamber up into the cave; the entrance is grand, but the cave continued only a short distance and on its walls is a kind of pitch or resin which is black and has a bitter but not disagreeable taste. In ascending the rock and near the summit, you encounter huge, broken rocks, but a passage is found through them, and the traveller soon arrives on the summit, and stands at the base of the flag-pole. Here a view meets the eye that cannot be surpassed by any on this coast, and it is conceded by all that for beauty and grandeur the views on this coast cannot be excelled.

The View from the Summit

Looking southward, at our feet and two hundred feet below, runs the road along the shore, until it becomes lost in the forest. One can trace along the shore, in the shoal water, the different-colored sand and the rocks at the bottom of the lake. Beyond is a wooded point, and in turn comes Zephyr Cove in all its loveliness; then another point projecting far into the water, with three or four solitary trees; and then another, fading away into the distant mountains at the head of the lake. On the opposite shore, to the southwest, rise the grandest peaks at the western summits, capped with a mantle of pure snow, contrasting strongly with the mighty precipices of jagged rock, on which is an irregular growth of tall forest trees; and in the ravines lie masses of snow, forming a white streak almost to the base of the chain. As one looks to the west, the mountains seem to be of less height and to have less snow, whilst those at the foot of the lake, to the northwest, are entirely clear of snow, which, however, may still be seen on some of the more distant peaks to the north. Looking at the shore as it stretches toward the foot of the lake, northward, cove after cove is seen stretching away, each one distinct and perfect, until they fade away behind some projecting point in the extreme distance. . . .

Inducements for Tourists

The steamers being in running order, parties can go to any part of the lake without trouble. As for hotels, if one wishes to spend money freely, and be exceedingly fashionable, he can be accommodated at the Lake House, or at the Glenbrook Hotel; board $21 per week. If one wishes to have a comfort, without much parade, there is the Logan House, board $15, or the Zephyr Cove House, board $12 per week. The fare from Sacramento, by the Pioneer Line, is $15, time eighteen hours; from Carson, $10, time six hours. From here there is a good road to the Big Trees, as one can go to Virginia and back by way of Donner Lake, making one of the most interesting trips in the country. Taking the boat from San Francisco, and the cars from Sacramento you soon speed over the plains and strike the foot-hills, then by stage up into the mountains, where everything is lovely at this time of the year; over the cragged summit of this glorious range of mountains, and then stopping at these lovely lakes; then over the eastern summit. Leaving the trees behind as you descend the eastern slope you behold the Washoe coun- try at your feet, with its rounded ranges of barren mountains, range beyond range, until you can distinguish no longer; then down to the valleys, then up the mountains to Silverland, where Virginia nestles close to the side of the giant Mount Davidson, thousands of feet above the level of the sea, where sage brush meets the eye everywhere—where an endless train of toiling teams ascend the steep grades cut around the mountainsides—where the clatter of the mills never stop—where Washoe zephyrs come so gently that you shut your eyes and hold fast to some solid object until the majestic column of sand marches by—where rows of donkeys driven by Celestial drivers look wistfully from under their burdens of gnarled scrub oak—where each man hopes soon to be by some lucky turn of the wheel of fortune a millionaire. Then back home again by the other route, through a succession of new and grand scenes which are characteristic of this land of gold—and tell me where can such a varied trip be found. Take the advice of one who has been there, and try it. The fare from Sacramento to Virginia by each road is $45, time twenty-four hours. Board is from $2 in California to $3.50 in Nevada. Persons who can spare a week or so from their business can make no trip which is as pleasant as the one which I have sketched. I do not think that one can be found in the United States to compare with this, either for those seeking health or those who wish to see the beauties of nature.

STEREOSCOPE.

≈≈≈

> White caps! . . . Why I've seen 'em running across here
> like a flock of sheep in a sweet potato patch.
> —"A Cruise on a Mountain Sea, Number Three,"
> *Sacramento Daily Union*, August 1, 1866

While Lake Tahoe tourism was expanding during the 1860s, the ability to easily circumnavigate the lake by land was not keeping pace. Except for the main thoroughfares and toll roads to the Washoe, public roads surrounding the lake were rude affairs or were temporary service paths for the flourishing timber operations. The first fully accessible road to circle Lake Tahoe was not completed until 1935. Prior to that, the best, and often the only, way to efficiently circle the inner perimeter of the lake was by boat.

The first verifiable, non-Indigenous vessels on the lake are considered to be two twenty-eight-foot whaleboats freighted over the heavily congested Johnson's Pass route from Sacramento in August 1860 for Lapham and Company on the south shore, and for Rufus Walton at Glenbrook. Other sailing vessels would follow.

In 1864 the first steamships arrived at Lake Tahoe, starting with the Governor Blasdel (1864) and followed by a flotilla of the most famous of the nineteenth-century Lake Tahoe steamers—Governor Stanford (1873), Meteor (1876), Tod Goodwin (1884), Tallac (1890), and the Tahoe (1896). Add to that list the rising number of commercial fishing boats, and Lake Tahoe had ever-increasing options for water transportation and commerce.

Despite tourist and resort advertisements ballyhooing the endless beauty and tranquility of Lake Tahoe's waters, plied by comfortable craft equipped with the latest safety equipment and passenger niceties, travelling around the lake by boat was not easy. The knowledgeable cautioned against complacency and issued warnings to be wary when navigating the unpredictable Gem of the Sierra.

The August 1, 1866, edition of the Sacramento Daily Union *reinforced this concern in an article entitled "A Cruise on a Mountain Sea, Number Three." The author, who identified himself as Winkle Jenkins, recounted his adventure aboard a schooner bound from Tahoe City to Emerald Bay in the company of his boisterous travelling companions—six-foot-two, 280-pound Ramsdale Buoy; Milton Tenderloin, a young man who, Winkle tells us, has just escaped a "severe sentence to a grocery business"; Mark Anthony Oldbuck, as "jolly and beaming" as a character from Dicken's* Pickwick Papers; *and Hardtack Carrigan, a relentless hardware drummer. Winkle is clear about the dangers of sailing on Lake Tahoe: "Smiling and lovely as she looks, Tahoe has fits of anger, when an old salt would prefer to encounter the wildest winds and the most threatening waves of the Atlantic to braving her perilous, freakish wrath." However, in this case, the problem was not inclement weather; it was lack of wind.*

A Cruise on a Mountain Sea

Number Three

Tahoe is a good name for the queen of mountain lakes; not because it is either high-sounding, musical or, in any of its several constructions, peculiarly appropriate, but because it is distinctive; there is but one Tahoe in the world. . . .

It would be a good day's work to cross the lake and journey to the edge of that snow by the shortest practicable route, and then the traveler would need a long day's rest. When such facts as these are learned, the mind begins to grasp the grandeur of Tahoe. There is much more which can only be learned by embarking, under the care of a skillful navigator and an intelligent guide, upon the sparkling water of this mountain sea. Smiling and lovely as she looks, Tahoe has fits of anger, when an old salt would prefer to encounter the wildest winds and the most threatening waves of the Atlantic to braving her perilous, freakish wrath.

A night's rest, while one of the pioneers of Lake Valley rowed over in the direction of Tahoe City to notify the Captain of the only available schooner that has been fitted up for the accommodation of tourists, refreshed Mr. Oldbuck and his companions. Next morning, as soon as the matin meal had been dispatched, the party gathered on the little wharf which had been built for a landing, and also as a protection for small boats against the breakers when the lake was in a tempestuous mood. The water was perfectly calm now, and near the shore shone like an emerald in the sunshine. On the adjacent beach the sand was thickly sown with jasper and cornelian, beautiful specimens of which were transferred to the pockets of Jenkins and Tenderloin. No schooner was in sight. She would not come into view until she should round Sugar-Pine Point, a long, low peninsula on the western shore, covered with valuable timber. Hours passed before the white sail was detected—a mere speck against the green—by the keen eye of Buoy, who knew exactly where to fix his gaze.

"Thar ain't enough wind here to snuff a candle," observed the big man, "but thar's a stiff breeze blowing over yonder. They've got Meeks' wind by this time."

"Whose wind?" inquired Hardtack.

"Meeks. The wind blowing out of the gorge at Meeks' creek. The winds to reckon on here blow out of Blackwood's, Meeks', Emerald Bay and Fallen Leaf Lake. If they don't blow, a sailing vessel might as well be anchored, for she can't make any headway. The schooner is heading for this point now, but if we don't see the white caps running out of Emerald Bay she won't get here till near two o'clock."

Jenkins looked at the waters of the lake, so quiet and unruffled as far as he could see, and couldn't help expressing a wonder whether it was possible for white-capped waves to show themselves on that calm surface.

"White caps!" responded Buoy; "why I've seen 'em running across here like a flock of sheep in a sweet potato patch."

Jenkins booked the simile, but thought it would hardly be of service to a poet smitten with the charms of Tahoe. He would take Tenderloin's opinion on that point.

"Yonder," said Buoy, pointing to a streak of smoke near the eastern shore, but far to the northward, "is the steamboat coming out of Zephyr Cove. She is an old schooner, with a steam engine aboard, and drives a fair business, carrying lumber across the lake for the sawmills. There's not many people around here now, and all kinds of trade are dull. But thar's the making of a great country here. Just look at it. Here we have plenty of the finest timber in the world, enough to keep fifty sawmills busy. And right over that ridge," pointing to the eastern range, "is a God-forsaken region that won't grow anything. Barren? Why, if a man owned seventy-five thousand million acres of it he couldn't pasture a whip-poor-will. But silver draws people thar, and they must have timber. Then that's mines near this lake that will be worth something one of these days, and at this end, where the Lake House stood, will be the Saratoga of the Pacific coast."

"Saratoga!" exclaimed Jenkins with a nauseating recollection of Congress Spring. "If they had such a lake as this anywhere in the Atlantic States, Saratoga, Newport and the White Hills would be deserted."

No white caps were running out of Emerald Bay. The schooner seemed to creep slowly along the western shore of the Lake, though far on her way across, and scarcely a ripple floated over the smooth, bright expanse of water between her and her destination. And when the vessel at last showed her hull and appeared to be within a mile of the landing, the party of tourists ascertained that they would have ample time to get dinner before she would be near enough to receive them and their traps. And they began to realize the magnitude of this Lake, where all apparent distance was a deception. . . .

It was the Captain's opinion that she couldn't reach Emerald Bay that night, although the entrance appeared to be within rifle shot, and therefore the tourists prepared to enjoy a sleep on the lake.

With night and the moon and stars came a gentle breeze, enough to ripple the water or rustle a leaf, but the schooner seemed to sleep upon the quiet bosom of the lake with heaven below and heaven above. The evening star, just over a western peak, made a pathway of light across the glassy surface, and all the bright hosts of the sky were mirrored in the lake. The mountains loomed up darkly, their summits being sharply defined against a sky o'erspread with silver radiance.

The night was delicious—the scene enchanting. But the temperature was unmistakably frosty. Tenderloin and Jenkins, with buttoned overcoats, seated upon the bow of the schooner, recalled the poetry applicable to the hour and scene, had intervals of silent communion with all this affluence of loveliness, during which it is to be supposed their thoughts were too deep to cast a spray of words, shivered, yawned and finally sank upon the deck to rest for the night, with a soft bundle of rope for a pillow, a spring plank for a mattress, and two thick blankets for a mutual quilt.

Winkle.

≈≈≈

Why should not California match her other excellences
and glories with the grandest aqueduct in the world?

—"Water from Lake Tahoe," San Francisco Daily
Alta California, October 17, 1866

While timber, fish, and tourism appeared to be the most exploitable resources at mid-nineteenth-century Lake Tahoe, one other important lake asset came to be viewed as essential to societal development by some—namely, the crystal-clear alpine water.

In the mid-1860s, it dawned upon civic leaders in San Francisco, two hundred miles west of the Lake Tahoe Basin, that water from the magnificent mountain lake could be diverted for use in the City by the Bay.

In 1865 civil engineer and surveyor Alexis Von Schmidt proposed to supply San Francisco by diverting lake water down the Truckee River Canyon via a series of tunnels and canals through the ridges above the North Fork American River. Von Schmidt proposed damming the outlet of the Truckee River at Tahoe City, raising the level of the lake by six feet, transforming Lake Tahoe into a massive reservoir, and siphoning the water for use in San Francisco. His calculations determined that these undertakings would provide about seventy million gallons of water per day to the San Francisco Bay Area. Alexis Von Schmidt argued that his plan would benefit both California and Nevada, should be noncontroversial, and would provide the greatest good to the greatest number.

Nevada disagreed. George A. Nourse, the attorney general of Nevada, questioned the legitimacy of the Von Schmidt project. In a sharply worded letter to the Sacramento Daily Union *on October 9, 1866, Nourse outlined his objections to the scheme on both legal and moral grounds:*

> *The Truckee river is now the only outlet of Lake Tahoe. Along its course mills have been erected, whose owners have a right to the use of its water by appropriation, and the owners of scores and hundreds of fine ranches along its hanks have, under the common law, the right to the full flow of the stream in its natural channel, undiminished. . . . It can hardly be expected that those thus interested in the water power of the Truckee will quietly allow the reservoir which supplies the water of that stream to be tapped and their water supply taken away for the benefit of the western slope of the Sierra—more particularly as the late law of Congress allowing patents to issue for mining claims specially recognizes and protects water rights acquired by appropriation.*

The following excerpt from the article "Water from Lake Tahoe," printed in the October 17, 1866, issue of the San Francisco Daily Alta California *presented Alexis Von Schmidt's pointed response to Nevada attorney general Nourse's opposition.*

Von Schmidt's 1865 water diversion plan did not come to fruition, but the issue was revisited many times in subsequent decades.

Water from Lake Tahoe

A. W. Von Schmidt, Chief Engineer of the Lake Tahoe Water Company, joins issue with the Attorney General of Nevada, in regard to the legality and feasibility of the scheme of carrying a portion of the waters of said lake into the territory of California. The following is an extract from his rejoinder:

The area of the lake is estimated at 240 square miles. One foot in depth of this surface would give a daily supply for the year of 13,748,252 gallons. If required, the lake can be raised six feet by placing a small dam at its outlet, and can be drawn six feet below its present surface, which would give us twelve feet of water from the entire surface of the lake, or 64,979,024 gallons per day. But should we take all the water that discharges itself from the outlet now running down the Truckee river, there still would be more water in the river below us than can possibly be used by the mills, for the reason that many large streams of water enter the river below the point of our dam.

It is also well understood that the mills that require water will be located one below the other, and that after one mill uses the water it runs again into the river and continues on to the next mill below, and so on down the stream.

In regard to irrigation I am satisfied there will always be sufficient water for all purposes required in that line.

In reference to the rights of the two States in which Lake Tahoe is situated, I think it would be well to consider their respective portion of the lake in each State. One-third of the lake is east of the line dividing Nevada from California. The other two-thirds are in California, as well as its outlet. . . .

The fact that California takes some of the water will not prevent Nevada, also, from receiving what she requires. And, under the circumstances of the case, it certainly should not be a bone of contention between the two States, as to who has or who has not the right to use the water. If there is to be any controversy, it should only be as to the most practicable method of tapping the lake, and how the greatest number of people are to be benefitted by the great work. . . .

In regard to Nevada, it will be time enough for her to complain when she finds that she will be injured by the loss of water. In any event, she cannot undertake to claim more than the one-third to which she is entitled. And why should she assume to prevent California from taking the two-thirds to which she is unquestionably entitled? Or does Nevada claim the right to take the whole lake and river?

The Act of Congress passed at the last session, has conferred all the privileges, under a general law, that the Lake Tahoe Water Company require for the right of way, and to the water; and as the Company is incorporated under the laws of this State, and intend to build its entire works within the limits of California, I cannot see how the Company can be stopped in its progress, or for what good reason any person can make opposition to it. Why should not California match her excellences and glories with the grandest aqueduct in the world?

≈≈≈

The most stupendous waterworks enterprise ever
undertaken on the American continent.

—Donald J. Pisani, "'Why Shouldn't California Have the
Grandest Aqueduct in the World?': Alexis Von Schmidt's Lake
Tahoe Scheme," *California Historical Quarterly*, 1974

"Whiskey is for drinking—water is for fighting!" This quotation is often falsely attributed to Mark Twain, but the mindset was anything but false in the mid-nineteenth-century American West. Water was especially crucial in the arid West, and with the onslaught of the California gold rush and the Comstock silver rush, the situation became acute. With a rapidly expanding population, mushrooming commercial activity, and the relentless demands of agriculture, developing settlements, and various forms of mining, the desire for an abundant and reliable source of water became a paramount concern. Lake Tahoe's unspoiled waters were a particularly valued potential resource. Prior to 1870, several major water projects were formulated that involved transporting Lake Tahoe water elsewhere, usually far away, via tunnels, canals, and pipes to the mines of the Mother Lode and the Comstock, to farm fields, to the new communities dotting the California and Nevada landscape, and, most famously, to the San Francisco Bay Area.

From the earliest days of the California gold rush, disputes arose as to water rights. Conflicts, sometimes heated, arose between those who felt water diversions should be freely available to those with an important economic need for water, such as miners, and entrepreneurs who argued that water and water supply was not a right, but a commodity—a product and service offered for sale and subject to market pressures. These disputes expanded to Nevada with the onset of the Comstock silver rush, and the battles became regional in scope. Many impassioned court cases were adjudicated, and numerous attempts at passing comprehensive water-rights legislation transpired, but it took years before a workable legal definition emerged. The issue is still hotly debated today.

It is generally conceded that most contentious Lake Tahoe water diversion plan was promulgated by San Francisco–based engineer Alexis Von Schmidt in 1865. Von Schmidt's massive blueprint to divert water from the Truckee River and Lake Tahoe to the San Francisco Bay Area was not the first Lake Tahoe water scheme, it certainly would not be the last, but it was the most famous.

In this excerpt from a 1974 article in the California Historical Quarterly *entitled "'Why Shouldn't California Have the Grandest Aqueduct in the World?': Alexis Von Schmidt's Lake Tahoe Scheme," historian Donald J. Pisani describes Von Schmidt's machinations and the subsequent California-Nevada legal skirmishes regarding Lake Tahoe water from 1863 to 1870.*

Donald J. Pisani was born and raised in Sacramento and received graduate degrees in history from the University of California, Berkeley, and the University of California, Davis. When this excerpted article was published in 1974, Pisani was a doctoral student at Davis. While at the Sacramento Valley campus, he worked with and was inspired by W. Turrentine Jackson, one of the deans of American western history. Donald J. Pisani is considered the preeminent scholar of natural resource development and use in the West. Dr. Pisani has served as the president of the both the American Society for Environmental History and the Agricultural History Society and has written four books and dozens of academic articles about water and governmental policy.

[Alexis Von Schmidt] revealed an interest in using Lake Tahoe as a water supply, though not for San Francisco. In the summer of 1863, a plan was submitted to Virginia City's Board of Aldermen. As one of six directors of the Lake Tahoe and Nevada Water Company, Von Schmidt suggested that Tahoe water could be piped over a low range of hills near Carson City, through the Washoe Basin, then up to a reservoir on the side of Mt. Davidson where it could be stored as a supply for the mines and towns of the Comstock Lode. But the aldermen doubted the feasibility of the project, since the 6,000-foot elevation of Virginia City would require an elaborate and expensive pump system, and they balked at granting the company an exclusive water franchise.

Two years later, on June 20, 1865, San Francisco's *Daily Alta California* announced that Von Schmidt had established the Lake Tahoe and San Francisco Water Works Company to bring the water of Lake Tahoe to the Bay Area, a distance of 163 miles across the interior of California. The *Alta* was confident the scheme would ". . . throw into the shade all similar works of either ancient or modern times, in the old or new world. The undertaking is so great that we can scarcely hope to see it finished in our time." The *Daily Morning Call* exuberantly declared that the project was ". . . decidedly the most stupendous waterworks enterprise ever undertaken on the American continent."

Initially, Von Schmidt's proposal to build "the grandest aqueduct in the world" attracted few investors, and the engineer turned to other projects. But the initial survey work done in 1865 and 1866 was enough to worry Nevada's attorney general who questioned whether Von Schmidt had any legal claim to Tahoe water. The Nevada official argued that Nevada's farms and mills were completely dependent on the Truckee River and held preeminent water rights through established usage. He expected that more water would be needed to drive quartz mills which would be constructed after the transcontinental railroad and a spur line connecting Virginia City and Truckee had been completed. Von Schmidt called the complaint groundless, since the dam he intended to build at the outlet of the lake, he maintained, would store enough water to supply both states. In any case, he emphasized that California had a superior claim to Tahoe water since two-thirds of the lake and its outlet were within its border.

The attorney general's fears turned out to be real but premature, for the project remained dormant until early 1870 when several circumstances contributed to its revival. The year 1869 had been very dry, and 1870 threatened to be even worse. Water rates in San Francisco rose to several times those paid by residents of New York, Boston, or Philadelphia. Everyone knew San Francisco did not have enough water, and Von Schmidt's revelation that [San Francisco's] Spring Valley Company shut down the water supply of certain parts of the city from midnight to dawn nursed public bitterness.

The engineer's attack on the Spring Valley Company coincided with the introduction of new water bills in both Sacramento and Washington DC. In the California bill, Von Schmidt's company pledged to supply San Francisco with 20,000,000 gallons of water daily. In return the Board of Supervisors was required to submit a $10,000,000 bond issue, at 7 per cent interest, to city voters at the next municipal election. The bonds would be paid off through water sales, and the act gave the board authority to buy out the Spring Valley Company at a price not exceeding the value of its capital stock. Undoubtedly Von Schmidt was confident that Tahoe water prices would undercut rates charged by the Spring Valley Company. As a result he could insure potential investors that if his project was accepted by the voters, ultimately the Lake Tahoe Company would establish its own water monopoly.

The provision of the federal bill would have given the Tahoe Company clear right-of-way over federal lands and a supply of earth, timber, and stone along the line of the aqueduct. Most important, a land grant was included. As each quarter of the aqueduct was completed, those ungranted odd checkerboard sections within twenty miles of both sides would become property of the water company. The California bill was sent to the San Francisco legislative delegation for consideration; the federal bill was referred to the Committee on Public Lands.

The project touched off a storm of controversy. Land-grant bills were under heavy attack in Congress, and the *Chicago Tribune* called the federal bill "alms-giving," arguing that the federal government had no business subsidizing private corporations by giving away public lands. Virginia City's *Daily Territorial Enterprise* echoed the arguments made by the Nevada attorney general in 1866 and warned that if the project was approved by the California legislature and San Francisco voters, ". . . we advise the incorporators to bring to the mountains an escort of twenty regiments of militia. They will need them all for we will not submit to the proposed robbery. That's all."

The controversy was more than one exclusively over water rights. Going straight to the point, the *Enterprise* charged that San Francisco capitalists had turned Nevada into an economic satellite of California. Thus, the Lake Tahoe scheme was given symbolic meaning:

San Francisco speculators have been plundering this state for many years almost without rebuke. They have ruined our best mines, compelled us to feed their extravagance, and played football with the vital interests of the whole Commonwealth. We have submitted to all this, and shall probably be forced to submit to it for some time to come; but our water supplies from Lake Tahoe must not be tampered with by these gentlemen. They may take the gold and silver from our hills, and bind us in vassalage to the caprices of their stock boards, but the pure water that comes to us from Lake Tahoe, that drives our mills and makes glad our waste places, is God's exhaustless gift, and the hand of man cannot deprive us of it.

The Truckee River flowing out of Lake Tahoe was Nevada's life-blood; its water was the promise of future industrial development and economic independence from California.

Reaction within California to the proposed bills was mixed. The Truckee River drove the machinery of the town of Truckee's factories and mills and supported its lumber industry by floating logs into Nevada. As it was, the river had sufficient volume only four months in the year to float timber across the border. If Nevada could not get the lumber it needed to build its towns and shore up its mines, Truckee would die, too. The Truckee *Weekly Republican* suggested violence would be used to prevent work on the project.

California's interior towns showed some support for the plan in the early 1870's. The *Marysville Union* was confident the project would "... cause millions of gold to be taken out that cannot be secured without this work, and hundreds of thousands of acres of the dry plains will be made into pleasant homes and add greatly to the taxable property of the State." The *Placer Herald* and Auburn *Stars & Stripes* maintained the project would allow miners to double or triple their operations. In Sacramento, a *Daily Bee* editor thought San Francisco could save capital residents the cost of building a new water system: "If San Francisco gives $10,000,000 to somebody to bring in the waters of Tahoe, they will have to come by our door and we can have them cheap, clear, and in abundance. . . ." However, he was skeptical the project could be completed soon enough to meet Sacramento's needs.

In San Francisco Von Schmidt's ambitious project faced heavy opposition. The engineer was attacked for not publishing full details of his construction plans and for appealing to the California legislature rather than allowing San Francisco's Board of Supervisors to rule on the plan's merit. Most public officials thought an adequate low-cost water supply could be found on the San Francisco peninsula, and they knew property taxes would have to be raised drastically to pay the $700,000 yearly interest on the bonds. Moreover, the water company, not the city, would own the completed water system and set its own rates. All this would have to be swallowed to get a water supply only twice as large as that provided by the Spring Valley Company. Some of the city's newspapers thought the bill was speculative, most thought it underhanded, and all smelled corruption.

These arguments hurt the bill's chance of passage, but it was the reputation of the 1870 legislature which killed it. There was nearly unanimous editorial agreement throughout Northern California that the 1870 legislature was the most corrupt in the state's history. Day after day editorials attacked one bill or another designed to subsidize a private company. The *Alta* pictured San Francisco as a medieval town under siege by robber barons roosting in Sacramento. The *Evening Bulletin* accused the legislature of trying to sell San Francisco by saddling the city with $40,000,000 in debt threatened by a half-dozen private bills. The *Chronicle* expected that the state legislature would find a way to assign to the city the state debt, "or, might it not be a good plan to confiscate the city altogether—sell her off at tax sale—give Sacramento and Oakland their just proportion of the proceeds, and hand the balance to the Tahoe Water Company? This would relieve many persons of anxiety upon the question, how to pay their taxes."

A rumor reached San Francisco in mid-March that certain members of the legislature were getting ready to sneak the Tahoe bill through before adjournment. In response, petitions against the bill were circulated throughout the city—Von Schmidt claimed the runners were hired by the frightened Spring Valley Company—and the signatures of over 1,000 prominent San Franciscans were forwarded to Sacramento. The chamber of commerce framed a bitter protest opposing any water bond-issue unless provision was made to transfer ownership of the completed works to the city. This opposition persuaded cautious members of the San Francisco legislative delegation to bury the bill. The federal bill remained bottled up in the Public Lands Committee.

≈≈≈

The water is tricolored.

—"Lake Tahoe," San Francisco *Daily Alta California*, November 18, 1867

The waters of Lake Tahoe have always been a source of fascination and mystery.

In the mid-nineteenth century, many legends involving the clarity, quality, and physical characteristics of the remarkably pristine lake water emerged. Some were borne out, while others were simply exaggerations or fables.

Reports circulated on the extraordinary clarity of the water, such as the anecdotes of unmistakable observations of large trout more than sixty feet below the surface. Those stories were true. There was the widely recounted conviction that drowned bodies never resurface. This was proven to be false. Some believed that the lake is bottomless—false. Descriptions existed about Lake Tahoe water lacking buoyancy, making it difficult to swim—also, false.

Legends told of intriguing and frightening creatures that dwelled in the lake, ranging from the Ong and Water Babies of the Washoe people to six-hundred-foot-long serpents to sightings of unexplainable and formidable ancient monsters. True? That is best left to your imagination. But founder of the University of California, Davis's Tahoe Research Group, Charles R. Goldman, attributes such sightings to pareidolia, or the tendency of the mind to visualize an object or pattern where none exists.

Many of these legends were disproven by scientific studies that began in earnest in the 1870s. But one legendary aspect of Lake Tahoe has remained constant: the dazzling multicolored water.

In an article entitled "Lake Tahoe," published in the November 18, 1867, issue of the San Francisco Daily Alta California, the lake's beauty, elevation, and surrounding terrain is described. Lake Tahoe is, the article notes, "a sheet of water, from the lovely bosom of which the roughest nature might draw inspiration."

However, the focus is on the awe-inspiring "tricolored" water. The article also mentions the legends regarding Lake Tahoe's depth, the belief that the drowned never reappear, and the lack of buoyancy.

It is unclear, but likely, that the Spirit of the Times referenced is the San Francisco newspaper California Spirit of the Times and Fireman's Journal, which was published from 1859 to 1870.

Lake Tahoe

We find in the *Spirit of the Times* a very interesting description of the scenery on the line of the Central Pacific Rail Road; and in the mountain regions beyond, by the editor of that journal. We quote from a description of the lake:

When we first saw this lake, we thought of all the different scenes of land and water view which we had ever visited, and none could compare in beauty to that before us, except Niagara, though the beauty of the falls and the lake are dissimilar, the former being stormy and gigantic in its grandeur, while the latter is as peaceful and placid as an infant's smile, though at times it is something like an infant in the suddenness of its squalls. Here, at an altitude of 6,218 feet above the level of the ocean, reposing in the strong embrace of dark and frowning mountains and laying at the feet of craggy hills, lies a sheet of water, from the lovely bosom of which the roughest nature might draw inspiration.

The water is tricolored, if we may use the expression in connection with it. For half a mile from the shore (which is of a soft, fine, sandy beach) the color is a most beautiful pea green, tinged with blue, and as clear as crystal, objects on the bottom being as distinct as if immediately before you. For half a mile further, it changes to a green about two shades darker, still with the bluish tinge, but as clear as before. One can hardly imagine that the bottom is so far removed, as it looks as if it could be stood on with the head out of water. From the last color it changes instantaneously to the deepest color of indigo blue. The density of this color is wonderful, but the lines of the three colors are as distinctly drawn across the lake, from north to south, as if painted there, and when the sun shines upon it in the afternoon they are more distinct than at any other time. The water of the lake is purity itself, but on account of the highly rarified state of the air it is not very buoyant, and swimmers find some little fatigue, or, in other words, they are compelled to keep swimming all the time they are in the water.

The depth of the water is very deceptive. From the northern shore and to a certain extent from the southern shore, a person may wade a long distance and not find it above the chin, but it makes depth very quickly. . . . The [depth] soundings, as a matter of course, do away with the idea that the lake is bottomless, and although the greatest depth in impenetrable and of a sufficiency to drown, there is a feeling of pleasure (!) to think that, though one may never return above from involuntary exploration of its hidden depths, the body will have a resting place, however "lowly" it may be.

The outlet of Lake Tahoe is the Truckee River. . . . The country surrounding the outlet is splendid in the extreme—the scenery equal to any on the lake, and well worth a visit from those who come to the locality. It in easily reached, and for all the trouble that may be taken to view it, the return will be a hundred fold. It is grand, interesting and delightful.

≈≈≈

> The lake went by many names that provoked controversy,
> sarcasm, contempt, and even a dash of whimsy.
> —Gary Noy, "Lake Bigler, Lake Tahoe, Etc."

For centuries, the magnificent blue lake high in the Sierra Nevada that we know today as Lake Tahoe had a different name. For generations, the dominant native nation in the region has been the Wá·šiw people. The Wá·šiw are better known as the Washoe. Their name for Lake Tahoe is dáʔaw.

But, in the 1840s, the newly arrived Euro-Americans first spied the stunning sheet of crystal-clear water and initiated decades of debate over how the lake should be designated. Originally ignoring the native appellation, the name of Lake Tahoe was far from certain or official for many years. The lake went by many names that provoked controversy, sarcasm, contempt, and even a dash of whimsy.

On a snowy February 14, 1844, an expedition led by "The Great Pathfinder" John C. Frémont crested a Sierra ridge and looked north at a breathtaking prospect: "We had a beautiful view of a mountain lake at our feet, about 15 miles in length, and so entirely surrounded by mountains that we could not discover an outlet." Frémont's party is generally considered the first non-native group to see Lake Tahoe. But neither dáʔaw nor Tahoe was assigned to the maps that were produced in the years immediately following Frémont's "discovery." Charles Preuss, Frémont's cartographer, simply called it Mountain Lake, and that label was commonly used to designate the lake until 1852. Frémont named it Lake Bonpland, after Aimé Jacques Alexandre Bonpland, the French botanist who had accompanied Baron von Humboldt on his Western Hemisphere explorations in the early nineteenth century. Lake Bonpland became the preferred term of European mapmakers; though not popular, it remained viable for years. Even as late as June 23, 1864, the San Francisco *Daily Alta California* commented on this naming dispute. In a filler for the newspaper's European Intelligence department, the *Daily Alta California* quoted the *Reese River Reveille* of Austin, Nevada, as promoting the official naming of the lake after Bonpland, whom the *Reveille* erroneously dubbed the "discoverer of the lake." The *Daily Alta California* vehemently disagreed with the suggestion, presenting a very strong and simple argument against the idea of a Lake Bonpland. The concept was absurd, the *Alta* noted, since "neither Humboldt nor Bonpland ever saw California."

Early California gold rush maps were notoriously inaccurate, and some did not show the lake at all. Some commercial maps sold to early gold seekers identified the lake as Frémont's Lake. In 1853 William M. Eddy, surveyor general of California, branded the lake as Lake Bigler, in honor of newly elected California governor John Bigler, who served from 1852 to 1856. In 1852 Bigler was credited with leading (or at least supporting) a party that rescued a snowbound wagon company south of the lake. Lake Bigler was a provocative choice, to say the least.

Other maps and emigrant guides of the era used a variety of names, such as Big Truckee Lake or the hybrid Lake Bigler Tahoe. Most confusingly, George Holbrook Baker's popular 1855 "Map of the Mining Regions of California" utilized several different alternatives on the same map—Mountain Lake, Lake Bigler (albeit for a different lake), and, at the location where Lake Tahoe should be, Mahlon Lake.

Of all the potential preferences, Lake Bigler stuck, sort of. When the Civil War began in 1861, former governor John Bigler was a controversial figure for his Confederate and proslavery sympathies, for possible involvement in a secession plot in California, for his rumored heavy drinking, and for what many considered an undeserved reputation as the savior of the trapped wagon train in 1852. Supporters of the Union cause called for the name Lake Bigler to be summarily expunged from the beautiful alpine lake. Union adherent and Yuba County assemblyman D. L. Haun unsuccessfully introduced Assembly Bill 437 in the 1861 California State Assembly to rechristen the lake Tula Tulia, which a few claimed was the appropriate Native designation.

In 1862, according to his personal papers, Robert Dean, who managed the Lake House resort on the south shore, wrote to the Union-sympathizing *Sacramento Union* suggesting a name change. Dean stated he was acquainted with a local Washoe leader named Gumalanga, known as Captain Jim by the white settlers, who had informed Dean that the Natives referred to the lake as "Tahoo," likely Dean's interpretation of the pronunciation of the Washoe term dáʔaw.

On May 28, 1863, the *Union* published a letter to the editor supporting Sierra Lake as the lake's appellation. The letter neatly distilled much of the objection to Bigler both as a politician and as the lake's name, and, in essence, reinforced the notion that any designation other than "Lake Bigler" would be desirable:

> A place so picturesque, so destined to become the greatest resort
> for health, novelty and enjoyment in the known world, ought not
> to bear the name of an individual; or if so, it should not take a
> name . . . [of] that species . . . which breathes nothing but con-
> demnation for the glorious defenders of our Government, and
> covert sympathy with treason. . . . The idea of naming a romantic
> body of water, as pure, transparent and beautiful as the diamond
> dews of morning, whose sides are embellished with the hues of
> our precious metals, and accumulated and held in a vast bowl of
> nature, scooped out of granite rocks, and faced with emerald, the
> idea of naming such a mirror of wonder after a politician, and of
> a very common class at that, is too absurd to be perpetuated. Let
> the name be changed, and when changed gives us one which shall
> be familiar, musical and appropriate . . . Sierra Lake.

The *Union* responded, "Sierra Lake would be very well, or the Indian
name of the lake, Teho," which was their adaptation of the Washoe
name suggested by Robert Dean.

In June 1863, the Territory of Nevada entered the debate. The *Nevada
Transcript* wrote, "It is proposed to drop the name of Bigler from the
lake among the Sierras and adopt the Indian name of Tahoe. Good idea.
Why the finest sheet of water in the mountains should be named after
a fifth-rate politician we have never been able to see." In the passionate
and partisan Civil War atmosphere, Lake Union was also proposed.

A few days later, the *Marysville Appeal* acidly suggested that Lake
Bigler be renamed Lago Beergler, as it "would stand always as a punning
allusion to the bibulous habits of 'Honest John' when he was Governor
of the State." The *Sacramento Union* soon objected to both Lake Bigler
and Lago Beergler unless "a lake of beer should be discovered." The
Union then offered its humble but sarcastic resolution to the Bigler
versus Tahoe challenge on July 27, 1863: "[Bigler should] apply to the
next Legislature for leave to call himself John Tahoe." Later in summer
1863, the Reverend Thomas Starr King, a renowned and influential
Unitarian preacher and an ardent Unionist who loathed Bigler, endorsed
the name Tahoe.

As counterpoint, in the September 4–5, 1863, edition of the *Virginia City Territorial Enterprise*, Samuel Clemens, then writing as Mark Twain, disparaged the lake being renamed Tahoe, which he called a "disgustingly sick and silly . . . name."

At the same time these assorted names were being contemplated, others were merely bewildered by the spelling and pronunciation of Tahoe. Many spelling variants were proposed over the decades, including Tah-ve, Tah-oo-e, Tah-ho-ee, Tahoo, Tah-jo, Ta-ho, Tajo, Pah-hoe, Ta-au, and Tahoe. Tongue-twisting pronunciations were bandied, such as "Tah-hoe," "Tay-hoe," "Daw-oh" and even "Tah-joe."

While a handful offered ongoing support for Lake Bigler, it appeared likely the tag would disappear due to widespread disapproval. But, in 1870, there was a surprise development. Following the Civil War, California Democrats regained control of the state legislature. On February 10, 1870, the Democrats, the party of John Bigler, overwhelmingly passed a law, Chapter 58 of the Statutes of California, stating "the lake shall be known as Lake Bigler . . . the only name to be regarded as legal." Despite the formal sanction of Lake Bigler in 1870, that name was rarely uttered as, by then, Lake Tahoe was commonly used. The lake would officially be known as Lake Bigler until July 18, 1945, when California Senate Bill 1265 repealed the 1870 act and authorized Lake Tahoe as the official designation.

The convoluted history of the naming of Lake Tahoe was largely forgotten as the years passed. Even today, most do not know this hidden history. In August 1983 the Chief Truckee Chapter, No. 3691, of the fraternal organization E Clampus Vitus, offered a remedy. On a boulder located near the beach at the Kings Beach State Recreation Area on the California side of the north shore, the Clampers placed a bronze plaque that reads as follows:

LAKE BIGLER

DURING 1852 THE NAME LAKE BIGLER CAME INTO COMMON USAGE MEMORIALIZING CALIFORNIA GOVERNOR JOHN BIGLER (1852–1858 [sic]), WHO GAINED NOTORIETY BY THE RESCUE OF A SNOWBOUND EMIGRANT PARTY AT LAKE VALLEY. CONTROVERSY WITH NEVADA OVER HIS SOUTHERN SYMPATHY LED THE CALIFORNIA LEGISLATURE TO LEGALIZE THE TITLE IN

1870. FOR 75 YEARS, UNTIL 1945, WHEN OFFICIALLY RECINDED [*sic*] THIS REMAINED THE LEGAL TITLE OF LAKE TAHOE.

The plaque is small. If E Clampus Vitus had attempted to present a comprehensive account of the ultimate designation of the Gem of the Sierra as Lake Tahoe, the plaque would have been the size of a freeway billboard.

≈≈≈

> We could not bear the thought of the finest body
> of water in the Sierra bearing and perpetuating
> the name of a person disloyal to the Union.
> —"Naming Lake Tahoe," *Sunset* magazine, January 1908

The Great Lake Tahoe Naming Debate sometimes was an occasion for good-natured joshing, but, much more often, the arguments were impassioned. This was especially true during the Civil War of 1861–1865 and its aftermath. Governor John Bigler, for whom the lake was formally named, was a Confederate partisan, and loyal Unionists could not abide the idea that the beautiful alpine lake would honor such a man.

In the January 1908 edition of Sunset *magazine, the perspective of R. G. Dean on the issue was presented. Robert Garwood Dean was born in New York in 1831 and orphaned at age sixteen. In 1849 R. G. Dean was a 49er, joining the mad rush to California in the earliest days of the gold rush. In 1859 Dean constructed a hotel at Lake Tahoe in Lake Valley (a.k.a. Bigler Lake Valley) at the south shore of the lake near the main road to the Comstock Lode. His establishment cycled through many names but was commonly called the Lake House and is considered the first tourist resort at the lake. Dean, a Union supporter, was angry that the magnificent body of water at his doorstep was named for Southern sympathizer Bigler. Dean originally suggested using the appellation Washoe, recognizing the Washoe people for whom the lake is their homeland. But he changed his mind after meeting with a Washoe elder named Gumalanga, known as Captain Jim by the white settlers, who informed R. G. Dean that the lake was referred to by the Washoe people as "Tahoo," in Dean's rendering. When a post office was established at the Lake House, the name, now spelled "Tahoe," was attached to the office. Dean and others, such as his uncle, Judge Seneca Dean of Genoa,*

Nevada, then persuaded the village that grew near the lake outlet of the Truckee River on the north shore to adopt the name Tahoe City. Soon, Lake Tahoe became the preferred name for many, but not all.

In the 1908 Sunset *magazine article that follows, R. G. Dean recounts his version of "Naming Lake Tahoe."*

Sunset *magazine first appeared in 1895 as a promotional vehicle for the Southern Pacific Railroad. It is still published today.*

The beginning of the article includes this cryptic reference: "Thinking it might interest the public as much as it did myself." The identity of myself *is uncertain, but it likely was Charles Sedgwick Aiken, editor of* Sunset *magazine in 1908.*

Thinking it might interest the public as much as it did myself to hear how Lake Tahoe obtained its name, the story is given here in the words of the man who named it, R. G. Dean, now a resident of Brentwood, Contra Costa county. He then lived in Lake Valley, conducting the Lake Hotel. Said he:

"John Bigler, Governor of California, was a pro-slavery Democrat and a strong southern sympathizer, and after the close of his term, identified himself with the political party that was scheming to establish a Pacific Confederacy, and to take California and Oregon out of the Union. The enmities engendered during that crisis in the political history of our state were deep-seated and bitter. The South was already fortifying itself in anticipation of seceding at the earliest opportunity, and the Democratic party was dominant and supreme.

"To this state had come a large percentage of northern men in quest of gold, rather than political preferment. They were busily engaged in mining or in commercial life, while our southern friends were largely in quest of office. The proposition to form a Pacific Confederacy was earnestly championed by the southern office-holders, and the possibility of having to shoulder our rifles was discussed around many a campfire in the mines. All this helps explain why the great lake was changed from Bigler to Tahoe.

"During the session of the legislature of 1851–52, an appropriation was made to assist the incoming immigration across the plains, during the coming summer. It was known to be very large—that many had left the Missouri river with inadequate outfits—that feed along the principal routes was scarce, and the possibility of alleviating the inevitable suffering, and assisting the immigrants across the desert and over the Sierra prompted the legislature of the state to place in Governor Bigler's hands a liberal fund to be disbursed as he thought proper.

"In the furtherance of the proposition, the Governor loaded a pack train with provisions and sent it forward via the Placerville route, to meet the immigrants, and he himself followed with a number of friends, and a splendid outfit, to Lake Valley. Here, on the south shore of the lake, then a nameless body of water, but beautiful as now, in her mirrored loveliness, the Governor and his party camped and hunted and fished and enjoyed a delightful outing.

"On the return of the party, the citizens of Hangtown, or Placerville, tendered them a banquet. It was at this feast that some one of the Governor's enthusiastic admirers proposed to christen the beautiful lake in his honor and amid the cheers of the banqueters it was formally named Bigler.

"For nearly ten years it carried this appellation only, but during the interval the events referred to had culminated in the Civil War. Men were dying by thousands on the eastern seaboard—our brothers and relatives—in support of the Union. Most Californians were intensely loyal. We could not bear the thought of the finest body of water in the Sierra bearing and perpetuating the name of a person disloyal to the Union and discussed the propriety of changing it. The Indian appellation was preferred if we could learn it. We consulted Captain Jim, a chief of the Walker river Indians, who came fishing to the lake.

"'Jim, what you call him—the lake?'

"'Oh! me call him Big Water.'

"'No, Jim. I want the name—your name, Jim—my name, Bob—his name, Sam. What Ingin name for the lake?'

"'Oh!' said Jim, throwing his head back, and pursing out his lips, 'Téhoo,' giving the long Italian sound of 'a' and breathing the hoo with a slightly aspirated accent on the 'h'—Tahoo!

"Returning to the hotel, the old Lake House, long since destroyed by fire, of which I was then proprietor, I exclaimed: 'I have it!' and gave the result of my interview with Captain Jim.

"With the concurrence of all present, a communication was written to the editor of the *Sacramento Union*, then the leading paper of the state, who immediately fell in with the proposition to change the name from Bigler to Tahoo.

"An editorial followed and the other Union papers of the state cheerfully seconded it and Tahoe—after changing the final 'o' to 'e' became the name it will always hear."

≈≈≈

Why, Mr. Knight, you have left off the name of Lake Bigler.
—William Henry Knight, "An Emigrant's Trip across the
Plains in 1859," *Publications of the Historical Society of
Southern California*, Volume 12, Part 3 (1923)

In 1862 H. H. Bancroft & Company, the publishing venture of prominent California historian Hubert Howe Bancroft, resolved to design and publish an updated map of the Pacific states, in light of the startling social and political changes wrought by the Comstock Lode silver rush.

Bancroft asked William Henry Knight, the manager of his publishing department, to spearhead the project. Knight and celebrated draftsman Vitus Wackenreuder worked on the map for over a year, gathering up-to-date information and making corrections where necessary. When it came to the depiction of Lake Tahoe, William Henry Knight concurred with objections to the designation of Lake Bigler. He instructed Wackenreuder to omit that name and substitute Lake Tahoe. The resultant 1864 map received the approval of the Department of the Interior and became the first map to confer federal government sanction on Lake Tahoe as the favored name of the lake. In 1870 Knight partnered with Bancroft to form Bancroft, Knight & Company publishers. Hubert Howe Bancroft later noted that the books, manuscripts, maps, and other documents collected by and for the use of Knight would constitute the nucleus of the world-renowned Bancroft Library at the University of California, Berkeley.

With his numerous connections in the literary and academic communities, William Henry Knight was influential in many civic and scientific advancements throughout California. Knight was important in the establishment of the California Academy of Sciences in San Francisco and the Southern California Academy of Sciences in Los Angeles. In the mid-1870s Knight influenced business magnate James Lick to finance the construction of Lick Observatory atop Mount Hamilton, east of San Jose. Alexis Von Schmidt had endeavored to convince Lick to station the observatory at Lake Tahoe. And for a time, it appeared that

Von Schmidt was successful; in fact, an 1874 Lick Trust Deed specified that the observatory be constructed at Lake Tahoe. However, the terrain was unsuitable, and the Lake Tahoe observatory was abandoned. Some older maps of Lake Tahoe label Observatory Point on the western shore, just north of Tahoe City on the southern perimeter of Carnelian Bay. Today, the location is known as Dollar Point.

In the 1923 edition of the Publications of the Historical Society of Southern California, *William Henry Knight detailed his 1859 journey to California. A portion of his memoir focused on his arrival at Lake Tahoe and his recollections of the decision to scrap Lake Bigler in favor of Lake Tahoe on* Bancroft's Map of the Pacific States, Compiled by William Henry Knight, 1864.

From Carson City our company climbed the eastern summit of the Sierra Nevada mountains and descended into a beautiful valley to the south end of what was then known as Lake Bigler, now Lake Tahoe, and camped there two nights, as there was good forage for our somewhat jaded animals. It was a little past the middle of August, and I broke a thin crust of ice in the morning to bathe my hands and face for breakfast.

Before descending to the Lake I mounted old Pete and climbed over a rough trail to the summit of a peak about 1,000 feet above the lake where I had a comprehensive view of the entire valley in which the deep blue waters of the lake was embossomed [*sic*]. Majestic forests of pine, fir and spruce clothed the mountain sides from the border of the lake to snow peaks 3,000 feet above. It was a bewilderingly beautiful sight, in strong contrast with the weary months I had experienced on the parched plains, and my eyes filled with tears of thankfulness in contemplating it. It is yet difficult for me to revert even today, to that wonderful scene which is deeply graven on the tablets of my memory, without emotion.

Four years later I was the means of changing the name of the lake from Bigler—a former governor of California—to Tahoe, a euphoneous Indian word meaning Big Waters, in contrast with many small lakes on the mountain sides. . . .

Note—Particulars of Naming Lake Tahoe

In 1862 I was manager of the publishing department of the large Bancroft establishment in San Francisco. Their business covered the entire region west of the Rocky Mountains from British Columbia to Mexico. Mr. Bancroft requested me to compile a map of this large region and I was a year in gathering the material from every county in the territory embraced, frequently addressing two or three letters before getting the requisite information. We hired an expert draftsman named Wackenreuder to draw the large map—some three feet wide by five feet high, embracing all the detail we had been able to gather.

Meantime I had learned that much dissatisfaction had been expressed regarding the name—Lake Bigler—which had been imposed upon the beautiful sheet of water lying on the eastern boundary of California at an elevation exceeding 6,000 feet. I fully sympathized with the prevailing sentiment and instructed the draftsman to omit that name from the lake. Consequently when I invited two prominent newspaper men— John S. Hittell, editor of the *Alta California*, then the leading republican organ of San Francisco; and Henry Degroot, traveling correspondent of the *Sacramento Union* and the *San Francisco Bulletin* to inspect and criticise the map, then ready to be sent to the copperplate engraver, Degroot, who had just returned from the Washoe region where the rich Comstock silver mines had been creating a world of excitement, suddenly turned to me and remarked, "Why, Mr. Knight, you have left off the name of Lake Bigler."

I then asked, knowing the prevailing objection to that name expressed by many California newspapers, what name either of the gentlemen would suggest for that beautiful lake lying between the double summits of the Sierras.

Neither of the gentlemen seemed surprised at my question, but began at once suggesting various names. I said I do not want hackneyed names that have been used for other geographical objects, and turning to Degroot I inquired if he knew what the Indians called it. He took a memorandum from his pocket and examined a list of Indian names of which he had made notes, and exclaimed, "Why, here it is; the Washoe tribe call it Tahoe, meaning Big Waters, for it is the largest body of water which those untraveled Indians know anything about." I was at once struck with the euphonious name and its significance, and I asked the gentlemen if they would support me in giving that name to the lake. They not only promised to do so but assured me that many of the country newspapers would gladly join them in fastening that name upon the lake.

I at once wrote to the Department of the Interior, saying that the name of the lake heretofore known as Bigler, had been changed in accordance with public sentiment to Tahoe, and requested them to substitute that name in all their future publications, which they did from that time on, thus giving the new name the U.S. Government sanction.

My map was sent to the engraver in 1863 and bore the following title: *Bancroft's Map of the Pacific States, Compiled by William Henry Knight, 1864.*

It was the first map ever issued having the name of Lake Tahoe, and every map published since that date has applied that name to the lake.

≈≈≈

> This sea is no more to be compared to Tahoe than
> a meridian of longitude is to a rainbow.
> —Mark Twain, *The Innocents Abroad*, 1869

Samuel Langhorne Clemens, better known by his pseudonym Mark Twain, was among the most famous of American humorists, writers, and lecturers. At his peak, he was probably the most celebrated American anywhere.

Samuel Clemens was born in Missouri in 1835 and did not arrive in the American West until 1861. By that time, he had served as newspaperman, printer, Mississippi River pilot, and even a Confederate soldier for two weeks at the start of the Civil War. He left the East to accompany his brother Orion, the newly appointed secretary of the Nevada Territory. Young Sam tried prospecting both in Nevada and California's Calaveras County and then worked as city editor of the Virginia City Territorial Enterprise, *where he first used the name of Mark Twain in 1862. Twain began as a writer of light humorous verse, an exemplar of what came to be called "California humor"—a potent combination of satire set in exaggerated real-life situations. In Nevada, this genre was known as the Sagebrush School, with primarily Nevada authors addressing Nevada themes.*

When Samuel Clemens first arrived in Nevada, he found the Great Basin to be desolate and dreary. But all that changed with his first visit to Lake Tahoe in 1861. Approaching the lake from Carson City to the east, Clemens and his compatriot John Kinney (whom Twain refers to as "Johnny" in Roughing It*), first spied Lake Tahoe, probably in*

September—Samuel Clemens loved the lake and could not stop talking or writing about it. In an October 25, 1861, letter to his sister Pamela Clemens Moffett, Sam tried to temper his enthusiasm. He wrote, "I had better stop about 'the Lake,' though,—for whenever I think of it I want to go there and die, the place is so beautiful. I'll build a country seat there one of these days that will make the Devil's mouth water if he ever visits the earth."

Mark Twain's first major work was The Innocents Abroad, or the New Pilgrims' Progress, *published in 1869. The book is a humorous travelogue chronicling Twain's five-month journey to the Holy Land and Europe with a group of memorable American travelling companions in 1867.* Innocents Abroad *transformed Twain from a relatively obscure newspaper correspondent to a best-selling author and international celebrity. It was the best-selling book of all Twain's catalog.*

In Innocents Abroad *Twain visits many famous lakes and bodies of water, and he cannot help but contrast them to Lake Tahoe. After all, Twain wrote in a sidenote, "I measure all lakes by Tahoe, partly because I am far more familiar with it than with any other, and partly because I have such a high admiration for it and such a world of pleasant recollections of it, that it is very nearly impossible for me to speak of lakes and not mention it."*

In this excerpt, Mark Twain compares Italy's Lake Como and the Holy Land's Sea of Galilee to Lake Tahoe.

Lake Como

It certainly is clearer than a great many lakes, but how dull its waters are compared with the wonderful transparence of Lake Tahoe! I speak of the north shore of Tahoe, where one can count the scales on a trout at a depth of a hundred and eighty feet. I have tried to get this statement off at par here, but with no success; so I have been obliged to negotiate it at fifty per cent, discount. At this rate I find some takers; perhaps the reader will receive it on the same terms—ninety feet instead of one hundred and eighty. But let it be remembered that those are forced terms—Sheriff's sale prices. As far as I am privately concerned, I abate not a jot of the original assertion that in those strangely magnifying waters one may count the scales on a trout (a trout of the large kind,) at a depth of a hundred and eighty feet—may see every pebble on the bottom—might even count a paper of dray-pins. People talk of the transparent waters of the Mexican Bay of Acapulco, but in my own experience I know they can not compare with those I am speaking of. I have fished for trout, in Tahoe, and at a measured depth of eighty-four feet. I have seen them put their noses to the bait and I could see their gills open and shut. I could hardly have seen the trout themselves at that distance in the open air.

As I go back in spirit and recall that noble sea, reposing among the snow-peaks six thousand feet above the ocean, the conviction comes strong upon me again that Como would only seem a bedizened little courtier in that august presence.

Sorrow and misfortune overtake the Legislature that still from year to year permits Tahoe to retain its unmusical cognomen! Tahoe! It suggests no crystal waters, no picturesque shores, no sublimity. Tahoe for a sea in the clouds: a sea that has character, and asserts it in solemn calms, at times, at times in savage storms; a sea, whose royal seclusion is guarded by a cordon of sentinel peaks that lift their frosty fronts nine thousand feet above the level world; a sea whose every aspect is impressive, whose belongings are all beautiful, whose lonely majesty types the Deity!

Tahoe means grasshoppers. It means grasshopper soup. It is Indian, and suggestive of Indians. They say it is Piute—possibly it is Digger. I am satisfied it was named by the Diggers—those degraded savages who roast their dead relatives, then mix the human grease and ashes of bones with tar, and "gaum" it thick all over their heads and foreheads and ears, and go caterwauling about the hills and call it mourning. These are the gentry that named the Lake.

People say that Tahoe means "Silver Lake"—"Limpid Water"—"Falling Leaf." Bosh. It means grasshopper soup, the favorite dish of the Digger tribe—and of the Piutes as well. It isn't worth while, in these practical times, for people to talk about Indian poetry—there never was any in them—except in the Fennimore Cooper Indians. But *they* are an extinct tribe that never existed. I know the Noble Red Man. I have camped with the Indians; I have been on the warpath with them, taken part in the chase with them—for grasshoppers; helped them steal cattle; I have roamed with them, scalped them, had them for breakfast. I would gladly eat the whole race if I had a chance.

But I am growing unreliable. I will return to my comparison of the Lakes. Como is a little deeper than Tahoe, if people here tell the truth.

They say it is eighteen hundred feet deep at this point, but it does not look a dead enough blue for that. Tahoe is one thousand five hundred and twenty-five feet deep in the centre, by the State Geologist's measurement. They say the great peak opposite this town is five thousand feet high: but I feel sure that three thousand feet of that statement is a good honest lie. The lake is a mile wide, here, and maintains about that width from this point to its northern extremity—which is distant sixteen miles: from here to its southern extremity—say fifteen miles—it is not over half a mile wide in any place, I should think. Its snow-clad mountains one hears so much about are only seen occasionally, and then in the distance, the Alps. Tahoe is from ten to eighteen miles wide, and its mountains shut it in like a wall. Their summits are never free from snow the year round. One thing about it is very strange: it never has even a skim of ice upon its surface, although lakes in the same range of mountains, lying in a lower and warmer temperature, freeze over in winter.

[Sea of Galilee]

The celebrated Sea of Galilee is not so large a sea as Lake Tahoe by a good deal—it is just about two-thirds as large. And when we come to speak of beauty, this sea is no more to be compared to Tahoe than a meridian of longitude is to a rainbow. The dim waters of this pool can not suggest the limpid brilliancy of Tahoe ; these low, shaven, yellow hillocks of rocks and sand, so devoid of perspective, can not suggest the grand peaks that compass Tahoe like a wall, and whose ribbed and chasmed fronts are clad with stately pines that seem to grow small and smaller as they climb, till one might fancy them reduced to weeds and shrubs far upward, where they join the everlasting snows. Silence and solitude brood over Tahoe; and silence and solitude brood also over this lake of Genessaret. But the solitude of the one is as cheerful and fascinating as the solitude of the other is dismal and repellant.

In the early morning one watches the silent battle of dawn and darkness upon the waters of Tahoe with a placid interest; but when the shadows sulk away and one by one the hidden beauties of the shore unfold themselves in the full splendor of noon; when the still surface is belted like a rainbow with broad bars of blue and green and white, half the distance from circumference to centre; when, in the lazy summer afternoon, he lies in a boat, far cut to where the dead blue of the deep water begins, and smokes the pipe of peace and idly winks at the distant crags and patches of snow from under his cap-rim; when the boat drifts shoreward to the white water, and he lolls over the gunwale and gazes by the hour down through the crystal depths and notes the colors of the pebbles and reviews the finny armies gliding in procession a hundred feet below; when at night he sees moon and stars, mountain ridges feathered with pines, jutting white capes, bold promontories, grand sweeps of rugged scenery topped with bald, glimmering peaks, all magnificently pictured in the polished mirror of the lake, in richest, softest detail, the tranquil interest that was born with the morning deepens and deepens, by sure degrees, till it culminates at last in resistless fascination!

It is solitude, for birds and squirrels on the shore and fishes in the water are all the creatures that are near to make it otherwise, but it is not the sort of solitude to make one dreary. Come to Galilee for that. If these unpeopled deserts, these rusty mounds of barrenness, that never, never, never do shake the glare from their harsh outlines, and fade and faint into vague perspective; that melancholy ruin of Capernaum; this stupid village of Tiberias, slumbering under its six funereal plumes of palms; yonder desolate declivity where the swine of the miracle ran down into the sea, and doubtless thought it was better to swallow a devil or two and get drowned into the bargain than have to live longer in such a place; this cloudless, blistering sky; this solemn, sailless, tintless lake, reposing within its rim of yellow hills and low, steep banks, and looking just as expressionless and unpoetical (when we leave its sublime history out of the question,) as any metropolitan reservoir in Christendom—if these things are not food for rock me to sleep, mother, none exist, I think.

Fig. 1. *Top:* Emerald Bay, ca. 1895. Photograph by R. J. Waters. Courtesy of the Carl S. Dentzel Photograph Collection of the American West, Huntington Museum, Library, and Botanical Gardens, San Marino, California. ID: photCL-98(1).

Fig. 2. *Bottom:* Tallac Point House, ca. 1870. Elias "Lucky" Baldwin acquired Tallac Point House in 1880 for use as a hotel and resort. Courtesy of the California History Room, California State Library, Sacramento. ID: 2007-0275.

Fig. 3. *Opposite top:* John Bigler, ca. 1850. John Bigler was the third governor of California, serving from 1852 to 1856. From 1870 to 1945, Lake Tahoe was officially designated as Lake Bigler. Courtesy of the California History Room, California State Library, Sacramento. ID: 2007-0341.

Fig. 4. *Opposite bottom:* Mark Twain, ca. 1870. Mark Twain (Samuel Clemens) first visited Lake Tahoe in 1861. From that point onward, Twain found every other lake he encountered to be inferior to Lake Tahoe. Courtesy of the California History Room, California State Library, Sacramento. ID: 2007-0023.

Fig. 5. *Above:* Tahoe City, ca. 1870. This image of the shoreline at Tahoe City was taken by the pioneering but eccentric photographer Eadweard Muybridge. Courtesy of the California History Room, California State Library, Sacramento. ID: Stereo-3498.

Fig. 6. Mount Tallac House (Yank's), ca. 1870. Photograph by Carleton Watkins. Courtesy of the California History Room, California State Library, Sacramento. ID: Stereo-4700.

Fig. 7. Cave Rock, ca. 1870. Cave Rock is considered sacred by the Washoe people. Courtesy of the California History Room, California State Library, Sacramento. ID: 2010-0602.

Fig. 8. *Opposite top:* At Aspen Point near Yank's Station, ca. 1870. Located at the site of the former Lake Valley House, Yank's Station was a popular hotel, stagecoach stop, and a Pony Express remount station in the 1860s and early 1870s, operated by Ephraim "Yank" Clement. In 1873 Yank's Station was renamed Meyers. Photograph by Carleton Watkins. Courtesy of the California History Room, California State Library, Sacramento. ID: Stereo-4687.

Fig. 9. *Opposite bottom:* Emerald Bay, ca. 1870. The island in the background is the only island in Lake Tahoe. It has been known by many names, including Coquette, Baranoff, Dead Man's, Hermit's, and Emerald Isle. But the most-used name is Fannette Island. Courtesy of the California History Room, California State Library, Sacramento. ID: Stereo-4713.

Fig. 10. *Above:* Storm on the lake, ca. 1870–1878. This dramatic landscape photograph of a storm sweeping across Lake Tahoe was taken by Carleton Watkins. Courtesy of the California History Room, California State Library, Sacramento. ID: 2005-0709.

Fig. 11. *Above: A Perilous Trip*, an illustration from *Harper's Weekly*, June 2, 1877. Courtesy of the Bancroft Library, University of California, Berkeley. ID: AP2 H3 v. 21, pp. 428–29.

Fig. 12. *Opposite:* Log chute on Truckee River, ca. 1890. Photograph By R. J. Waters. Cut timber would slide down a log chute to the Truckee River for transport to nearby sawmills. The log chute is on the right of the photograph. Courtesy of the California History Room, California State Library, Sacramento. ID: 1992-6632.

Fig. 13. *Mining on the Comstock*, a drawing of Philip Deidesheimer's square-set mine-timbering method, which revolutionized mining in the Comstock Lode. Drawn by T. L. Dawes, the illustration was first published, engraved, and printed in 1876. Courtesy of the Library of Congress, Prints and Photographs Division, Washington DC. LC-DIG-pga-01999.

Fig. 14. Glenbrook Bay, Lake Tahoe, with lumber mills in full operation, ca. 1876. Photograph by Carleton Watkins. Courtesy of the J. Paul Getty Museum. Digital image courtesy of the Getty's Open Content Program. ID: 85.XM.36.

Fig. 15. A portrait of the famous Washoe basket maker Dabuda, also known as Louisa Keyser or Dat-So-La-Lee, ca. 1900. Courtesy of the Library of Congress, Prints and Photographs Division, Washington DC. LC-USZ62-117637.

Fig. 16. *Cave Rock, Lake Tahoe, View from the Road, # 676*, ca. 1865.
From 1865 until 1931, the road at Cave Rock, on the eastern shore of
Lake Tahoe, used a hanging bridge and rock wall on the outer edge of the
landmark. In 1931, to accommodate the Lincoln Highway, a tunnel was
bored through the rock. A second tunnel was added in 1957. Cave Rock is
considered sacred by the Washoe people. They were not consulted about
the construction of either tunnel. Photograph attributed to Lawrence &
Houseworth. Courtesy of the California History Room, California State
Library, Sacramento. ID: Stereo-3280.

Fig. 17. *Above:* Warm Springs Hotel at Carnelian Bay, ca. 1870. Photograph by Carleton Watkins. Originally named Cornelian Bay after the semiprecious stones found in the area, Carnelian Bay became a well-known location for health resorts by the end of the nineteenth century. Located at the north end of Lake Tahoe, Carnelian Bay features both cold and hot mineral springs. Courtesy of the California History Room, California State Library, Sacramento. ID: Stereo-4723.

Fig. 18. *Opposite:* The steamer *Governor Stanford* at Warm Springs, ca. 1875. The *Governor Stanford* was a double-decker steamer named after Leland Stanford, Central Pacific Rail Road magnate, and governor of California from 1862 to 1863. The steamer operated from 1872 to 1883. Photograph by Carleton Watkins. Courtesy of the J. Paul Getty Museum. Digital image courtesy of the Getty's Open Content Program. ID: 85.XM.36.

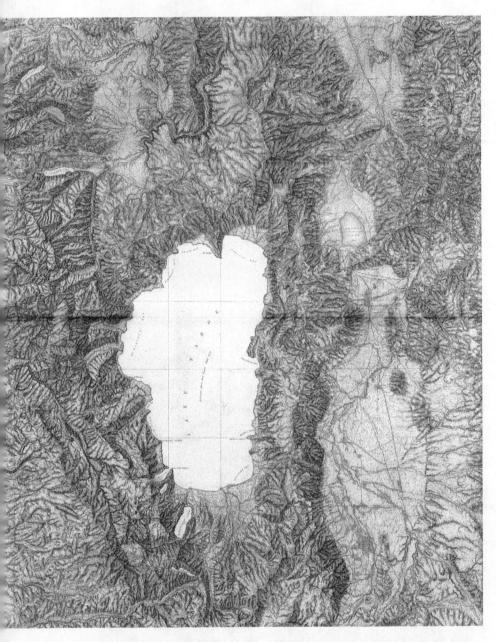

Fig. 19. *Topographical Map of Lake Tahoe Region.* Originally published in 1877, it was reprinted as part of the *Report upon United States Geographical Surveys West of the One Hundredth Meridian, 1889.* Call number: G1380. U56 1873 Vault. Courtesy of the Library of Congress, Prints and Photographs Division, Washington DC.

Fig. 20. Miners of the Comstock Lode, ca. 1890. In the early 1860s, many
who passed through Lake Tahoe were headed to the mines of the Comstock
Lode. These are portraits of miners at the Ophir Mine and Gould and Curry
Mines. The inset shows the Bickell Brothers, who lost their lives in a fire at
the Gold Hill Mine on April 7, 1869. Courtesy of the Library of Congress,
Prints and Photographs Division, Washington DC. ID: LC-USZ62-107525.

Fig. 21. *Above:* Grand Central Hotel, Tahoe City, ca. 1886. Photograph by R. J. Waters. Courtesy of the Carl S. Dentzel Photograph Collection of the American West, Huntington Museum, Library, and Botanical Gardens, San Marino, California. ID: photCL-98(12).

Fig. 22. *Opposite top: View from Sierra Rocks–Eastern Shore of Lake Tahoe, Looking South Towards Cave Rock,* ca. 1865. This image shows the typical quality of roads surrounding Lake Tahoe in the 1860s. Photograph by Charles Leander Weed. Courtesy of the J. Paul Getty Museum. Digital image courtesy of the Getty's Open Content Program. ID: 84.XC,870.91.

Fig. 23. *Opposite bottom:* Custom House and Embarcadero, Tahoe City, ca. 1870. Custom houses served as offices for government officials charged with regulating imports and exports. In this case, the location also served as a post office, billiard hall, and general store. Photograph by Carleton Watkins. Courtesy of the California History Room, California State Library, Sacramento. ID: Stereo-4832.

Fig. 24. *Opposite top:* Marlette Lake, ca. 1895. Water from the Lake Tahoe Basin and surrounding region was highly prized. Marlette Lake, located on a ridge above the eastern shore of Lake Tahoe was a primary water source for Virginia City and the Comstock Lode. Photograph by R. J. Waters. Courtesy of the Carl S. Dentzel Photograph Collection of the American West, Huntington Museum, Library, and Botanical Gardens, San Marino, California. ID: photCL-98(1).

Fig. 25. *Opposite bottom:* The Truckee River Outlet Dam in Tahoe City, ca. 1890. A rock and lumber dam originally constructed in 1870 as part of Alexis Waldemar Von Schmidt's blueprint to divert water from Lake Tahoe to San Francisco via tunnels and canals. Although Von Schmidt's plan was unsuccessful, the dam remained until 1913, when it was replaced by the current Lake Tahoe Dam. Courtesy of the Special Collections and University Archives Department, University of Nevada, Reno. ID: UNRS-P2432-1.tif.

Fig. 26. *Above:* Along the Placerville-Carson Road, ca. 1866. The Placerville-Carson Road was the main thoroughfare to the Comstock Lode. It was often congested. Photograph attributed to Lawrence and Houseworth. Courtesy of the Library of Congress, Prints and Photographs Division, Washington DC. ID: LC-USZ62-107525.

Fig. 27. The terminus of a Lake Tahoe V-flume in Carson City, ca. 1880. Timber and lumber were offloaded at Carson City for transport to the Comstock Lode. Photograph by Carleton Watkins. Courtesy of the California History Room, California State Library, Sacramento. ID: Stereo-2113.

Fig. 28. *Right:* John C. Frémont, c. 1856. Frémont's surveying expedition in 1844 is considered the first non-Indigenous group to see Lake Tahoe. Courtesy of the California History Room, California State Library, Sacramento. ID: 2008-1534.

Fig. 29. *Below: Eagle Cañon, from Eckley's Island, Emerald Bay, Western Shore of Lake Tahoe,* ca. 1864–1865. Eckley's Island was one of many names attached to what is commonly known today as Fannette Island in Emerald Bay. Photograph attributed to Lawrence and Houseworth. Courtesy of the J. Paul Getty Museum. Digital image courtesy of the Getty's Open Content Program. ID: 84.XC.979.4484.

Fig. 30. *Above:* Zephyr Cove with Mount Tallac in the background, ca. 1875. Photograph by Carleton Watkins. Courtesy of the J. Paul Getty Museum. Digital image courtesy of the Getty's Open Content Program. ID: 85.XM.36.

Fig. 31. *Opposite top: Friday's Station, Valley of Lake Tahoe,* ca. 1864–1865. Friday's Station was established in 1858 as a stage station on the Placerville–Carson City route. It later became a remount station for the Pony Express. The station was located at what is today known as Edgewood, Nevada. Photograph by Charles Leander Weed. Courtesy of the California Historical Society, San Francisco. ID: PC-RM-Lawrence-Houseworth_0651.

Fig. 32. *Opposite bottom: The Lake House, Lake Tahoe,* ca. 1864–1865. Established by R. G. Dean in 1859 on the south end of Lake Tahoe in Lake Valley, the Lake House is considered the first tourist resort at the lake. Photograph by Charles Leander Weed. Courtesy of the California Historical Society, San Francisco. ID: PC-RM-Lawrence-Houseworth_0653.

Fig. 33. *Above:* Trains of the Lake Tahoe NGRR descend into the Carson Valley, ca. 1877. Railroad cars carrying lumber from Lake Tahoe ran constantly as timbering expanded dramatically during the 1870s. Photograph by Carleton Watkins. Courtesy of the J. Paul Getty Museum. Digital image courtesy of the Getty's Open Content Program. ID: 87.XM.72.4.

Fig. 34. *Opposite top:* Tahoe House and Bar in Tahoe City, ca. 1873. Constructed by William Pomin (or Pomine) in 1868. Some historical reports credit Pomin for surveying and establishing Tahoe City in 1863. William Pomin's family is standing on the porch. Photograph by Carleton Watkins. Courtesy of the California History Room, California State Library, Sacramento, ID: Stereo-5347.

Fig. 35. *Opposite bottom:* Fallen Leaf Lake, ca. 1870. Fallen Leaf Lake is a mountain lake located about one mile southwest of Lake Tahoe in El Dorado County, California. Hiking to Fallen Leaf Lake was a frequent excursion for visitors to Lake Tahoe. Photograph by Carleton Watkins. Courtesy of the California History Room, California State Library, Sacramento. ID: 2010-0499.

Fig. 36. *Above:* Swift's Station on Carson and Lake Bigler Road, ca. 1865. Swift's Station was located about two miles east of Spooner Summit on the main road from Lake Tahoe to Carson City. Courtesy of the Library of Congress, Prints and Photographs Division, Washington DC. LC-USZ62-11012.

Fig. 37. *Opposite top: View on the Summit of the Sierra Nevada, Leading Down into Lake Valley,* ca. 1866. A wintertime scene on the crowded Placerville-Carson Road. Photograph by Charles Leander Weed. Courtesy of the California History Room, California State Library, Sacramento. ID: Stereo-3721.

Fig. 38. *Opposite bottom:* Elias Jackson "Lucky" Baldwin, ca. 1895. Lucky Baldwin was the owner of the Tallac House Resort on the southwest shoreline of Lake Tahoe, which was considered one of the finest at the lake. Baldwin was also a bit of a scoundrel. Courtesy of the California History Room, California State Library, Sacramento. ID: 2008-0882.

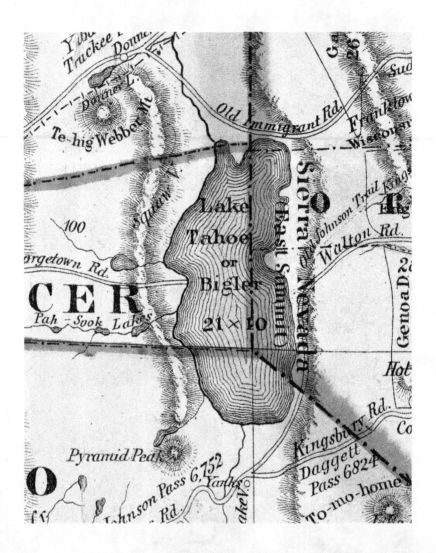

Fig. 39. For decades, there was vigorous debate as to the correct designation of Lake Tahoe. During the California gold rush and the Comstock Lode silver rush, the argument centered on Lake Tahoe versus Lake Bigler. Detail from *DeGroot's Map of Nevada Territory*, 1863. Courtesy of the California History Room, California State Library, Sacramento. ID: Basement Maps; 912 C15 1863.

Fig. 40. A family portrait of the Washoe people, ca. 1866. Photograph attributed to Lawrence and Houseworth. Courtesy of the J. Paul Getty Museum. Digital image courtesy of the Getty's Open Content Program. ID: 84.XC.902.157.

Fig. 41. The Carson and Tahoe Lumber and Fluming Company (CTLF), lumber and wood yard in Carson City, ca. 1880. During its twenty-three years of operation, the CTLF transported 750 million board feet of lumber from the Lake Tahoe Basin to Carson City. In the distance on the left is the Nevada State Capitol Building. Just over the ridge on the horizon is Lake Tahoe. Photograph by Carleton Watkins. Courtesy of the California History Room, California State Library, Sacramento. ID: Stereo-2112.

THREE

Delights and Damages

1870–1879

Tourism, timber, and transformation characterized Lake Tahoe from 1870–1879.

The completion of the transcontinental railroad in 1869 opened the Lake Tahoe Basin to increased visitation and magnified exploitation of resources. A cornucopia of travel guidebooks extolled the wonders and beauty of the lake (although a few observers were not impressed with Lake Tahoe), scientific studies examined the quality of the water and the impact of widespread logging, company records were jammed with profit statements and ledgers awash with black ink, and the beguiled rhapsodized on the spiritual rewards of their Lake Tahoe encounters.

Tourism reached another level, as more luxurious resorts were constructed and "older" establishments expanded. Preeminent was the Grand Central Hotel in Tahoe City, the grandest resort on the lake, opened in 1869. Some newer ventures, such as Dr. George Bourne's Hygienic Health Resort in Carnelian Bay (which he dubbed the Cornelian Bay Sanatoria), were tied to the touted health benefits of Lake Tahoe's air, lake water, and hot and cold mineral springs. Beyond the physical advantages, Lake Tahoe was promoted as a religious retreat—a heavenly place where, as Mark Twain memorably stated in *Roughing It*, "The air up there in the clouds is very pure and fine, bracing and delicious. And why shouldn't it be?—it is the same the angels breathe."

Meeting the daily needs of visitors and permanent residents remained a crucial component of the region's economy.

At least twenty-five commercial fishers operated at the lake on the principle that the best strategy was to remove as many trout as possible in the shortest time span. Fishers used a wide variety of techniques, including long seine nets, specially equipped trawlers, fish traps, dams, grab hooks, and even dynamite. Since the 1860s, laws had been passed to regulate the wasteful Lake Tahoe fishing trade—the fishers were hobbled but not harnessed. Tons of fish were shipped from the Truckee railhead in iced railroad cars to markets in San Francisco and as far east as New York. The Lake Tahoe fishery was rapidly being depleted.

In the watersheds on the California side of Lake Tahoe, large flocks of sheep were common, and streambed and hillside erosion resulted. Cattle ranches multiplied. More than a dozen dairies flourished, providing products for local consumption and export. Basin hay production reached hundreds of tons annually.

Everything old was new again, as the scheme to siphon Lake Tahoe water for use in San Francisco rematerialized. In 1870 Alexis Von Schmidt, who had first proposed the water diversion plan in 1865, purchased land at the Lake Tahoe outlet in Tahoe City and built a dam, effectively transforming the lake into a reservoir.

Initial research on the Lake Tahoe biosphere was undertaken. Analyses of the impact of overfishing, the effects of logging on water quality, and the consequences of large-scale timber operations on the environment in general commenced. Scientific reports indicated that determined settlement on the lakeshore and the residue of logging threatened the remarkable clarity of the lake water. These conclusions were spearheaded by the pioneering 1873 investigations of the biological, chemical, and physical features of Lake Tahoe water by Dr. John LeConte.

Large swaths of timber were efficiently severed from the ridges and valleys. While there was selective harvesting, most trees were clear-cut, leaving a sprawling landscape of stumps, a massive graveyard peppered with biological tombstones. The expansion of logging was breathtaking. Ringing the lake were dozens of timber claims and logging enterprises; some were independent contractors, while most were tied to large lumber companies such as the Carson Tahoe Lumber and Fluming Company, the El Dorado Wood and Lumber Company, the Sierra Nevada Wood and Lumber Company, the Nevada Lumber Company, the Truckee Lumber Company, and the Donner Lumber and Boom Company. These loggers controlled tens of thousands of acres in the Lake Tahoe Basin and harvested hundreds of millions of board feet of lumber that was used in railroad construction, for domestic and commercial structures, and to shore up mine shafts in the Comstock Lode. An estimated two-thirds of Lake Tahoe's timber resources were cut. Just one company—the Carson and Tahoe Lumber and Fluming Company—would, in its history, process 750 million board feet of lumber and stack five hundred thousand cords of wood in the Lake Tahoe Basin.

To facilitate the undertaking was an enormous infusion of capital, hundreds of loggers (many of whom were Chinese), wood camps, sawmills, lumberyards, reservoirs, inclined tramways, and the creation of a transportation spider web of narrow-gauge railroad spurs, timber rafting outfits, log booms, wagon and skid roads, and flumes—all of which significantly refashioned the Lake Tahoe natural environment.

Change is inevitable. After all, as the ancient Greek philosopher Heraclitus noted in 500 BCE, "There is nothing permanent except change." In the 1870s the transformations and resource exploitation at Lake Tahoe were mostly embraced as a muscular manifestation of the nineteenth-century desire to conquer nature and as partial fulfillment of national resolve. But some were troubled. They asked, should the most powerful amenity drawing people to Lake Tahoe—the virtues of clean air; deep blue, translucent waters; abundant wildlife; verdant forests; the appeal of solitude and reflection; and the opportunity to refresh one's spirit—be sacrificed on the altar of commerce and Manifest Destiny? Can the changes be stopped or, at least, slowed? Can Lake Tahoe be protected? These questions grew in importance in the years and decades that followed.

≈≈≈

So now everybody can come up and be steamboated.
—"San Francisco Markets, Etc.," *Sacramento Daily Union,* July 20, 1870

Lake Tahoe in the 1870s dawned with puffs of smoke from railroad engines and steamships. The decade was characterized by many notable activities, such as logging, commercial fishing, and the rapid growth of tourism. But new modes of transportation also left an indelible mark on the Gem of the Sierra.

In 1869 the transcontinental railroad was completed, and the station at Truckee provided improved access to Lake Tahoe that increased visitation dramatically. But, on the lake itself, the most visible transportation advancement was the presence of increasing numbers of steamships.

The first steamships arrived at Lake Tahoe in 1864, followed in subsequent decades by many additional steam vessels offering passenger ferry transport, express-delivery services, commercial freighting and fishing expansion, and support for the flourishing logging industry.

In an article in the July 20, 1870, edition of the Sacramento Daily Union, *a correspondent from Tahoe City took notice of the impressive, albeit slow, wagon delivery of the steamer* Emerald *from the railhead in Truckee to the north shore hamlet of Tahoe City. The fourteen-mile journey took seven days. The* Emerald *hauled passengers and freight and towed log booms until 1881.*

Steamers were welcomed as the next step in Lake Tahoe's commercial evolution. As the Sacramento Daily Union *correspondent observed, "This steamer is just what has been wanted for years to make it convenient for visitors to get around."*

In the article, Ben Holladay Jr. is referenced as the owner of the Emerald. *Holladay was an important figure in the history of the American West and Lake Tahoe. In the 1860s Ben Holladay owned the Overland Stage Line. He secured the exclusive government contracts to deliver mail throughout the West, and Holladay's Overland Stage became one of the largest employers in the United States. As his business prospered, Holladay reinvested the profits to acquire and eliminate competing freight and passenger companies. Holladay, who became known as the "Stagecoach King," sold his stage line to Wells Fargo in 1866 for $1.5 million ($29 million in 2023 money).*

Ben Holladay Jr. first visited Lake Tahoe in 1862; soon afterward, he obtained title to the lands surrounding Emerald Bay. Holladay built an estate at Emerald Bay—it is recognized as the first private estate at Lake Tahoe.

From Lake Tahoe

A correspondent of the Union, writing from Tahoe City, July 18th, gives these items of interest:

The little steamer *Emerald*, belonging to Ben Holladay, Jr., arrived safe at Tahoe last Monday. From the cars at Truckee she was put on heavy logging trucks, and with twelve yoke of cattle was hauled to Tahoe, occupying seven days in the trip. She was unloaded from the trucks on the Lake shore directly in front of the Tahoe House, where she was completely fitted up, her machinery put in place, and repainted. On Saturday she was launched, and Sunday she steamed up and made two trips across the lake to the Glenbrook House, bringing over a large party of Virginia City folks to Tahoe and returning with them in the evening. This steamer is just what has been wanted for years to make it convenient for visitors to get around. She runs twelve miles an hour, is comfortably fitted up, and strong and safe in any kind of weather. Captain Mackey superintended the getting of her here and fitting her up, and now she will be turned over to Captain Scott, who will run her. While on the steamboat question, it will be gratifying to the public to know that they will not be bound down to one only. Howland & Cay have their new hull about completed. Cay has just returned from San Francisco, where he has purchased a steam engine of John Lochhead's make, and it will be here within eight days; so now everybody can come up and be steamboated.

≈≈≈

A few weeks spent here in summer, is worth
more than a year squandered in Europe.

—Harvey Rice, *Letters from the Pacific Slope; or First Impressions*, 1870

The completion of the transcontinental railroad in 1869 unlocked the floodgates for tourist visitation to Lake Tahoe. Those with the means and the motivation to travel often made a point to include the two jewels of California scenery—Lake Tahoe and Yosemite—on their itineraries. Almost immediately after the transcontinental line opened, there were books, newspaper correspondence, and guidebooks touting both the beauty and the bounty of exploitable natural resources at Lake Tahoe.

An early case in point was provided by Harvey Rice in his 1870 book Letters from the Pacific Slope; or First Impressions. *Rice and his wife, Emma, crossed the country by rail in 1869, soon after the transcontinental railroad was fully operational.* Letters from the Pacific Slope *is Rice's account of his trip. While Harvey and Emma mostly stuck to the transcontinental route, they did make side excursions to Salt Lake City, Carson City, and Lake Tahoe.*

Harvey Rice was a prominent Cleveland, Ohio, lawyer, politician, and newspaper publisher. He made his greatest mark in 1828 when Rice and some partners purchased a small Cleveland newspaper called the Independent News-Letter, *which after reorganization in 1842, would be renamed the* Cleveland Plain Dealer. *This award-winning newspaper has been published continuously ever since.*

In this excerpt from Letters from the Pacific Slope; or First Impressions, *Harvey Rice described his visit to "wild and romantic" Lake Tahoe. He extolled the "pure, cool, and exhilarating" mountain air; delighted in his dinner of a fresh-caught, six-pound Lake Tahoe trout; and marveled at the "immense statue" of Shakespeare Rock. Rice noted that the lake's "waters are as clear and pure as crystal" and that the lake was not "made in vain" for the water might be siphoned for use in San Francisco.*

Lake Tahoe is certainly a beautiful gem—the most beautiful that ever glittered in the crown of a mountain monarchy. Its waters are as clear and pure as crystal. It is said to be more than two thousand feet deep; and though it receives several streams, it has no outlet. You can see fish and pebbles glimmering in its depths, as in a mirror. It is quite a large lake, being thirty miles long and ten or twelve broad; nor was it made in vain. San Francisco is agitating the question of monopolizing its waters for the use of its citizens, by conducting it in iron pipes to the city, a distance of a hundred and fifty miles, and at a cost estimated at twelve millions of dollars. Its borders are wild and romantic. It is surrounded by snow-capped mountains, which are reflected in the mirror of its waters. Ragged rocks, looking like armed giants, stand out here and there along its margin, as if to guard the spot from intrusion. Though located in a region of perpetual frost and snow, its waters never freeze; but why they should not, is a mystery. In summer it is a place of popular resort. The mountain air is pure, cool, and exhilarating. No invalid can breathe it without feeling its invigorating influence. Indeed its restorative influence is like the fabled elixir of life, it makes one, however old he may be, feel youthful, if not absolutely frolicsome. There is a small steamboat that plies on the lake, for the benefit and pleasure of visitors, and on both sides of the lake there are several first-class hotels, which furnish excellent accommodations for summer guests and pleasure parties. We stopped at the Glenbrook House, which commands a fine view of the lake and its scenery. The lake abounds in silver trout, so called because they are dotted with silver stars; a fresh-caught one, weighing six pounds, supplied us with an excellent dinner. The table was loaded with all kinds of luxuries, including the best of California fruits, and attended by a Chinese waiter.

Glenbrook gives name to the hotel, and runs dashing by its door, giggling and laughing like a mountain maid. On the opposite side of the glen rises Shakespeare Rock, two hundred feet high, looking like an immense statue, chiseled by human hands. It is in itself a marvel. Its apex resembles very distinctly the head of Shakespeare. The features of the face are like his in expression.

The brow is crowned with a wreath of golden moss; and the eyes, nose, mouth, and chin, fully delineated. There he stands facing the lake, and gazing in mute rapture upon its placid waters. No artist could improve this portraiture of genius, which has been thus lithographed by the hand of Nature, and placed on exhibition in this lofty granite hall of her own Mountain Home.

Not far from the Shakespeare statue appears Cathedral Rock, which is so named from its resemblance to a Roman church. It looks so much like a magnificent church, that you imagine you can see the worshipers inside, through the gothic windows, engaged in their devotions. About three miles from Glenbrook there is a wonderful cave in a rock, which presents a bold, perpendicular front, overlooking the lake and rising to a height of four hundred and eighty feet. The cave opens at its base and extends into the rock, like an arched passage-way, a hundred feet or more, and is high enough to admit of standing erect in it. We entered and advanced to its termination, but saw nothing except blackened, vitrified walls, and some specimens of jasper and agates. The cave was probably produced by volcanic action, and is well worth a visit.

There are many other interesting spots along the borders and in the vicinity of Lake Tahoe, which every excursionist should visit, who enjoys communion with Nature and admires her wonderful works. A few weeks spent here in summer, is worth more than a year squandered in Europe, or at a fashionable watering place in the Eastern States, so far as regards pleasure, or the attainment of health.

≈≈≈

He who cannot content himself for a time at Tahoe,
could not be satisfied in any place on earth; he
would need to find a new and better world.

—George Crofutt, *Crofutt's Trans-Continental Tourist's Guide*, 1871.

The opening of the transcontinental railroad line in 1869 fostered major growth for an already popular publication genre—travel guides and railway guides.

Riding the rails in the 1870s could be problematic. Weather was unpredictable, railroad maintenance could be spotty, no standardized time zones existed, and equipment could malfunction. And sometimes just knowing where one was and what was nearby could be a mystery. Guidebooks could plug the gaps.

Travel guides and railway guides had been in existence since the railroads first made their appearance in the 1830s, but with the transcontinental railroad now connecting the coasts, more information was increasingly desirable. In the 1870s dozens of guidebooks cataloging timetables, ticket prices, attractions, weather forecasts, lodgings, maps, and scenic information were published.

Arguably, the most popular guides were produced by George Andrews Crofutt, one of the most widely read and least-known authors of the nineteenth century. Born in Connecticut in 1827, Crofutt was a struggling journalist, editor, and publisher in New York City and Philadelphia. Bankrupted by the Panic of 1857, Crofutt joined the Pikes Peak gold rush in 1860. While he failed as a prospector in Colorado, George Crofutt found the American West irresistible.

On May 10, 1869, Crofutt attended the Golden Spike Ceremony at Promontory Summit, Utah, celebrating the joining of the Central Pacific Rail Road and the Union Pacific Railroad and inaugurating the transcontinental line. This momentous event rekindled Crofutt's passion for journalism. He began publishing tourist's guides to the American West and was immediately successful. Capitalizing on traveler fascination with the West and the economic windfall offered by transcontinental tourism, George Crofutt sold thousands of his guides. The guidebooks featured comprehensive research and were groundbreaking in their use of engravings of natural wonders.

Crofutt's tourist guides were unabashedly promotions for westward expansion. In 1872 George Crofutt commissioned one of the most famous paintings in nineteenth-century American West history—an allegory on Manifest Destiny entitled American Progress *by John Gast. The painting was widely reproduced at the time and is a frequent illustration in current histories of the American West.*

Following is an excerpt from the 1871 edition of Crofutt's Trans-Continental Tourist's Guide. *In this passage, Crofutt circles Lake Tahoe and spotlights such locales as Friday's Station, Tahoe City, Carnelian Bay, Emerald Bay, Sugar Pine Point, and several sawmills. George Crofutt strongly urges his readers to "go there and spend a short time . . . you will be in no hurry to leave."*

Lake Tahoe, or Bigler, as it is called on some of the official maps. Tahoe is an Indian name, signifying "big water," and is pronounced by the Indians "Tah-oo," while the "pale faces" pronounce it "Tahoe." It is located 12 miles south of Truckee. A splendid road affords one of the best and pleasantest drives to be found in the State. The road follows the river bank, under the shade of waving pines or across green meadows, until it reaches Tahoe City, at the foot of the lake. Here are excellent accommodations for travellers, a good hotel, boats, and a well-stocked stable, from whence you take a carriage (if you come by stage) and travel around the lake.

The latest attraction is a steamboat, placed upon the lake by B. Hollady [*sic*], Jr., for the accommodation of pleasure seekers.

According to the survey of the State line Lake Tahoe lies in two States and five counties. The line between California and Nevada runs north and south, through the lake, until it reaches a certain point therein, when it changes to a course 17 degs. east of south. Thus the counties of El Dorado and Placer, in California, and Washoe, Ormsby and Douglas, in Nevada, all share in the waters of the Tahoe. Where the line was surveyed through the lake it is 1,700 feet deep.

Starting on our exploring tour we will commence with the eastern shore. The first object of interest met with is a relic of the palmy days of staging:

Friday's Station, an old stage station, established by Burke in '59, on the Placerville and Tahoe stage road. Ten miles further on we come to the Glenbrook House, a favorite resort for tourists. Four miles further on we come to The Cave, a cavern in the hillside, fully 100 feet above and overhanging the lake. There are also two saw mills on the eastern shore of the lake. From Glenbrook House there is a fine road to Carson City.

Following around to the north end of the lake, and but a short distance away, are the celebrated Hot Springs, lying just across the State line, in Nevada. Near them is a splendid spring of clear cold water, totally devoid of mineral taste. The next object which attracts our attention is Carnelian Bay, a beautiful indenture in the coast, with fine gravel bottom. Thus far there has been scarcely a point from which the descent to the water's edge is not smooth and easy.

Passing on around to the west side we return to **Tahoe City**, which contains two hotels, two stores, one saloon, two livery stables and several private dwellings. Four miles from Tahoe City is Saxon's saw mill, and two miles beyond this we come to more saw mills, and finally we reach Sugar Pine Point, a spur of mountains covered with a splendid forest of sugar pine, the most valuable lumber, for all uses, found on the Pacific coast. There are fine streams running into the lake on each side of the point.

We now arrive at **Emerald Bay**, a beautiful placid inlet, two miles long, which seems to hide itself among the pine-clad hills. It is not over 400 Yards wide at its mouth, but widens to two miles inland, forming one of the prettiest land-locked harbors in the world. It is owned by Ben Holliday [*sic*]. At the south end of the lake is the site of the Old Lake House, burned a short time ago. . . . Around the lake the land is generally level for some distance back, and covered with pine, fir, and balsam timber, embracing at least 300 sections of as fine timbered land as the State affords. It is easy of access and handy to market, the logs being rafted down the lake to the Truckee, and thence down to any point on the railroad above Reno.

So much for the general appearance of Lake Tahoe. To understand its beauties, one must go there and spend a short time. When once there, sailing on the beautiful lake, gazing far down its shining, pebbly bottom, hooking the sparkling trout that make the pole sway and bend in your hand like a willow wand, you will be in no hurry to leave. If you become tired of sailing and angling, take your gun and tramp into the hills and fill your game pouch with quail and grouse, and perhaps you may start up a deer or bear. He who cannot content himself for a time at Tahoe, could not be satisfied in any place on earth; he would need to find a new and better world.

We have now circled the lake and can judge of its dimensions, which are 22 miles in length and ten in width. We are loath to leave it, but we will return to Truckee, and thence to **Donner Lake.**

≈≈≈

How can San Francisco seriously entertain a similar project.

—*Report of the Special Committee of the Board of Supervisors,*
. . . on the Water Supplies for the City of San Francisco, 1871

In 1871, Alexis Von Schmidt tried again. Six years earlier, in 1865, Von Schmidt had proposed a massive water plan to transfer Lake Tahoe water from the Truckee River to the San Francisco Bay Area via a series of tunnels and canals through the Sierra Nevada and an aqueduct bisecting the Central Valley. The notion was abandoned after fierce opposition, primarily from Nevada interests.

Alexis von Schmidt was not discouraged. On October 1, 1871, he resurrected the project and issued Report to the Lake Tahoe and San Francisco Water Works Company on Its Sources of Supply; Proposed Line of Works; Estimated Cost and Income. *The new proposition was essentially the same as the 1865 project but with one added wrinkle.*

In 1870, to thwart an aqueduct, the California Legislature had granted the Donner Lumber and Boom Company the right to construct a small dam at the Lake Tahoe–Truckee River outlet.

Undaunted, Von Schmidt sprang into action. By the end of 1870 the Lake Tahoe and San Francisco Water Works Company purchased land at the lake outlet in Tahoe City and planned to construct its own dam, with a second diversion dam downstream. Alexis von Schmidt claimed that the main dam would raise the lake level by six feet and provide as much as 820 million gallons of water daily for San Francisco. The project would channel water from the Truckee River to Squaw Valley (today's Palisades Tahoe), construct a tunnel to the North Fork of the American River and eventually, through an aqueduct, deliver the water to San Francisco. The Lake Tahoe and San Francisco Water Works Company would have a monopoly on the water delivery. The cost would be $10 million ($235 million in 2023 money).

In 1871 Alexis Von Schmidt and his water company formally proposed the project to the County of San Francisco Board of Supervisors. Von Schmidt's blueprint was approved by the Board of Supervisors, but it was vetoed by San Francisco mayor Thomas Selby over misgivings regarding the water company's monopoly and the threat of lawsuits. After a lively discussion, the Board of Supervisors sustained the veto.

As part of the debate over the project, an 1871 report entitled Report of the Special Committee of the Board of Supervisors, Together with Communications of Gen. B. S. Alexander, USA, and Prof. George Davidson, USCS, on the Water Supplies for the City of San Francisco *was issued. The report's conclusion was that Von Schmidt's "scheme" was fanciful at best (or "chimerical," to use the report's term) and much too expensive for the project's anticipated benefits. A portion of the argument compared the proposed Lake Tahoe–San Francisco water project to a similar project slated for London.*

Lake Tahoe

The Lake Tahoe project in particular embraces a scheme of tunnelling at the outstart, to tap the proposed supply of water, nearly equal in magnitude to the famous Mont Cenis Tunnel under the Alps, which has cost about $15,000,000, and required fourteen years of active work, backed by the cheap labor and mechanical resources of two great nations to complete. Such a scheme as this for our water supply has been well referred to as "chimerical;" and when we further consider that this costly mountain labor—for which this city has been modestly requested to pay $6,000,000 as a starter, with the prospect of having the privilege of paying unlimited millions more in future to keep the ball in motion—is to bring us forth a veritable mouse of twenty millions gallons of water for our people as the projectors may see fit to supply, it may deserve a harsher epithet.

Disadvantages of Seeking a Water Supply from Very Distant Sources

Another important question for consideration is the risk of frequent interruptions of the water supply from sources so distant, requiring so long a line of works, crossing in their route as projected, broad plains, large rivers, and our still larger bay.

In this connection we think it may not be improper for us to quote from the report of the Royal Commissioners, on the water supply of London, page 126, which says:

> As to the plans for obtaining water from the mountainous districts of England and Wales, we are of opinion that Mr. Bateman's scheme is, in an engineering point of view, feasible and practicable, and that by it a large supply of water might be obtained for the metropolis, but that experience warrants great caution in judging of the sufficiency of a gravitation scheme of such magnitude.
>
> That the quality of the water would be satisfactory as regards its purity.
>
> That the outlay for the scheme would be very large, amounting, according to the evidence laid before us, to about £11,000,000; but in the absence of detailed surveys, and in a project involving works of such great magnitude and novelty, and subject to such large contingencies and elements of uncertainty, we do not consider that it is possible to arrive at any trustworthy estimate of the cost.—
>
> That even assuming that the work could be carried out for the estimated amount, the cost to the metropolis of obtaining water by this scheme would be much greater than is incurred by the present plan, and would continue to be so up to any quantity likely to be required within a reasonable lapse of time.
>
> That grave doubts may be entertained whether it is desirable that the metropolis should be dependent on one source of supply so far removed, and which might be liable to accidental interruption.

The same reasoning, perhaps slightly modified, will apply to obtaining a water supply from the lakes on the western slope of the Sierras, or the head waters of the American, the Mokelumne and other rivers heading in the Sierra Nevada mountains. *If London with its vast population of nearly four millions of people and its almost fabulous wealth, hesitates to go one hundred and eighty miles for a water supply, how can San Francisco seriously entertain a similar project.*

≈≈≈

It must surely be the fairest picture the whole earth affords.
—Mark Twain, *Roughing It*, 1872

Written between 1870 and the end of 1871 and published early in 1872, Mark Twain's second major work was titled Roughing It. *It is about Twain going west to dig for wealth on and in the rocks of California and Nevada and ultimately finding prosperity as a journalist and entertainer. The book was based on the trials and escapades Twain (then known as Samuel Clemens, of course) had experienced between 1861 and 1866. Among its most famous passages is Twain's description of his 1861 arrival at Lake Tahoe with his friend and business partner John Kinney, referred to as "Johnny" by Twain.*

We had heard a world of talk about the marvelous beauty of Lake Tahoe, and finally curiosity drove us thither to see it. Three or four members of the Brigade had been there and located some timber lands on its shores and stored up a quantity of provisions in their camp. We strapped a couple of blankets on our shoulders and took an axe apiece and started— for we intended to take up a wood ranch or so ourselves and become wealthy. We were on foot. The reader will find it advantageous to go horseback. We were told that the distance was eleven miles.

We tramped a long time on level ground, and then toiled laboriously up a mountain about a thousand miles high and looked over. No lake there. We descended on the other side, crossed the valley and toiled up another mountain three or four thousand miles high, apparently, and looked over again. No lake yet. We sat down tired and perspiring, and hired a couple of Chinamen to curse those people who had beguiled us. Thus refreshed, we presently resumed the march with renewed vigor and determination. We plodded on, two or three hours longer, and at last the Lake burst upon us—a noble sheet of blue water lifted six thousand three hundred feet above the level of the sea, and walled in by a rim of snow-clad mountain peaks that towered aloft full three thousand feet higher still! It was a vast oval, and one would have to use up eighty or a hundred good miles in traveling around it. As it lay there with the shadows of the mountains brilliantly photographed upon its still surface I thought it must surely be the fairest picture the whole earth affords.

We found the small skiff belonging to the Brigade boys, and without loss of time set out across a deep bend of the lake toward the landmarks that signified the locality of the camp. I got Johnny to row—not because I mind exertion myself, but because it makes me sick to ride backwards when I am at work. But I steered. A three-mile pull brought us to the camp just as the night fell, and we stepped ashore very tired and wolfishly hungry. In a "cache" among the rocks we found the provisions and the cooking utensils, and then, all fatigued as I was, I sat down on a boulder and superintended while Johnny gathered wood and cooked supper. Many a man who had gone through what I had, would have wanted to rest.

It was a delicious supper—hot bread, fried bacon, and black coffee. It was a delicious solitude we were in, too. Three miles away was a saw-mill and some workmen, but there were not fifteen other human beings throughout the wide circumference of the lake. As the darkness closed down and the stars came out and spangled the great mirror with jewels, we smoked meditatively in the solemn hush and forgot our troubles and our pains. In due time we spread our blankets in the warm sand between two large boulders and soon feel asleep, careless of the procession of ants that passed in through rents in our clothing and explored our persons. Nothing could disturb the sleep that fettered us, for it had been fairly earned, and if our consciences had any sins on them they had to adjourn court for that night, any way. The wind rose just as we were losing consciousness, and we were lulled to sleep by the beating of the surf upon the shore.

It is always very cold on that lake shore in the night, but we had plenty of blankets and were warm enough. We never moved a muscle all night, but waked at early dawn in the original positions, and got up at once, thoroughly refreshed, free from soreness, and brim full of friskiness. There is no end of wholesome medicine in such an experience. That morning we could have whipped ten such people as we were the day before—sick ones at any rate. But the world is slow, and people will go to "water cures" and "movement cures" and to foreign lands for health. Three months of camp life on Lake Tahoe would restore an Egyptian mummy to his pristine vigor, and give him an appetite like an alligator. I do not mean the oldest and driest mummies, of course, but the fresher ones. The air up there in the clouds is very pure and fine, bracing and delicious. And why shouldn't it be?—it is the same the angels breathe.

Samuel Clemens and John Kinney only enjoyed their initial Lake Tahoe reverie for several days. After surveying and provisioning a "wood ranch" of several hundred acres, flames escaped their campfire. The roaring blaze that followed destroyed their dreams and a sizeable portion of the forest.

By and by our provisions began to run short, and we went back to the old camp and laid in a new supply. We were gone all day, and reached home again about nightfall, pretty tired and hungry. While Johnny was carrying the main bulk of the provisions up to our " house" for future use, I took the loaf of bread, some slices of bacon, and the coffee-pot, ashore, set them down by a tree, lit a fire, and went back to the boat to get the frying-pan. While I was at this, I heard a shout from Johnny, and looking up I saw that my fire was galloping all over the premises!

Johnny was on the other side of it. He had to run through the flames to get to the lake shore, and then we stood helpless and watched the devastation.

The ground was deeply carpeted with dry pine-needles, and the fire touched them off as if they were gunpowder. It was wonderful to see with what fierce speed the tall sheet of flame traveled! My coffee-pot was gone, and everything with it. In a minute and a half the fire seized upon a dense growth of dry manzanita chapparal six or eight feet high, and then the roaring and popping and crackling was some-thing terrific. We were driven to the boat by the intense heat, and there we remained, spell-bound.

Within half an hour all before us was a tossing, blinding tempest of flame! It went surging up adjacent ridges—surmounted them and disappeared in the canyons beyond—burst into view upon higher and farther ridges, presently—shed a grander illumination abroad, and dove again—flamed out again, directly, higher and still higher up the mountain-side—threw out skirmishing parties of fire here and there, and sent them trailing their crimson spirals away among remote ramparts and ribs and gorges, till as far as the eye could reach the lofty mountain-fronts were webbed as it were with a tangled network of red lava streams. Away across the water the crags and domes were lit with a ruddy glare, and the firmament above was a reflected hell!

Every feature of the spectacle was repeated in the glowing mirror of the lake! Both pictures were sublime, both were beautiful; but that in the lake had a bewildering richness about it that enchanted the eye and held it with the stronger fascination.

We sat absorbed and motionless through four long hours. We never thought of supper, and never felt fatigue. But at eleven o'clock the conflagration had traveled beyond our range of vision, and then darkness stole down upon the landscape again.

Hunger asserted itself now, but there was nothing to eat. The provisions were all cooked, no doubt, but we did not go to see. We were homeless wanderers again, without any property. Our fence was gone, our house burned down; no insurance. Our pine forest was well scorched, the dead trees all burned up, and our broad acres of manzanita swept away. Our blankets were on our usual sand-bed, however, and so we lay down and went to sleep. The next morning we started back to the old camp, but while out a long way from shore, so great a storm came up that we dared not try to land. So I bailed out the seas we shipped, and Johnny pulled heavily through the billows till we had reached a point three or four miles beyond the camp. The storm was increasing, and it became evident that it was better to take the hazard of beaching the boat than go down in a hundred fathoms of water; so we ran in, with tall white-caps following, and I sat down in the stern-sheets and pointed her head-on to the shore. The instant the bow struck, a wave came over the stern that washed crew and cargo ashore, and saved a deal of trouble. We shivered in the lee of a boulder all the rest of the day, and froze all the night through. In the morning the tempest had gone down, and we paddled down to the camp without any unnecessary delay. We were so starved that we ate up the rest of the Brigade's provisions, and then set out to Carson [City] to tell them about it and ask their forgiveness. It was accorded, upon payment of damages.

The exact location of the Twain's timber claim and conflagration has been the subject of lively debate for some time. Some historians believe the site is in Nevada on the eastern shore of Lake Tahoe adjacent to today's Thunderbird Lodge, while others argue for various spots on the northern end of the lake in or near Carnelian Bay or Agate Bay. In 2011 a proposal to label a portion of the eastern Lake Tahoe shoreline between the Thunderbird Lodge and Sand Harbor as Clemens Cove was submitted to the United States Board on Geographic Names by the Nevada State Board on Geographic Names. It was rejected, with the primary objection from the Lake Tahoe Basin Management Unit of the U.S. Forest Service.

In December 2013 the Clemens Cove naming was briefly revived by the Nevada State Sesquicentennial Commission, with the unanimous backing of the commission board, including then Nevada lieutenant governor Brian Krolicki, chair of the commission. On this occasion, the principal opposition was lodged by the leadership of the Washoe Tribe of Nevada and California. The Washoe people objected to Clemens Cove based upon Clemens's (Twain's) racist descriptions of the Lake Tahoe Native population and his disparagement of the designation of Tahoe for the lake. An example of Twain's comments is found in his 1869 book, Innocents Abroad: "*Tahoe means grasshoppers. It means grasshopper soup. It is Indian, and suggestive of Indians. They say it is Piute—possibly it is Digger. I am satisfied it was named by the Diggers—those degraded savages who roast their dead relatives, then mix the human grease and ashes of bones with tar, and 'gaum' it thick all over their heads and foreheads and ears, and go caterwauling about the hills and call it mourning. These are the gentry that named the Lake.*"

In May 2014 consideration for Clemens Cove was indefinitely suspended by the Nevada State Board on Geographic Names.

≈≈≈

I was more disappointed with the lake than
I should otherwise have been.

—J. W. Boddam-Whetham, *Western Wanderings; A
Record of Travel in the Evening Land,* 1874

Most who visited Lake Tahoe found it beyond compare, but there were a handful who were tepid about its charms—case in point, John Whetham Boddam-Whetham of England.

Born in 1843 at Kirklinton Hall, Country Cumbria, in northwest England, Boddam-Whetham was known as a first-class cricketer in his youth. In his late twenties, J. W. Boddam-Whetham embarked on world travel, visiting such spots as Fiji, Samoa, Australia, and Central and South America. In the early 1870s Boddam-Whetham toured the United

States, which resulted in his 1874 book Western Wanderings: A Record of Travel in the Evening Land. *His excursion took him to New York, Chicago, Omaha, Salt Lake City, Virginia City, Oregon, Washington, British Columbia, and Hawaii. In California, Boddam-Whetham visited San Francisco, Mount Shasta, the Modoc Plateau, Yosemite Valley, and Lake Tahoe.*

J.W. did not much care for America. In the final chapter of Western Wanderings, *he states,*

> *The Old World offers many attractions that are wanting in the New World. In the first place, the social attractions afforded by the capitals of Europe are vastly superior to those of America. Then there are the charms of antiquity, of historical and artistic association; the wonderful picture-galleries, the museums, the sculpture; everything, in short, to gratify the tastes of the merest tyro as well as those of the most cultivated connoisseur. . . . After having seen Rome, Naples, and Athens he is not likely to care for Chicago or San Francisco.*

Boddam-Whetham did appreciate California, however, noting that the Golden State was "a most charmingly attractive country to those who have once had experience of its delights."

J.W. was lukewarm regarding Lake Tahoe. While he enjoyed most of the "charming scenery," he found the lake inferior to Italy's Lake Como and was thoroughly disappointed with the lack of game and good hunting which he had been led to believe was a Lake Tahoe trademark.

From Carson a capital road, but a very steep one, took me to Glenbrook House, a pleasant little inn, situated on Lake Tahoe. Mark Twain, in one of his amusing books—' Innocents Abroad,' I think—says that this lake is superior to the Italian lakes. I suppose he means its situation is higher, as, although very beautiful, it wants the variety of scene and the lovely islands and villas which give such wondrous views to those delightful lakes.

Entirely surrounded by mountains covered with sad forests of gigantic pines, Lake Tahoe would present rather a sombre aspect if it were not for its marvellously clear and sparkling water, in which you may 'try and drown many worms,' as the poacher said when caught fishing in preserved waters. Perhaps I was more disappointed with the lake than

I should otherwise have been from having been told there was capital shooting amongst the surrounding hills, but finding, after many long trudges and many conversations with wood-cutters, &c. on the subject, that there was no game at all worth speaking of, as all birds and animals had been driven away by the advance of civilization. There is a singular natural curiosity on the face of a high rock in full view of the lake. It is a profile of Shakespeare, and not at all a bad likeness. It has been formed by depressions in the stone like a gigantic natural intaglio.

A little steamer carried me to Tahoe City, on the opposite side of the lake, crossing the line on its way, as the division between Nevada and California runs—north and south through the lake. The lake is about twenty miles long and ten broad, and there are many points of interest around it. Caves, hot-springs, and beautiful little bays and inlets abound, and the valley of Lake Creek is one of the most fertile in the Sierras, and is dotted over with farms and milk ranches. The shores of Lake Tahoe have been chosen for the site of the Lick Observatory, the princely gift of Mr. Lick to the State. Another point of interest will soon, therefore, be added to the charming scenery.

From Tahoe City, a drive of about twelve miles along the river-bank and across green meadows brought me to Truckee station, whence, after visiting Donner Lake, which is a miniature Tahoe, I proceeded on my journey.

≈≈≈

Sunday at Tahoe! I wish I could spend it in perfect
quiet. But my underclothes must be changed.
—Joseph LeConte, *A Journal of Ramblings through*
the High Sierra of California, 1875

Joseph LeConte was born in Georgia in 1823 but is best known for his experiences in California.

LeConte earned his medical degree in New York and set up a practice in his home state of Georgia but soon discovered that his specialty was not medicine, but geology. LeConte went back to school, studying geology at Harvard under Louis Agassiz, a prominent but controversial pioneer of natural history scholarship and scientific methodology. Upon graduation, LeConte taught natural science, chemistry, and geology at numerous colleges in the South. In 1869 Joseph moved to Berkeley, California, where he joined the faculty of the recently created University of California. He was accompanied by his brother John, a physics professor, a future president of the University of California, and an early scientific researcher of Lake Tahoe limnology.

In 1870 LeConte embarked on a five-week horseback trip to the Sierra Nevada with a party that included University of California students and professors. The trek famously included outings to Yosemite and Lake Tahoe. Joseph LeConte's recollections of the journey would ultimately be published as A Journal of Ramblings through the High Sierra of California. Also stemming from this excursion and other subsequent visits were a campaign to establish today's Yosemite National Park, calls to promote more recreational use of the Sierra, and the establishment of the Sierra Club in 1892. Joseph LeConte died of a heart attack during a 1901 Sierra Club outing in Yosemite.

The legacy of Joseph LeConte has been revised over the years. In 1903 the Sierra Club built the LeConte Memorial Lodge in Yosemite Valley in his honor. The lodge was renamed the Yosemite Conservation Heritage Center in 2016 after the unearthing and reevaluation of Joseph LeConte's white supremacist writings. An unapologetic Confederate and slaveholder, LeConte considered Reconstruction indefensible and frequently used racist descriptions in his publications, most notably in his posthumously published 1903 The Autobiography of Joseph LeConte.

Despite LeConte's indefensible bigotry, his commentaries provide useful insight into the prevailing nineteenth-century fashion of Sierra Nevada scientific writing—a fusion of scientific precision and pensive musing. In this passage from his A Journal of Ramblings Through the High Sierras of California, Joseph LeConte recalls a lazy two days at Lake Tahoe in August 1870. LeConte noted that Lake Tahoe was a "lovely lake" where "I could dream away my life here with those I love."

August 21[1870]. Sunday at Tahoe! I wish I could spend it in perfect quiet. But my underclothes must be changed. Cleanliness is a Sunday duty. Some washing is necessary. Some of the party went fishing today. The rest of us remained in camp and mended or washed clothes.

At 12 M. I went out alone, and sat on the shore of the Lake, with the waves breaking at my feet. How brightly emerald-green the waters near the shore, and how deeply and purely blue in the distance! The line of demarcation is very distinct, showing that the bottom drops off suddenly. How distinct the mountains and cliffs all around the Lake; only lightly tinged with blue on the farther side, though more than twenty miles distant!

How greatly is one's sense of beauty affected by association! Lake Mono is surrounded by much grander and more varied mountain scenery than this; its waters are also very clear, and it has the advantage of several very picturesque islands; but the dead volcanoes, the wastes of volcanic sand and ashes covered only by interminable sagebrush, the bitter, alkaline, dead, slimy waters, in which nothing but worms live; the insects and flies which swarm on its surface, and which are thrown upon its shore in such quantities as to infect the air,—all these produce a sense of desolation and death which is painful; it destroys entirely the beauty of the lake itself; it unconsciously mingles with and alloys the pure enjoyment of the incomparable mountain scenery in its vicinity. On the contrary, the deep-blue, pure waters of Lake Tahoe, rivaling in purity and blueness the sky itself; its clear, bright emerald shore-waters, breaking snow-white on its clean rock and gravel shores; the Lake basin, not on a plain, with mountain scenery in the distance, but counter-sunk in the mountain's top itself,—these produce a never-ceasing and ever-increasing sense of joy, which naturally grows into love. There would seem to be no beauty except as associated with human life and connected with a sense of fitness for human happiness. Natural beauty is but the type of spiritual beauty. Enjoyed a very refreshing swim in the Lake this afternoon. The water is much less cold than that of Lake Tenaya or the Tuolumne River, or even the Nevada River.

The party which went out fishing returned with a very large trout. It was delicious. . . .

August 22. Nothing to do to-day. . . .

I went down alone to the Lake, sat down on the shore and enjoyed the scene. Nothing to do, my thoughts to-day naturally went to the dear ones at home. Oh! how I wish they could be here and enjoy with me this lovely Lake! I could dream away my life here with those I love. How delicious a dream! Of all the places I have yet seen, this is the one I could longest enjoy and love the most. Reclining thus in the shade, on the clean white sand, the waves rippling at my feet, with thoughts of Lake Tahoe and of my loved ones mingling in my mind, I fell into a delicious doze. After my doze I returned to camp, to dinner.

About 5 p.m. took another and last swim in the Lake.

≈≈≈

M. C. Gardner alone has a contract to supply 60,000,000 feet of logs during the next six years.

—Charles F. McGlashan, "Resources and Wonders of Tahoe," *Sacramento Daily Union*, May 29, 1875

In 1875 two articles appeared in the Sacramento Daily Union *that detailed the resources and scientific discoveries at Lake Tahoe in mid-decade. The stories were written by one of the most consequential and reprehensible figures in Lake Tahoe Basin History.*

The articles were "Resources and Wonders of Lake Tahoe" (May 29, 1875) and "Scientific Fun on Lake Tahoe" (July 24, 1875). They were published under the byline of C. F. McGlashan.

Charles Fayette (C. F.) McGlashan, was a lawyer, journalist, chronicler of the Donner party, butterfly collector, member of the California State Assembly, and, in his later years, champion of anti-Chinese suppression.

Born in Wisconsin in 1847, McGlashan and his family moved to Placerville, California, in 1854. In the early 1870s McGlashan settled in Truckee. A few years later, he hung his shingle as a lawyer and became publisher and editor of the most influential regional newspaper in the Lake Tahoe–Truckee district—the Truckee Republican.

During his nearly seventy years in Truckee, Charles McGlashan chronicled the daily comings and goings in the growing tourist and railroad center. He also become known as a recognized expert on butterflies. With his daughter Ximena, McGlashan operated a butterfly hatchery, which they called a "farm," and published twelve well-received issues of a magazine entitled The Butterfly Farmer.

In 1879 Charles F. McGlashan wrote The History of the Donner Party, *which is considered the first comprehensive historical examination of the Donner party tragedy of 1846–1847. McGlashan relied on newspaper articles, diaries, survivor interviews, and the unpublished memoirs of Donner party members. Perhaps his most famous survivor interview was with the reviled Louis Keseberg, who was accused of a gruesome litany of offenses, including theft, murder, and cannibalism.*

But these accomplishments were eclipsed by McGlashan's racism. In the 1880s Charles F. McGlashan was elected to the California State Assembly and became a leader in the anti-Chinese movement sweeping the American West. McGlashan fervently advocated the "Truckee method" that used starvation, boycotts, and denial of services to attack Chinese immigrants and residents. On January 13, 1886, McGlashan noted in a Truckee Republican *editorial, "Either the whites will rule Truckee and the Chinese must leave, or the Chinese must rule and the whites will leave. There will be no compromise, no flag of truce, no cessation of hostilities until the final surrender is made." Within a few weeks, the Truckee method led to hundreds of Chinese abandoning Truckee. McGlashan was named chairman of the Anti-Chinese League of San Jose and, also in 1886, he took the reins of the State Anti-Chinese Non-Partisan Association, headquartered in San Francisco.*

When Charles F. McGlashan died on January 6, 1931, many California newspapers noted his passing. The death notices declared him "one of the state's most notable figures," a "famous California journalist, attorney, and scientist" and a "pioneer historian." Not a single obituary mentioned that McGlashan had been a leader in the anti-Chinese movement.

The May 29, 1875, article "Resources and Wonders of Lake Tahoe" was likely inspired by the trailblazing 1873 investigations of the biological, chemical, and physical features of Lake Tahoe water by Dr. John LeConte. McGlashan's story highlights many aspects of the Lake Tahoe's economy, including the lumber industry, dairy farming, hay harvesting, and commercial fishing. Charles McGlashan also relates the tales of some Lake Tahoe characters, most notably Captain Dick, "the Hermit of Tahoe."

In this excerpt, McGlashan begins with his arrival at Glenbrook, a lumber mill compound on the eastern shore. Glenbrook is "noisy, dusty, smoky, and, withal, busy, [and] reminds us that profit as well as pleasure lurks around the shores of the lake." And one of the major profit engines is lumbering, which Charles McGlashan describes in detail. Given McGlashan's anti-Chinese sentiments, the passage on lumber industry personnel concludes with his unsurprising comment: "Four gangs of Chinamen are working on the narrow gauge, but white labor is preferred."

Glenbrook, noisy, dusty, smoky, and, withal, busy, reminds us that profit as well as pleasure lurks around the shores of the lake, and we are at once inquiring about

The Resources of Tahoe.

We find them numerous and exceedingly interesting. Nearly a dozen hotels do a thriving summer business in attending to the wants of tourists, yet tourists bring only a small portion of the cash to Tahoe. The lubering [lumbering] interests are immense. The high mountain walls which encircle the lake are covered luxuriantly with forests. The Carson and Tahoe Lumbering and Fluming Company are letting exceeding large contracts. M. C. Gardner alone has a contract to supply 60,000,000 feet of logs during the next six years. He supplies six million feet this year and at the rate of 12,000,000 per annum thereafter.

Logging by Railroad

It is generally understood that the Carson and Tahoe Company are building a narrow gauge railway from Glenbrook to the Summit beyond, to connect with the head of their lumber flume. It is not so generally known, however, that Gardner is building a broad gauge railroad through Lake Valley to haul saw logs to the lake. The road when completed will be from four to nine miles, and will extend to the very shore. The heavy logs will be loaded on the cars in the woods, and drawn by regular locomotive engines to the lake, and from thence will be towed by steamers in rafts to the Glenbrook mills. Maine lumbermen, with all their boasted laurels, must look to it lest California be the first to substitute railway cars for logging trucks, and engines for ox teams.

There are three sawmills now running, and by the first of June two more will start. The Carson and Tahoe Company are building a magnificent first class mill at Glenbrook, and Spooner and Patten are erecting a good sawmill two miles southeast of Glenbrook, and have a contract for cutting 20,000,000 feet of lumber. To Mr. Rigby, of Glenbrook, I am indebted for the following estimates of the daily capacity of the mills and the amount they are to saw during 1875. The new mill at Glenbrook is called a double mill. One side squares up the logs in readiness for the saws of the other side to convert it into lumber: Carson Company's old mill, daily capacity, 50,000 feet; amount to cut in 1875, 6,000,000 feet; Carson Company's new mill, daily capacity, 75,000 feet; amount to cut in 1875, 11,000,000 feet; Captain Bragg's mill, daily capacity, 40,000 feet; amount to cut in 1875, 4,000,000 feet; Glenbrook (F. Davis) mill, daily capacity, 50,000 feet; amount to cut in 1875, 6,000,000 feet; Spooner and Patten, amount to cut in 1875, 2,000,000 feet. Total to be cut in 1875, 29,000,000 feet.

In addition to the above amount of timber which is contracted to be sawed this year, there are 3,000,00 or 4 000,000 feet of hewn timber on the northern shore of the lake ready for market. This increases the figures of the actual Tahoe lumber trade of 1875 to

Thirty-Three Million Feet.

This does not include the shingle business nor getting out lagging. Davis and Noteware have about 2,000,000 shingles on hand which were sawed at Bay City this last winter. The engines and machinery of the steamer *Truckee* were taken out last fall, placed in the Bay City Shingle Mill, and this spring were replaced in the vessel. There is little market for shingles. Davis and Scott are erecting a shingle mill about two miles from Hot Springs, and will cut enough to supply the Carson yard of the Glenbrook Mill Company. Perhaps they will cut 1,000,000 this summer.

Logging is used in the mines for braces. It is seven or eight feet in length, four inches wide and three inches thick. It is principally carried on at the western side of the lake by McCumber and Fozner. About 75,000 is the annual amount cut and split, and the market price is ten cents apiece.

The Supply of Timber

In the lake basin is by no means inexhaustible, but will supply the present demands for ten or twelve years. The best timber is at the foot of the lake, and in the largest quantities. Twelve thousand feet of logs will come this year from the south end of the lake, six from Sugar Pine Point, five from Tahoe City and seven from Bay City and Griffs.

The boating and rafting business employs about forty or fifty men. The steamers *Emerald*, *Truckee* and *Blasdell* tow rafts of lumber which average about 200,000 feet. There is a great variety of small boats and sailing craft, and boatmen's wages will average during the business season from $40 to $50 per month and board. Lumbermen get $50, $75 and even as high as $150. The mills above mentioned employ about 250 white men; over 150 are working on the railroad, and there are engaged in the logging business around the lake about 130 men. Four gangs of Chinamen are working on the narrow gauge, but white labor is preferred.

≈≈≈

By coercion they are made subservient to
the intellect of the superior race.
—*Report of Explorations across the Great Basin of the*
Territory of Utah for a Direct Wagon-Route from Camp Floyd
to Genoa, in Carson Valley, in 1859, by Captain J. H. Simpson,
appendix O, United States Department of War, 1876

Until 1861, Nevada was part of the huge Utah Territory. The Utah Territory was established in 1850 and included land that became the present-day areas of Utah, western Colorado, a small sliver of Wyoming, and northern Nevada. In 1861 Nevada Territory was carved from Utah Territory primarily to permit greater governmental control of the Comstock Lode–Washoe silver resources. Nevada was admitted as the thirty-sixth state in 1864.

An ongoing concern of the United States and territorial governments was the threat (perhaps more accurately, the perceived threat) presented by the Indigenous nations of the region. Formulating a policy and course of action became a priority. Government and military authorities relied on the testimony and analyses of those considered experts on the Native communities.

While the attitudes of the so-called experts, government officials, and military leaders were often in harmony, there were the occasional disagreements. These differences led to variations in the oversight of the Native population, regularly to the detriment of the Indigenous nations. Beyond the indignity of their situation, Native people were frustrated and burdened with uncertainty. While some government advisors might argue for more charitable treatment of the original inhabitants, these recommendations were frequently swept away by the dominant culture's lust for Native lands and their mineral and commercial resources. A classic example occurred in 1851 with the case of the secret treaties.

In that year the federal government appointed three commissioners to negotiate treaties with California Indians. By 1852 the commission-

ers claimed eighteen treaties had been negotiated with 139 tribes. The eighteen treaties set aside over seven million acres of land for Native use and would fund programs for Indian self-sufficiency. Upon learning of the treaties, the California public was furious. The California State Legislature instructed the United States senators from California to oppose ratification of the treaties.

In February 1852 President Millard Fillmore submitted the eighteen treaties to the United States Senate for ratification. The Senate adjourned to a secret session to consider the treaties. During this session, the Senate failed to ratify any of the eighteen treaties. The Senate ordered the treaties to be sealed and kept secret for the next fifty-three years.

An additional illustration of the differing opinions regarding the parameters of territorial, state, and federal Indian policy is presented here. In 1859 an exploration of the Utah Territory was undertaken by Captain James H. Simpson of the Corps of Topographical Engineers. Coming on the heels of the short-lived Utah War of 1857–1858, a series of armed confrontations between Mormon settlers and the U.S. military, Simpson's company was to survey a wagon road and provide reconnaissance across the eastern section of the Utah Territory.

The subsequent 1859 expedition report (which was not published until 1876) also included an evaluation of the Native population of the Utah Territory by Dr. Garland Hurt. Hurt was the Indian agent for the Utah Territory and was considered one of the more sympathetic figures vis-à-vis the Native peoples of the Utah Territory. However, Hurt advocated that Indigenous people largely abandon their traditional culture and become farmers, perhaps through coercion, presaging the tenets of the Dawes Severalty Act of 1887. Dr. Garland Hurt was a lonely voice in the Anglo-American-ruled American West for his proposition that, while the Native population in his charge was indigent and inferior to whites, the Indigenous people were originally equal to the white population in the eyes of God, with the potential to regain equality under "the province of moral authority."

In the following excerpt from his May 2, 1860, letter to Captain James H. Simpson, Dr. Garland Hurt detailed his opinion of the tribes of the Utah Territory, which included Lake Tahoe. The Native peoples surrounding Lake Tahoe are the Washoes, the Paiutes, and the Shoshones—Hurt spells these nations as "Wah-shoes," "Py-Utes," and

"Sho-sho-nees." Hurt claimed to have no special knowledge of the Washoe and Paiute people, but he lumps them into his analysis, nonetheless.

Captain Simpson's response is enveloped in the elaborate religiosity common to the era. However, his most telling phrase is straightforward: "I agree with you in all you say, except [to note] . . . the impossibility of [the Native population's] restoration to the same level of physical, mental, moral, and religious condition [as whites]."

The Washoe people were victims of the ambiguous policies and forsaken promises. From the onset of the Comstock Lode silver rush in 1859, the Washoe Nation sought protection via government agencies regarding fishing rights, pine nut harvesting, and loss of hegemony. Washoe leadership protested and petitioned local, state, and federal governments for the remainder of the nineteenth century. These efforts frequently fell on deaf ears, or government pledges were abandoned.

In 1892 a dramatic step was taken. Resolving to directly confront the federal government leadership in the nation's capital, the venerated Washoe leader Gumalanga, known as Captain Jim by white settlers, raised money and acquired supportive petition signatures from Carson Valley white residents. Along with friend and interpreter Dick Bender, Gumalanga traveled to Washington DC to plead the Washoe people's case for a reservation and protection of pine nut groves. During their thirteen-day visit, they met with United States senators from Nevada and California and appeared before the Federal Indian Commission. Washoe oral histories assert that Gumalanga and Dick Bender had an audience with President Benjamin Harrison and believed they had reached agreements for substantial benefits and compensation. However, upon returning home, Gumalanga and the Washoe people learned that the only approved government provision was $1,000 in aid (almost $34,000 in 2023) for the elderly and incapacitated tribal members. The Washoe people never received these funds. It is alleged that C. C. Warner, the Federal Indian Agent for Nevada, mismanaged the money.

Indians of Utah

By Dr. Garland Hurt

The following communication from Dr. Garland Hurt, who for several years was an Indian agent under the General Government in Utah, will be of interest to all who take an interest in ethnological subjects. I cannot agree, however, with the doctor in the idea which he appears to hold forth as to the original disparity of the races, and that any mode of treatment of the Indian tribes which ignores this doctrine, or rather which is based on the doctrine of the original unity of the race, must be attended with failure. I know it is the habit of many excellent and scientific men, as the doctor has done, to leave out in their philosophy a great truth—the greatest that has been divulged to the world—that the great I AM has spoken to man in his ignorance, and has given to him certain primary truths, which if he regard, he will assuredly live in light; but which if he disregard, he will as assuredly walk in darkness himself, and lead others into darkness. Among these great primary truths, I hold, is the unity of the race; and before any one, in my judgment, has a right to disbelieve it, he must first show that the source of knowledge of the Holy One, the Bible, which unbelievers have as yet only served to strengthen by their cavils and objections, is untrue, and therefore unworthy of being received as the grand text-book of individuals as well as of nations. This the history of that work through the ages which are gone, its internal evidences, and its acknowledged bearing on the happiness of the nations of the earth which have sincerely embraced it, show they will never be able to do. So far from it, it is the belief of the writer (however it may be the fashion of the mere moralist to deny it and sometimes to deride it) the greatest specimen of statesmanship is yet to be exhibited in the condition of a kingdom whose controlling officers shall be like Joseph and Daniel of Bible history and Washington of modern times, whose only fear seems to have been lest they should do wrong and run counter to the Divine mind.

Dr. Garland Hurt to Captain Simpson.

Washington DC, May 2, 1860.

Dear Sir: In reply to your inquiries for information concerning the Indians in the Territory of Utah, I would remark that numerous tribes are designated by persons living in the Territory, which, in my opinion, are susceptible of the following divisions and subdivisions, viz:

Utahs: Pah-Utahs, Yamp-Pah-Utahs, Cheveriches, Pah-Vantes, San-pitches, Py-eeds.

Sho-sho-nees: Snakes, Bannacks, To-si-witches, Go-sha-Utes, Cum-um-pahs.

Py-Utes.

Wah-shoes.

The two latter tribes inhabit the country along the eastern base of the Sierra Nevada Mountains, and are not sufficiently understood by me to enable me to speak of them in detail. . . .

They have no literature, and can scarcely be said to have a history of their own tribes or families. The few traditions that have descended to them are too vague, indistinct, and disconnected to be relied on as a history beyond the first preceding generation.

They are firm believers in charms, legerdemain, and necromancy, and in the management of their sick these superstitious devices constitute their principal treatment, which their patients submit to with the most unbounded faith.

Each band has its medicine-man, whom they treat with great respect and partiality.

Among all the tribes of this region there is the same indisposition to habits of industry, indolence being the rule and industry the exception, and nothing but the keenest impulses of necessity can impel them to action.

But this characteristic they, I believe, only possess in common with all the inferior tribes of our species, and, with a view to their civilization, is an item worthy of much consideration. Intellectually they appear to be as well-endowed as most of the native tribes of this continent; yet there seems to be a want of some of those higher intellectual endowments which render our own race progressive and so eminently fit us for the enjoyment of an enlightened government. The discussion of this subject involves a comparison of the races and invites an inquiry into the causes of the disparity that now exists between them, whether that disparity arises out of mental or physical inequality, or both; to what extent that inequality is capable of retarding their progress in the advancement of civilization, arts, and science. It appears to be the opinion of a large number of our modern philanthropists that all beings possessing the human form were originally endowed with an equality that ever forbids the idea of inferiority.

With an eye single to this similarity in physical form, they seem to overlook the mental inequality, or attribute it to a want of culture; and hence the misguided zeal for the improvement of many of the colored races, whose mental inferiority is a fixed and demonstrable fact, which must ever and inevitably define their position in the scale of political importance, and renders the idea of their future elevation to an equality with the Caucasian race utterly preposterous, and can only exist in the misguided wanderings of a perverted imagination. They have shown from their earliest generations their incapacity for any except the most simple forms of government, such as would assimilate them to some species of the gregarious animals, whom they approximate to in this respect and imitate as much as they do the higher orders of their own species.

The conclusions, then, to which we must arrive by this course of reasoning are obvious.

First. That by becoming the constant recipients of our care and sympathy their condition is temporarily ameliorated, but only so during the application of that care and sympathy.

Secondly. By amalgamation we elevate them at the expense of the degradation of the superior race.

Thirdly. By coercion they are made subservient to the intellect of the superior race, and made to bear the burden of their own subsistence, by controlling and directing their physical energies into the channels of usefulness. There is a misguided philanthropy which seems to be constantly directing our energies to the accomplishment of what in the nature of things is utterly impossible, and which it is the province of moral philosophy to correct.

These errors are exemplified in the attempt of our Government, at the expense of millions of treasure, to improve the moral and social condition of the aborigines of the country, who continue to sink lower in degradation and want, and are annually diminishing in numbers. While a small African colony, in the Southern States of the confederacy, under what some are pleased to style tyranny and oppression, have swelled to a powerful nation, infinitely more happy than the Indians or than themselves could be without the controlling influence of the superior race.

These Africans, we repeat, are infinitely more happy and

prosperous than it were possible for them to be without the controlling influence of the superior race; while at the same time, instead of diminishing they contribute to swell the sources of the national revenue.

Very respectfully, your obedient servant,
Garland Hurt.
Capt. J. H. Simpson, U. S. A.

Washington DC, May 5, 1860.

Dear Sir: Your very valuable letter, in relation to the Indians in Utah Territory, I have just received and read with a great deal of interest. It will constitute an important portion of my forthcoming report. I agree with you in all you say, except as to the original disparity of the races, and the impossibility of their restoration to the same level of physical, mental, moral, and religious condition. The same God who has for wise purposes permitted the degradation of some portions of the human family, can also by His Spirit so breathe upon mankind as to cause them, through the purchased redemption of His only beloved Son, to see each other eye to eye, and to delight themselves in the common blessings of one united family. This view is perfectly consistent to my mind with the coercion, for a time, of the inferior races to labor, of which you speak, and which I believe is one of the divinely appointed means to that end.

Very respectfully, yours,
J. H. Simpson,
Captain Topographical Engineers.
Dr. Garland Hurt.

≈≈≈

Where tall pines now shade all the shores and wave
on all the mountain slope, naught will shortly be seen,
save decaying stumps and naked granite rocks.

—Dan De Quille, *History of the Big Bonanza*, 1876

The Lake Tahoe timber industry was relentless.
In the 1870s tens of millions of board feet of timber were harvested annually in the Lake Tahoe Basin. Hundreds of thousands of cords of

wood were consumed each year for domestic and commercial use. The lake was surrounded by increasingly bare ridges and grim expanses of tree stumps.

This disfigurement was evident to all but was often discounted as the price paid for a booming economy and the desirable expansion of mines, railroads, housing, and a merchant class. But there were critics who decried the environmental devastation inflicted by logging. One trenchant eyewitness was William Wright, an author, journalist, and humorist better known by his pseudonym Dan De Quille. Wright (De Quille) became renowned for his accounts of the events and personalities during the Comstock Lode silver rush, which began in earnest in 1859.

William Wright was born in Ohio in 1829. In 1849, he moved to Iowa, married, and then, in 1857, left Iowa to be an argonaut in the final stages of the California gold rush. Failing in the California gold fields, Wright crossed the Sierra Nevada to Virginia City, Nevada Territory, in 1859, upon news of the silver strike in the Washoe. William Wright struck out in the Comstock as well and was hired as a reporter for the Virginia City Territorial Enterprise *in 1862. Soon afterward, he adopted the pen name Dan De Quille.*

Dan De Quille was on the Territorial Enterprise *staff for over thirty years and, during his tenure, developed a reputation for energetic prose and humorous observations. In 1863 De Quille hired and mentored a struggling young writer named Samuel Clemens, who later became internationally famous as Mark Twain. Dan De Quille is often credited with helping Twain develop his writing style of incisive social commentary imparted with a clever and comical flair.*

In 1874 some of the Comstock mine owners hungered for a history book about the Washoe and Comstock Lode. De Quille was the favored author and called upon his old friend Twain for advice. With Mark Twain's support, Dan De Quille's invaluable chronicle of the Comstock was published in 1876 by the American Publishing Company. It was entitled History of the Big Bonanza.

The book featured a varied assortment of technical chapters on mining and logging, descriptions of historical events and locales, and often humorous character sketches of Washoe Territory and Comstock Lode denizens.

In this memorable excerpt from History of the Big Bonanza, *Dan De Quille details some of the practices and the aftermath of the extensive, destructive, and brutally efficient logging in the Lake Tahoe Basin. He focuses on log booms and the construction of flumes. The passage ends with the chilling observation: "The time is not far distant when the whole of that part of the Sierra Nevada range lying adjacent to the Nevada silver-mining region will be utterly denuded of trees of every kind."*

Not less than eighty million feet of timber and lumber are annually consumed on the Comstock lode. In a single mine—the Consolidated Virginia—timber is being buried at the rate of six million feet per annum, and in all other mines in like proportion. At the same time about 250,000 cords of wood are consumed.

The pine-forests of the Sierra Nevada Mountains are drawn upon for everything in the shape of wood or lumber, and have been thus drawn upon for many years. For a distance of fifty or sixty miles all the hills of the eastern slope of the Sierras have been to a great extent denuded of trees of every kind; those suitable only for wood as well as those fit for the manufacture of lumber for use in the mines. Already the lumbermen are not only extending their operations to a greater distance north and south along the great mountain range, but are also beginning to reach over to the western slope—over to the California side of the range.

Long since, all the forests on the lower hills of the Nevada side of the mountains that could be reached by teams, were swept away, when the lumbermen began to scale the higher hills, felling the trees thereon, and rolling or sliding the logs down to flats whence they could be hauled. The next movement was to erect saw-mills far up in the mountains, and to construct from these, large flumes leading down into the valleys, through which to float wood, lumber, and timber. Some of these flumes are over twenty miles in length, and are very substantial structures, costing from $20,000 to $250,000 each. They are built on a regular grade, and, in order to maintain this grade, wind round hills, pass along the sides of steep mountains, and cross deep canons; reared, in many places, on trestle-work of great height.

These flumes are made so large that timbers sixteen inches square and twenty or thirty feet in length may be floated down in them. In a properly constructed flume, timbers of a large size are floated by a very small head of water; and not alone single logs, but long processions of them. Timbers, wood, lumber—in fact, all that will float—is carried away as fast as thrown in. When a stick of timber or a plank has been placed in the flume, then ends all the expense of transportation, as, without further attention, it is dumped in the valley—twenty miles away, perhaps. By means of these flumes, tens of thousands of acres of timber-land are made available, that could never have been reached by teams.

In some places, where the ground is very steep, there are to be seen what are called gravitation flumes, down which wood is sent without the aid of water. These, however, are merely straight chutes, running from the top to the bottom of a single hill or range of hills. In places, they are of great use, as through them wood may be sent down within reach of the main water-flume leading to the valley. Nearly all of the flumes have their dumps near the line of the Virginia and Truckee Railroad, or some of its branches or side-tracks, and in these dumps are at times to be seen thousands upon thousands of cords of wood and millions of feet of lumber. . . .

Logs are rafted across Lake Tahoe to the mills, from all points. The lake being of great size, and all of its shores and the slopes of the surrounding mountains being heavily timbered, the company have command of a vast area of pine-forests. Through the waters of the lake and its numerous bays, they reach out and up into the mountains in all directions, gathering the pines into their mills, carrying them, in the shape of lumber, up their railroad, and then shooting them through their big flume down over all the hills till they land in Carson Valley.

This is all very well for . . . the mining companies, who must have lumber and timber, but it is going to make sad work, ere long, with the picturesque hills surrounding Lake Tahoe, the most beautiful of all the lakes in the Sierra Nevada Mountains. Where tall pines now shade all the shores and wave on all the mountain slope, nought will shortly be seen, save decaying stumps and naked granite rocks. But timber and lumber are imperatively demanded, and the forests of not only these hills but of a thousand others, will doubtless be sacrificed.

The rafts of logs are towed across the lake by small steamboats. This rafting is of a novel character. The logs forming the raft are not pinned or in any way fastened together. The steamboat runs up to a bay or other place where logs are lying, and casts anchor. A boat is then sent out which carries a long cable strung full of large buoys. This cable is carried round a proper fleet of logs, as a seine is carried round a school of fish. The steamer then weighs anchor and starts across the lake, towing along all the logs about which the cable has been cast. No matter how rough the lake may be, the logs remain in a bunch, being attracted the one to the other, and clinging together as bits of stick and chips are often seen to do when floating on a lake or stream.

Other large mills . . . are engaged in devouring the forest surrounding Lake Tahoe. About five million feet of lumber per month are turned out by the several mills at the lake, and each summer about three million feet of timbers are hewn in that locality. Many of the sugar-pine trees about Lake Tahoe are five, six, and some even eight feet, in diameter; all are very tall and straight.

At a point in the Sierra Nevada Mountains, about eleven miles from the town of Reno, on the Central Pacific Railroad, Messrs. Mackay & Fair have a lumber-flume over twenty miles in length. This flume was built through an exceedingly rugged region, and cost $250,000. It taps a tract of twelve thousand acres of heavy pine-forest owned by the parties named. The land is estimated to contain 500,000 cords of wood, 100,000,000 feet of saw-logs, and 30,000,000 feet of hewn timber; all of which will be brought down to the Virginia and Truckee Railroad, through the flume. . . .

No means of transporting wood, lumber, and timber is or can be cheaper than these flumes. When once a plank or stick of wood has been dropped in at the head of the flume it is already as good as at the other end, twenty or thirty miles away. The flumes are far ahead of railroads of any gauge, broad or narrow, as a means of cheap transportation for wood and lumber.

Each season, from 80,000 to 100,000 cords of wood are floated down the Carson River. This wood is cut high up in the Sierras, at the headwaters of the Carson and its tributaries, and is sent down from the mountain slopes for many miles, in flumes of the same kind as those in use for the transportation of lumber. The wood is collected on the banks of the river, ready to be launched at the proper and auspicious moment. . . .

The time is not far distant when the whole of that part of the Sierra Nevada range lying adjacent to the Nevada silver-mining region will be utterly denuded of trees of every kind.

≈≈≈

This bracing air, this unique spot, this wonderful
lake, this rich, healthful aroma of deep pine-forests,
this grand scenery, all combined, make it one of the
best of places for religious summer resort.

—Reverend A. H. Tevis, *Beyond the Sierras, or,*
Observations on the Pacific Coast, 1877

Lake Tahoe has always been a spiritual center. For centuries, the Indigenous people at the lake revered the deep blue waters and the natural bounty available to them. For the Washoe people, Lake Tahoe was their touchstone, their worldly and sacred homeland. Their identity and beliefs were inextricably linked to the lake.

Euro-Americans who arrived in midcentury initially viewed the lake through the prism of economic opportunity as they rushed to the Comstock, but they also took notice of the splendor and the sense of emotional otherworldliness it could create.

A few came to envision Lake Tahoe as the perfect location for religious retreats, an escape from secular woes, a refuge where one could relish the "very pure and fine, bracing and delicious" air—"the same the angels breathe," as Mark Twain famously observed in Roughing It. *One such recommendation came from the Reverend Augustus H. Tevis, author of the 1877 book* Beyond the Sierras; or, Observations on the Pacific Coast.

Rev. Augustus Havens Tevis was born to a farming family in Indiana in 1841. He left college to enlist in the Union Army during the Civil War. After three years' service, Tevis was mustered out, returned to college, and received a divinity degree in 1868. After several years of ministry in Missouri and Indiana and missionary work throughout the world, including Palestine and Peru, Rev. A. H. Tevis was transferred to Carson City, Nevada. Tevis was in Carson City for two years, serving his own congregation and as chaplain for both the Nevada State Legislature and State Prison. During this time, Tevis wrote Beyond the Sierras; or, Observations on the Pacific Coast.

While in Carson City, A. H. Tevis spent six weeks "Summering at Lake Tahoe," a wondrous place he described as "charming, silvery, unique Tahoe, or Pearl of the Sierras." Although he found the Lake Tahoe Basin to be the "Land of Sabbath-breaking," Tevis also exclaimed, "How often have I wished this place—mountains, lake, and all—could be the place of one of the grand Eastern camp-meetings!"

Tevis's wish for Lake Tahoe religious and spiritual sanctuaries was fulfilled, but it was mostly in the twentieth century. Today, in numerous locations circling the lake, denominational and nondenominational retreats rejuvenate many. However, for most, no institutions such as these are necessary. These individuals would certainly agree with the words of Claire MacDonald, who wrote in her 1929 book Lake Tahoe: *"There is plenty of religion up here, without any ambassador to present it. Lofty feelings food souls, for which no human touch is needed to translate."*

Following his tenure at Carson City, Tevis served in Santa Barbara and San Diego and returned to Indiana in 1879, where he obtained a medical degree and became Rev. A. H. Tevis, MD. *After transfer to Springfield, Missouri, Tevis retired in 1883. Some biographies note that Tevis was President James Garfield's likely nominee for the Jerusalem consulate, but, following Garfield's assassination six months into his term in 1881, the appointment never occurred.*

And of the many curiosities that nature has scattered over the length and breadth of this coast, Lake Tahoe is one of the most charming.

This is a land of wonders, certainly of curiosities. Providence has made this vast area, between the Rocky Mountains and the sea, his chief receptacle of the wealth of the country. And what folly to travel in foreign countries to see the sights until you have at least seen some of the wonders and treasures of our own great Commonwealth! You can spend your life in exploring these various wonders, and then not find an end,—petrified forests; lost rivers, whose *termini* no one knows, and of whose source there is great doubt; brackish lakes, whose waters are worse than the Dead Sea, and in which no living thing can exist; bubbling, hissing, thundering geysers, whose awfulness presses the hardest heart; roaring cataracts, that with a band of silver seem to bind together earth and sky; boiling springs, hither and yon in almost countless profusion, that send their breath of steam as through the throats of some great furnace from Vulcan's forge; geographical and topographical features that are marvelous in themselves; the big trees, whose magnitude is a wonder, and whose age links the present almost to the days of Solomon; Yosemite, unlike anything of the kind in the known world, whose sublimity is beyond description; and charming, silvery, unique Tahoe, or Pearl of the Sierras.

There is no patent on the name, hence we have chosen to christen it thus.

And who will say it is a misnomer that has seen its grandeur and enjoyed the beauty of its surroundings?

Its name belongs to the Indian tongue and signifies *clear water*.

This lake in its greatest length is twenty-three miles, and greatest width eleven miles; hence it has an area of two hundred and fifty-three square miles. Its altitude is six thousand two hundred and twenty feet above the level of the sea. Here, spread out before me, like the finest of burnished silver, is a lake unlike any other body of water in the world, save one in Switzerland, and that has only a few marks of similarity.

This lies nestled away, like a very jewel, in the summit of the Sierras,— the Alps of America,—at an altitude of a mile and a quarter above the level of the sea. Think of it! A body of water containing an area of more than two hundred and fifty square miles, and deep enough to float the largest vessel that ever traversed the sea, and then have almost immeasurable depths below the keel; think of this being in the very summit of the greatest range of mountains in America!

It has been sounded along the line between Nevada and California, which runs through the lake, to the distance of two hundred and fifty-three fathoms, or fifteen hundred and eighteen feet. But other places have been sounded to the great distance of nearly twenty-five hundred feet. The character of the water is almost incredible to one who has never looked upon it. Coming down from the springs that burst from the canons, and the everlasting snows that crown the mountaintops, where "*'Tis felt the presence of the Deity*," the water is almost perfectly pure.

I have leaned over the side of the boat and watched the play of the trout a hundred and fifty feet below the surface. I have dropped a small, shining, metallic button, and watched distinctly its oscillations in sinking for three or four minutes.

The transparent nature of the Water is best seen in the morning, when the lake is perfectly calm; not even the small surface ripples that nearly always exist on ordinary streams and lakes are visible.

The various angles of vision present the most charming scene. Yonder the lake looks like a quiet mass of molten silver; yonder, where the rays of the sun meet you, is a gorgeous array of crimson and gold; then there is a range of purest emerald, deepening into blue-black as the scene stretches away from you, bespangled in the distance by the rising whitecaps. This, fringed with the green of the deep pine-forests that skirt the mountains and capped with the everlasting snows, made radiant with the flood of sunlight, furnishes a picture of incomparable beauty, and worthy of a master's brush.

But here by you, right at your feet, is one of the most pleasing features of all; so still in the morning quietness, and such air-like purity withal. You think you can reach down and pick up those shining pebbles, and yet they are twenty, thirty, or forty feet beneath you. And that boat or skiff seems to be poised in mid-air. You can count the small indentures and nail-heads in the very keel.

You cringe with fear as your boat glides towards that huge bowlder, as large as a church, thinking surely your vessel will be wrecked; but there is no danger, as the rock is many feet beneath you. The transparency of the water makes the danger seem so near.

How often have I wished this place—mountains, lake, and all—could be the place of one of the grand Eastern camp-meetings! This bracing air, this unique spot, this wonderful lake, this rich, healthful aroma of deep pine-forests, this grand scenery, all combined, make it one of the best of places for religious summer resort.

Yonder is a quaint spot, a veritable Gibraltar on a small scale, a lonely, rocky island in the centre of Emerald Bay. Some foolish man built a tomb in the solid rock on its summit, intending to be buried there, where the marks of decay come slowly over his grave, and where he might sleep undisturbed amid the incomparable grandeur that would have surrounded him. His sarcophagus and all were prepared, but the treacherous billows of the lake, that occasionally foam and roar with fury, seized him, and he lies buried at the bottom,—no man knows where, for no one going down ever comes up again from these waters.

≈≈≈

Lake Tahoe is not only an abundant reservoir,
but it is preeminently a safe reservoir.

—George H. Mendell, *Report on the Various Projects
for the Water Supply of San Francisco, Cal.*, 1877

The idea that Lake Tahoe could be tapped for use in the San Francisco municipal water supply had more lives than a cat.

Several proposals had been offered in the 1860s and 1870s to construct massive infrastructure to transfer water from the Lake Tahoe and Truckee River outlet to the City by the Bay. Mostly promoted by Alexis von Schmidt and the officers of the Lake Tahoe and San Francisco Water Works Company, these propositions had come to naught due to concerns over costs and lawsuits.

However, San Francisco still needed water. In 1877 George H. Mendell, the engineer to the Board of Water Commissioners of San Francisco, issued a report detailing fourteen potential water sources for the city. Entitled Report on the Various Projects for the Water Supply of San Francisco, Cal., *the report itemized an interesting assortment of streams, rivers, and lakes scattered across Northern California, including Silver Lake in El Dorado County, the Mokelumne River, South Yuba River, San Joaquin River, Clear Lake, Feather River, Rubicon River, Tuolumne River (site of Hetchy Hetchy Valley), and even conceivable water resources on the San Francisco Peninsula. Also on the list was Lake Tahoe.*

George Henry Mendell was born in Pennsylvania in 1831 and graduated from West Point in 1852. Mendell joined the U.S. Army Corps of Engineers and participated in several topographical surveys prior to the Civil War. He was involved in the war from the outset, beginning with the Manassas Campaign of 1861 and concluding with the supervision of harbor protection in Massachusetts in 1865. He rose to the rank of colonel during the Civil War. Following the war, George H. Mendell was supervising engineer for the construction of military fortifications on Alcatraz Island, the San Francisco harbor, and on the Columbia River. He served on commissions that studied the potential for additional fortifications on the Pacific Coast and for irrigation systems in the San Joaquin, Tulare, and Sacramento Valleys. In civilian life, Mendell was the engineer to the Board of Water Commissioners of San Francisco from 1876 to 1878 and the consulting engineer for the State of California from 1878 to 1880.

In this excerpt from Report on the Various Projects for the Water Supply of San Francisco, Cal., *George H. Mendell details the process and parameters by which Lake Tahoe water can be transported to San Francisco. The summary is largely a recapitulation of older plans, such as those offered by Alexis von Schmidt, but it demonstrates the persistence of the Lake Tahoe water diversion plan.*

Lake Tahoe

This lake lies partly in California and partly in Nevada. It is, however, on the eastern slope of the Sierra Nevada, and its altitude above the sea is something over 6,200 feet. Its greatest length is 22 miles, and the greatest width 12 miles. Its area is 192 square miles, more or less, and its drainage basin, including in this its own area, is 500 square miles. These dimensions are taken from the published map, which is the only definite and available source of information. The lake is stated to have a depth of 1,500 feet. It is never frozen over, and this fact is probably due to the great depth. . . .

To take 100 millions of gallons per day, for every day in the year, would lower the level of the lake less than one foot, disregarding evaporation and drainage.

To restore one foot to the lake would require the drainage basin to deliver less than five inches of rain. The lowest fall of which we have any record at Truckee, a few miles distant, and 600 feet below the latter, is 16 inches.

The dam at the lake raises the water six feet, or thereabouts, above the lowest level, and will serve to distribute the excess of one winter over the next year, should its accumulation prove below the average.

This lake is to be regarded as a reservoir, which can always be relied upon to furnish any desired amount of water, and its relative value, as compared with other projects having their source of supply in similar regions, is to be studied in the light of the expense necessary to make the reservoir available for our purposes. The dam at the outlet of the Truckee is made of timber, and it will be inexpensive to replace, when it becomes necessary. It is supplied with gates, by which the flowage of the Truckee River can be regulated. A large but unknown quantity of water is now, and will be required for the service of the mills along the river.

It is proposed to take the water for city supply from the Truckee River, 3¾ miles below the lake. At this point there is a dam, by means of which the water can be diverted into a canal, which will deliver it, in a length of 15 miles, at the mouth of the tunnel to be constructed through the Sierra Nevada.

This tunnel will be 24,172 feet in length, of which, 18,496 feet will require to be excavated from two points, one at each end, the height of the mountain being considered, over this distance, as too great to admit the use of inter-mediate shafts. The remaining part of the tunnel, 5,676 feet in length, can be excavated in convenient intervals, by shafts about 100 feet deep. . . .

Here the water will be discharged into the south branch of the North Fork of the American, from which it will be again taken out by a canal, twelve miles below. This canal is estimated to be 60 miles long or thereabouts, and it will terminate at the reservoir north of Auburn.

The North Fork of the American will give a sufficient supply of water for a large part of the year, and it is only when this supply becomes deficient, that it will be necessary to draw upon the reservoir of the lake. . . .

Lake Tahoe is not only an abundant reservoir, but it is preeminently a safe reservoir. The dam, as has been remarked, raises the water only six feet, and therefore it is not exposed to danger.

≈≈≈

A huge cod-line, armed with a hook large enough
to kill a shark, was the rude and unsportsmanlike
implement used for killing the speckled beauties.

—Major Sir Rose Lambart Price, *The Two Americas:*
An Account of Sport and Travel. With Notes on Men
and Manners in North and South America, 1877

Foreign visitors to nineteenth-century Lake Tahoe were usually people of means. The reality was that Lake Tahoe tourist amenities were expensive for anyone—foreign or domestic. But those from far-flung countries had the added burdens and costs of long-distance travel and the obligatory cluster of baggage and personal accoutrements. As a result, most overseas sightseers tended to be upper crust or nouveau riche.

The British found the American West especially intriguing and, with the completion of the transcontinental railroad in 1869, less demanding and more cost-effective to visit. Frequently, British travelers embarked on a tour of North America, using the new transcontinental train depots and trackside hotels to hopscotch across the continent. British males seemed particularly interested in fishing and hunting in the West, and their travel journals regularly focused on those outdoor activities.

In 1874 Major Sir Rose Lambart Price, the 3rd Baronet Price of Treng-

wainton Estate, near Penzance in County Cornwall, England, took the standard tour a bit farther. Price expanded his journey to include South America, Central America, Canada, and the United States. His 1877 travel narrative was entitled The Two Americas: An Account of Sport and Travel. With Notes on Men and Manners in North and South America. *On his multicontinental trek, Sir Rose Lambart Price visited many American locales, including Los Angeles, San Diego, Sacramento, San Francisco, Yosemite Valley, and Virginia City. He also dashed through Utah, Wyoming, the Dakota Territory, Nebraska, and Illinois. A memorable, but short, stop on his itinerary was Lake Tahoe.*

Sir Rose Lambart Price came from old money. How his family gained its wealth is disturbing. In the early nineteenth century, Sir John Price (Rose Lambart Price's grandfather) owned and managed a successful sugar plantation in Jamaica called Worthy Park. The plantation's success was built on slave labor. For years after slavery was abolished in the British Empire in 1807, the elder Price is alleged to have used enslaved people as servants on his Cornish manor. The Price family would later sell Trengwainton but retain its royal titles.

Ironically, Sir Rose Lambart Price first rose to public notice as a lieutenant in the Royal Marine Light Artillery, serving in Africa on missions to suppress slavery and the slave trade. Having attained the rank of major, he then served in the Royal Marine Battalion in the 1857–1858 Indian Rebellion. In late December 1857 Rose Lambart Price fought with the joint British-French forces at the Battle of Canton, China, during the Second Opium War. He was shot through the leg at that battle. Six months later, Major Sir Rose Lambart Price was present at the surrender of Beijing (then called Peking) that ended the Second Opium War.

In this excerpt from The Two Americas: An Account of Sport and Travel. With Notes on Men and Manners in North and South America, *Rose Lambart Price recounts his whirlwind stopover at Lake Tahoe. In a mainly elitist, patronizing tone, Price commented on the unsatisfactory quality of the accommodations ("a second or third rate kind of inn" in Truckee), mourned a deadly stagecoach accident ("the stage was pitched about sixty or eighty feet down an almost precipitous declivity"), belittled "Truckee City" ("almost every town of half-a-dozen streets, or even houses, in America is called a city"), shuddered at an ungentlemanly method of Lake Tahoe trout angling ("A huge cod-line, armed with a hook large enough to kill a shark, was the rude and unsportsmanlike implement used for killing the speckled beauties"), criticized the dreadful condition of the stage connection between Lake Tahoe and Carson City ("The road between Lake Tahoe and Carson is far and away the dirtiest in the West, which is saying a very great deal"), and noted his happiness at avoiding a night's lodging in Carson City ("an event . . . devoutly to be dreaded").*

I was rather glad when at 10 p.m. our train arrived at a station called Truckee, where, at a second or third rate kind of inn attached to the railway station, we were obliged to pass the night.

Our drive next morning from Truckee to Lake Tahoe, along the banks of the River Truckee, was one to be remembered. A well-kept road followed the river's bank through forest and meadow, forming a kind of cañon. On each side rose steep mountains, in some places showing extraordinary rock formations, whose fantastic outlines and queer conformation added considerably to the general effect of all around us. The river was clear as crystal and formed a very beautiful piece of water, spoiled, however, for trout fishing by the numberless saw-mills and mill-dams that are established along its banks; this part of Nevada being the great lumber region of the state, and Truckee City (almost every town of half-a-dozen streets, or even houses, in America is called a city) the principal depôt and chief market.

On our road we were pointed out the scene of a recent coach disaster, in which a couple of people were killed, and a few more badly injured. It seems that in going down a steep incline with a high bank on one side and a precipice on the other, the brake had carried away. The horses became unruly, and finally the stage was pitched about sixty or eighty feet down an almost precipitous declivity, killing and wounding the people mentioned. The horses were, I believe, all killed, and on examining the place, my only surprise was that the whole party had not suffered the same fate.

Our intention had been to cross Lake Tahoe at once and go on to Virginia City, but while waiting for the steam-boat which was to convey us across the lake, K. became so enamoured of a beautiful dish of trout, some of them running about five pounds, that he determined on staying to try his luck, a local fisherman promising to provide the necessary equipment, and I was only too glad of the delay. Lake Tahoe is really very beautiful. The water is singularly clear. Even on coral banks in the

Indian Ocean, atolls rising from an almost unfathomable depth nearly perpendicularly, and celebrated for the extraordinary translucency of the blue water that surrounds them, have I never seen to greater depths. On a calm, clear, bright day, when the surface of the lake is unruffled, a white plate can easily be discerned a hundred feet beneath its tranquil waters. The counties of Eldorado and Placer in California, and Washoe, Ormsby, and Douglas in Nevada, share it between them. Its greatest depth is 1700 feet, its length twenty-two miles, and width about ten miles.

After a swim we repaired to the boat, where our fisherman awaited us, and judge of our surprise when the means of capture met our astonished gaze. A huge cod-line, armed with a hook large enough to kill a shark, was the rude and unsportsmanlike implement used for killing the speckled beauties, whose good looks we had both so much admired. No play and no sport could possibly be obtained, as neck and crop by main force the wretched fish is bundled into the boat. Of course fishing under such circumstances was a "dead sell," and not having our own gear with us, nothing could be done. The Tahoe hotel was exceedingly comfortable, and I can hardly recommend a pleasanter or more charming spot for any one willing to linger a week amid delightful scenery with the certain knowledge of returning each day after his wanderings to a good dinner; but should he be an angler, let him remember to bring his own rod.

Our next day was somewhat eventful. It was polling day for California, and instead of being conveyed directly across the lake to meet the coach for Carson, we were trotted round to accommodate the different voters whose patriotism demanded their presence at the poll. The cruise was certainly pleasant enough, and one could hardly fail to admire the beauty of all around, but the delay nearly necessitated our spending the night in Carson, an event, under the peculiar circumstances of our being pressed for time, devoutly to be dreaded. . . .

The road between Lake Tahoe and Carson is far and away the dirtiest in the West, which is saying a very great deal; and the blacks gathered on the engine, lying over the coating of dust picked up during our drive with Hank Monk, rendered us simply filthy. H. also carried his portmanteau himself, a thing very few free-born Americans ever dream of doing, and the remarks that greeted us on passing through a somewhat disreputable portion of the town were, if not complimentary, at least good-natured and amusing. "Where are you poor beggars going to?"

"Pretty well played out I guess?" and "Have a drink?" were the various comments of the sympathising "innocents," who evidently took us for discharged miners or workmen on the tramp. At last we succeeded in getting comfortably settled in an [*sic*] hotel, and were glad enough to turn in after our adventurous but somewhat fatiguing journey.

≈≈≈

I passed several hours of the afternoon in listening,
alone, to the murmur of the pines, while the waves were
gently beating the shore with their restlessness.
—Thomas Starr King, "Living Water from Lake Tahoe," *Christianity
and Humanity: A Series of Sermons (Sermon 19)*, 1877.

In 1860 the Reverend Thomas Starr King, a thirty-six-year-old Unitarian Universalist minister from Boston, became pastor of San Francisco's First Unitarian Church. That summer, King visited Yosemite and the Sierra Nevada and wrote eight letters to the Boston Evening Transcript *chronicling his adventure and his impressions of the environment.*

The reverend's letters were considered especially credible due to his reputation as a respected observer of mountain landscapes, resulting from his 1859 book on the White Mountains of New Hampshire, entitled The White Hills: Their Legends, Landscapes, and Poetry. *King's writings and sermons often utilized Sierra Nevada settings as examples of God's divine plan. Lake Tahoe was a favorite subject.*

The Reverend Thomas Starr King was a zealous campaigner for California remaining in the Union during the Civil War. King traveled far and wide to promote the cause of the Union. Exhausted, King died unexpectedly of diphtheria and pneumonia in 1864 at the age of forty. From 1931 to 2009, a statue of Thomas Starr King was one of California's two representatives in the U.S. Capitol's Statuary Hall. In 2009, King's statue was replaced by one of Ronald Reagan.

In 1877 a collection of the Reverend Thomas Starr King's most popular lectures and sermons were collected in two volumes, entitled Substance and Show *and* Christianity and Humanity. *The books were produced under the direction of prominent author Bret Harte. In 1863 Harte's first of many short stories was published in the* Atlantic Monthly *upon the recommendation of Thomas Starr King.*

Sermon 19 in Christianity and Humanity *is "Living Water from Lake Tahoe," King's meditation on the bond between Christianity and the physical manifestation of a miracle that many considered Lake Tahoe. It is also a classic example of nineteenth-century oratory.*

Living Water from Lake Tahoe

When one is climbing from the west, by the smooth and excellent road, the last slope of the Sierra ridge, he expects, from the summit of the pass, . . . to look off and down upon an immense expanse. He expects, or, if he had not learned beforehand, he would anticipate with eagerness, that he should be able to see mountain summits beneath him, and beyond these, valleys and ridges alternating till the hills subside into the eastern plains. How different the facts that await the eye from the western summit, and what a surprise! We find, on gaining what seems to be the ridge, that the Sierra range for more than a hundred miles has a double line of jagged pinnacles, twelve or fifteen miles apart, with a trench or trough between, along a portion of the way, that is nearly fifteen hundred feet deep if we measure from the pass which the stages traverse, which is nearly three thousand feet deep if the plummet is dropped from the highest points of the snowy spires.

Down into this trench we look, and opposite upon the eastern wall and crests, as we ride out to the eastern edge of the western summit. In a stretch of forty miles the chasm of it bursts into view at once, half of which is a plain sprinkled with groves of pine, and the other half an expanse of level blue that mocks the azure into which its guardian towers soar. This is Lake Tahoe, an Indian name which signifies "High Water." We descend steadily by the winding mountain-road, more than three miles to the plain, by which we drive to the shore of the Lake; but it is truly Tahoe, "High Water." For we stand more than a mile, I believe more than six thousand feet above the sea, when we have gone down from the pass to its sparkling beach. . . .

To a wearied frame and tired mind what refreshment there is in the neighborhood of this lake! The air is singularly searching and strengthening. The noble pines, not obstructed by underbrush, enrich the slightest breeze with aroma and music. Grand peaks rise around, on which the eye can admire the sternness of everlasting crags and the equal permanence of delicate and feathery snow. Then there is the sense of seclusion from the haunts and cares of men, of being upheld on the immense billow of the Sierra, at an elevation near the line of perpetual snow, yet finding the air genial, and the loneliness clothed with the charm of feeling the sense of the mystery of the mountain heights, the part of a chain that link the two polar seas, and of the mystery of the water poured into the granite bowl, whose rim is chased with the splendor of perpetual frost, and whose bounty, flowing into the Truckee stream, finds no outlet into the ocean, but sinks again into the land.

Everything is charming in the surroundings of the mountain Lake; but as soon as one walks to the beach of it, and surveys its expanse, it is the color, or rather the colors, spread out before the eye, which holds it with greatest fascination. I was able to stay eight days in all, amidst that calm and cheer, yet the hues of the water seemed to become more surprising with each hour. The Lake, according to recent measurement, is about twenty-one miles in length, by twelve or thirteen in breadth. There is no island visible to break its sweep, which seems to be much larger than the figures indicate. And the whole of the vast surface, the boundaries of which are taken in easily at once by the range of the eye, is a mass of pure splendor. When the day is calm, there is a ring of the Lake, extending more than a mile from shore, which is brilliantly green. Within this ring the vast center of the expanse is of a deep, yet soft and singularly tinted blue. Hues cannot be more sharply contrasted than are these permanent colors. They do not shade into each other; they lie as clearly defined as the course of glowing gems in the wall of the New Jerusalem. It is precisely as if we were looking upon an immense floor of lapis lazuli set within a ring of flaming emerald. . . .

I must speak of another lesson, connected with religion, that was suggested to me on the borders of Lake Tahoe. It is bordered by groves of noble pines. Two of the days that I was permitted to enjoy there were Sundays. On one of them I passed several hours of the afternoon in listening, alone, to the murmur of the pines, while the waves were gently beating the shore with their restlessness. If the beauty and purity of the Lake were in harmony with the deepest religion of the Bible, certainly the voice of the pines was also in chord with it. . . .

How few human eyes have yet rested upon it in calmness, to drink in its loveliness! There are spots near the point of the shore where the hotel stands, to which not more than a few score intelligent visitors have yet been introduced. Such a nook I was taken to by a cultivated friend. We sailed ten miles on the water to the mouth of a mountain stream that pours foaming into its green expanse. We left the boat, followed this stream by its downward leaps through uninvaded nature for more than a mile, and found that it flows from a smaller lake, not more than three miles in circuit, which lies directly at the base of two tremendous peaks of the Sierra, white with immense and perpetual snow-fields. The same ring of vivid green, the same center of soft deep blue, was visible in this smaller mountain bowl, and it is fed by a glorious cataract, supported by those snow-fields, which pours down in thundering foam, at one point, in a leap of a hundred feet to die in that brilliant color, guarded by those cold, dumb crags.

Never since the creation has a particle of that water turned a wheel, or fed a fountain for human thirst, or served any form of mortal use. Perhaps the eyes of not a hundred intelligent spirits on the earth have yet looked upon that scene. Has there been any waste of its wild and lonely beauty? Has Tahoe been wasted because so few appreciative souls have studied and enjoyed it? If not a human glance had yet fallen upon it, would its charms of color and surroundings be wasted charms?

≈≈≈

> They make the descent in thunder and smoke,
> and each log, as it strikes the water, will send up a
> beautiful column of spray a hundred and fifty feet,
> resembling the effect of a submarine explosion.

—Benjamin Parke Avery, *Californian Pictures in Prose and Verse*, 1878

The Lake Tahoe Basin was an inviting target for newspaper reporters and traveling correspondents in the nineteenth century. Sometimes it seems as if every aspiring writer visited the Gem of the Sierra and crafted a portrait of the natural or human landscape.

One such figure was Benjamin Parke Avery. Avery was a journalist, a poet, an essayist, and, for a short time at the end of his life, a diplomat.

Benjamin Parke Avery was born in New York City in 1828. He was a 49er, arriving in California in 1849 after a voyage from Nantucket, Massachusetts, around Cape Horn aboard the sailing ship Aurora. *As was true of many, Avery was unsuccessful as a prospector during the California gold rush. Abandoning his search for the elusive golden quarry, he opened a drugstore and started a newspaper in the mining*

camp of North San Juan, Nevada County. Making journalism his trade,
Benjamin Parke Avery became part owner and editor of the Marysville
Appeal, *an influential Sacramento Valley journal. Subsequently, he*
became the Sacramento correspondent for the San Francisco Bulletin. *In*
the early 1860s Avery was the official printer for the State of California.

In 1873, in failing health, Benjamin took an extended hiatus in the
Sierra Nevada. His health seemingly restored; Avery was appointed
editor of the Overland Monthly *magazine in 1874. After only six months*
on the job at the magazine, Avery was selected as minister to China
during the administration of President Ulysses S. Grant.

After less than a year as minister to China, Benjamin Parke Avery
died in Beijing (then called Peking) on November 8, 1875, at the age of
forty-eight. Posthumously, in 1878, a collection of Avery's writings was
issued as Californian Pictures in Prose and Verse. *Many of what Avery*
described as "word-sketches" and "scenery-studies" were previously
published in the Overland Monthly.

In this excerpt, Benjamin Parke Avery's word-sketch of Lake Tahoe
conveyed the "exquisite purity and beauty of color" of the water, so
"wonderfully transparent, and the sensation upon floating over and
gazing into its still bosom, . . . is almost akin to that one might feel in
a balloon above the earth." Avery notes the "informal and picturesque"
shoreline and the overpowering and "awful spiritual presence" of the
lake. He also described the road from Truckee to Tahoe City and the array
of "timber-ways"—chutes hundreds of feet long cascading downward
from the mountain ridges to the Truckee River—that hurtle cut logs
at such breakneck speed that when they enter the river a "submarine
explosion" occurs.

Lake Tahoe [is] only fifteen miles southwardly from Donner Lake
and the line of the Central Pacific Railroad. Its elevation above the
sea, exceeding six thousand feet; its great depth, reaching a maximum
of more than one thousand five hundred feet; its exquisite purity and
beauty of color; the grandeur of its snowy mountain walls; its fine
beaches and shore groves of pine, make it the most picturesque and
attractive of all the California lakes. Profound as it is, it is wonderfully
transparent, and the sensation upon floating over and gazing into its still
bosom, where the granite boulders can be seen far, far below, and large
trout dart swiftly, incapable of concealment, is almost akin to that one

might feel in a balloon above the earth. The color of the water changes with its depth, from a light, bluish green, near the shore, to a darker green, farther out, and finally to a blue so deep that artists hardly dare put it on canvas. When the lake is still, it is one of the loveliest sights conceivable, flashing silvery in the sun, or mocking all the colors of the sky, while the sound of its soft beating on the beach is like the music of the sea-shell. When the wind angers its surface, its waves are dangerous to buffet. The sail that would float over its still face like a cloud is then driven like fate, and is lucky to escape destruction. Sometimes the dense ranks of tall pines, firs, and cedars extend to the shore and are reflected in the placid sheet. There is always some new beauty to see, and one scarcely knows which is most delightful,—to float over the deep blue element that kisses his bark, or to wander along the sandy beach and through the surrounding woods, thinking of the power that reared this noble range and gemmed its deep gorges with such scenes of witchery. . . .

The favorite road follows for fifteen miles the banks of its outlet, Truckee River,—a rapid stream of remarkably clear water. . . . The heavily timbered ridges, putting down in nearly straight lines from the summit, rise on either side of this stream to a height of from one thousand to two thousand feet. . . . Extensive logging operations are conducted along the Truckee, and it is one of the sights of the trip to witness the shooting of the logs along timber-ways for one thousand two hundred feet down the side of the ridge. They make the descent in thunder and smoke, and each log, as it strikes the water, will send up a beautiful column of spray a hundred and fifty feet, resembling the effect of a submarine explosion. . . . The first sight of the lake is very striking as one breaks from the sombre-hued forests of pine and fir, and gazes on a wide expanse of blue and gray water, sparkling in the sun, and relieved by a distant background of violet-colored mountains. There is an exciting freshness in the air, and the spirits are elate with freedom and joy. It is a treat to watch the alternations of color on the water. . . . Near the southern and eastern shores the white sandy bottom brings out the green color very strikingly. . . . Sailing or rowing over the translucent depths, not too far from shore, one sees the beautiful trout far below, and sometimes their shadows on the light bottom. It is like hovering above a denser atmosphere. But the surface of the lake easily ruffles into dangerous waves under a sudden wind, and a number of incautious persons have been lost in these cold depths which never give up their dead. The beaches of white sand, or clean, bright pebbles, rich in polished agate, jasper and carnelian, margined with grassy meads where the strawberry ripens its luscious fruit, and running close to park-like groves of pine, fir, and cedar, afford delightful rambles. The shorelines are informal and picturesque, opening into green coves and bays, where sometimes a cascade comes foaming down from the snow-peaks, or pushing out sharp points of timber and long strips of reedy marsh, leading to valleys where smaller lakes are found glassed amid a close frame-work of rocky heights. . . . The afternoon haze over mountain and lake is a delicate, pearly gray. Later, this color shades off into violet, and, as the sun sinks, the mountains take on the most delicious crimson flush, deepening into purple, while the lake is wonderful in its play of reflected color, and at a certain hour looks like an opal set in rubies. The moon at night converts the surface into a shield of flashing silver. By day or night the musical lapse of the wavelets on the beach charms and soothes; and when all the solitude of its original loneliness seems to come over the scene again, we have the sensation of an awful spiritual presence, "felt in the heart and felt along the blood."

≈≈≈

It seems to me that miracles of cure might
be wrought on these shores.

—Helen Hunt Jackson, *Bits of Travel at Home*, 1878

As the 1870s progressed, travel literature of the American West developed an increasingly familiar premise. While commending, even worshipping, the natural splendor, writers also grumbled about the accommodations, the cost, and the physical discomfort of sightseeing. An example related to Lake Tahoe is found in the 1878 book Bits of Travel at Home *by Helen Hunt Jackson.*

Born Helen Fiske in 1830 in Massachusetts, she married Captain Edward Hunt in 1852. Helen endured a string of tragedies during the marriage. Her infant son Murray died in 1854, Captain Hunt died in 1863, and, two years later, her second son Warren died at age nine. Bereft, Helen Hunt dulled her pain through writing poems and travel articles. In May 1872 Helen boarded the transcontinental railroad for a trip to San Francisco. After completing her western journey, Helen Hunt contracted a respiratory ailment, most likely tuberculosis. Seeking treatment, she wintered in Colorado in 1872. There, Helen met and married William Sharpless Jackson, an affluent banker and railroad executive. Subsequently, she was known as Helen Jackson or Helen Hunt Jackson. However, during her prolific writing career, Helen Hunt Jackson usually published under the pseudonym H.H.

While H.H. continued to write travel narratives, she also explored the theme of the oppression of Native Americans. In 1881 Helen Hunt Jackson wrote A Century of Dishonor, a nonfiction examination of the injustices committed against Indigenous people throughout American history. In 1884 Jackson published the romantic novel Ramona. Set in post–Mexican War Southern California, Ramona is an emotional tale of racial discrimination faced by Ramona, a mixed-race Scottish–Native American orphan girl. Ramona was enormously popular, was reprinted hundreds of times, and has never been out of print. Ramona spurred tourism to Southern California and would ultimately spawn motion picture and television adaptations. Many historians believe that the public adulation for Ramona influenced to some degree the passage of the Dawes Severalty Act of 1887 (also known as the General Allotment Act), the first American law to address Native American land rights and authorized the dissolution and redistribution of tribal communal territory. At the time, the Dawes Act was applauded as humane reform, but current historical scholarship considers the act injurious to Native culture and self-determination. The Dawes Act certainly had a deleterious impact on the Washoe people, as their land claims at their homeland of Lake Tahoe were routinely denied.

In this passage from Bits of Travel at Home, Helen Hunt Jackson describes her evocative, albeit slow, arrival at Lake Tahoe and her fascination with the brilliant and everchanging colors of the lake, bemoans the plodding nature of Lake Tahoe steamship voyages, offers a curious reference to the Edward Lear nonsense poem "The Quangle Wangle's Hat," and praises Fred and his rowboat.

You are three hours going from Truckee to Lake Tahoe, and it is so steadily up hill that you begin to wonder long before you get there why the lake does not run over and down. At last you turn a sharp corner, and there lies the lake, only a few rods off. What color you see it depends on the hour and the day. It has its own calendars—its spring-times and winters, its dawns and darknesses—incalculable by almanacs.

It is apt to begin by gray, early in the morning; then the mountains around it look like pale onyx and the sky, too, is gray. Then it changes to clouded sapphire, and the mountains change with it also to a pale, opaque blue; then to brilliant, translucent, glittering sapphire, when the right sort of sun reaches just the right height. And, when there is this peculiar translucent sapphire blue in the water then the mountains are of opal tints, shifting and changing, as if heat were at work in their centres.

Then, if at sunset the mountains take on rose or ruby tints, the water becomes like a sea of pink pearl molten together with silver; and as the twilight wind cools it changes to blue, to green, to steel-gray, to black. This is merely one of its calendars of color; one which I happened to write down on a day when, lying all day by a second-story window, I saw no interval of foreground at all,—only the sky arching down to the lake, and the lake reaching, as it seemed, up to my window-sill. I felt as one might who sailed in a hollow globe of sapphire or floated in a soap-bubble.

There are two tiny steamboats on Lake Tahoe. Every morning one lies at the little wharf opposite the hotel, and rings its miniature bell and whistles its gentle whistle; but it will wait while the head waiter puts up more lunch, or the bridegroom runs back for the forgotten shawl. The twenty or thirty people who are going off in her all know this, and nobody hurries. There are several small villages on the shore of the lake; there are some Hot Springs; there is Cornelian Beach, where tiny red and yellow cornelians can be picked up by handfuls; there is Emerald Bay, where are sharp cliffs many hundred feet high, and water of a miraculous green color. It takes all day to go anywhere and come back in one of these boats, for the engines are only of one tea-kettle power. In fact, as the little craft puffs and wriggles out from shore, it looks as if it had the Quangle Wangle for steersman. . . . The row-boats are better; and, if you take a row-boat, Fred is the man to row you. Everybody at Lake Tahoe knows Fred. He it was who rowed us out to one Sunday service we shall not forget. It was four o'clock in the afternoon. Summer afternoons on Lake Tahoe are warm till sunset—never has the mercury been known to rise above 75 degrees in this magic air; and it rarely, during July and August, falls below 62 degrees. The delight and the stimulus of this steady, clear, crisp air, snow-cooled, sun-warmed; water-fed, cannot be told. Day after day of warm sunlight, such as only rainless skies can show; and night after night of the sleep which only cool nights can give; almost it seems to me that miracles of cure might be wrought on these shores.

≈≈≈

Lake Tahoe is king of them all, not only in size, but in the surpassing beauty of its shores and waters.

—John Muir, "Lake Tahoe in Winter," *San Francisco Bulletin*, April 3, 1878

John Muir is most associated with Yosemite, but Lake Tahoe provided a critical moment in his journey of environmental activism.

Born in Dunbar, Scotland, in 1838, Muir emigrated to Wisconsin in 1849. A budding inventor, John Muir won a prize for his clever devices at the 1860 Wisconsin State Fair. Soon afterward, he entered the University of Wisconsin. Muir attended the college for four years but did not receive a degree. As Muir noted, he departed the University of Wisconsin to attend the "University of the Wilderness." Nearly blinded in an industrial accident in 1867, John Muir recovered and lit out for the territories. Leaving Wisconsin, Muir walked to the Gulf of Mexico and then headed west to California, arriving in March 1868. For the next twelve years, Muir sauntered through the Sierra Nevada, established a nest in Yosemite, and wrote and wrote. Muir filled more than sixty journals with hundreds of notes and enjoyed the publication of dozens of his articles during this period of his life. His notebooks bulged with natural observations and often lyrical praise for the entrancing merits of his beloved Sierra Nevada.

And then, he stopped—for a while. In 1880, Muir married Louisa Wanda Strentzel and devoted most of the next decade to fruit farming in Martinez, a community near the San Francisco Bay. He was very successful and became financially independent, but the strain of managing the family business nearly killed him. Muir's writing was still in demand, but he found balancing farm management with publication increasingly draining. He lost weight, his literary output suffered, he grew weary. In a February 23, 1887, letter to family friend Janet Dou-

glass Moore, whom as a child twenty years earlier had sat and read to Muir as he recovered from his eye injury, John Muir described himself as careworn. When he looked in the mirror, Muir wrote, "I see but little more than the marks of rough weather and fasting. Most people would see only a lot of hair, and two eyes, or one and a half, in the middle of it, like a hillside with small open spots, mostly overgrown with shaggy chaparral." Six months later, in a letter to his brother David, Muir confessed that "I am all nervo shaken and lean as a crow—loaded with care, work, and worry. The care and worry will soon wear away, I hope, but the work seems rather to increase." Seemingly endless farm responsibilities and pressing commitments to produce books on Alaska and Yosemite weighed heavily on Muir.

Concerned for his health and mental well-being, Muir's perceptive wife Louie prevailed upon him to take a vacation. In 1888 John Muir visited Lake Tahoe for the first time in ten years in the company of fellow artists and naturalists. Muir was appalled by what he encountered. The lumber industry was fully engaged, devouring hundreds of acres of forest and leaving desolation in its wake. In a brief journal entry from June 1888, Muir despairingly noted, "The road from Truckee dusty. The ground strewn with fallen trunks burned or tops of trees felled for lumber." Muir, now fifty years old but feeling much older, was disconsolate. He wrote to Louie that he was considering cutting short his Lake Tahoe respite.

Louisa Strentzel Muir's response to her husband's gloom proved to be a turning point in his life. In a letter, Louie wrote, "A ranch that needs and takes the sacrifice of a noble life ought to be flung away beyond all reach and power for harm. . . . The Alaska book and the Yosemite book, dear John, must be written, and you need to be your own self, well and strong, to make them worthy of you. There is nothing that has a right to be considered beside this except the welfare of our children."

John Muir took his wife's sage advice and encouragement to heart and devoted the rest of his life to conservation and preservation causes. In the years that followed, Muir traveled the world promoting his environmental vision. He explored Nevada, Utah, the Pacific Northwest, Alaska, Siberia, Manchuria, Japan, Egypt, Australia, and New Zealand. Muir wrote dozens of articles in support of eco-friendly issues, strengthening of the national park system, in opposition to exploitation of natural resources, and in strong support of preserving and protecting part of Lake Tahoe as a national park. Despite repeated and intensive efforts,

Lake Tahoe never became a national park, a deep regret Muir endured until his dying day. In 1892 Muir founded the Sierra Club and remained its president until 1914. John Muir died on Christmas Eve 1914 at the age of seventy-six.

In an April 3, 1878, article for the San Francisco Bulletin, *John Muir described Lake Tahoe in winter. Despite the stripping of at least one hundred million board feet of lumber by this juncture, Muir noted, "The destructive action of man in clearing away the forests has not as yet effected any very marked change in general views." Ten years later, John Muir's opinion would be strikingly different.*

The winter glory of the Sierra! How little is known of it! Californians admire descriptions of the Swiss Alps, reading with breathless interest how ice and snow load their sublime heights, and booming avalanches sweep in glorious array through their crowded forests, while our own icy, snow-laden mountains, with their unrivaled forests, loom unnoticed along our eastern horizon. True, only mountaineers may penetrate their snow-blocked fastnesses to behold them in all their white wild grandeur, but to every healthy man and woman, and even to children, many of the subalpine valleys and lake-basins, six or seven thousand feet above the sea, remain invitingly open and approachable all winter. With a friend and his two little sons I have just returned from a week of bracing weathering around Lake Tahoe, in which we enjoyed glorious views of winter, fine rolling and sliding in the snow, swimming in the icy lake, and lusty reviving exercise on snow-shoes that kept our pulses dancing right merrily. All the weather was hearty and exhilarating, though varying almost from hour to hour: snowing, blowing, clear and cloudy, but never rigorously cold. . . .

This winter has been remarkably mild, the mercury having seldom made a very near approach to zero, even during the coldest nights around the lake, while the average noonday temperature was considerably above the freezing-point. The snow lies deep on the surrounding mountains and about the shores, solid white contrasting with the dark-blue water of the lake, while the forests and canons and the upper glacial fountain hollows are well filled, assuring abundance of summer water for the lakes and streams. . . .

Down in the forested region, at about the elevation of Lake Tahoe, the greater portion comes gently to the ground, light and feathery, some of the flakes in mild weather being nearly an inch in diameter, and is evenly distributed and kept from drifting to any great extent by the shelter of the woods. Every tree is loaded with the fairy bloom, bending down the branches, and hushing the singing of the elastic needles. When the storm is over and the sun shines, the dazzling snow at once begins to settle and shift and fall off the trees in miniature avalanches; then the relieved branches spring up and shake themselves dry, and the whole green forest, fed and refreshed, waves and sings again rejoicing. . . .

Few even among Californians have any fair conception of the marvelous abundance of glacier lakes hidden in the fastnesses of our mountains. The snow and some of the glaciers make a telling show, even from the distant lowlands; but not a single stream is visible, nor a hollow where one might hope to find a lake. Nevertheless, wild rivers are falling and sounding in every canon, and all their upper branches are fairly laden with lakes like orchard-trees with fruit. They nestle in rocky nooks and hollows about all the high peaks and in the larger canons, reflecting their stern, rugged beauty and giving charming animation to the bleakest and most forbidding landscapes. . . . Lake Tahoe is king of them all, not only in size, but in the surpassing beauty of its shores and waters. It seems a kind of heaven to which the dead lakes of the lowlands had come with their best beauty spiritualized. It lies embosomed in mountains of moderate height near the northern extremity of the high portion of the range, between the main axis and a spur that puts out on the east side from near the head of the Carson River. Though it is twenty-one miles long by ten wide, and from about five hundred to sixteen hundred feet deep, its basin was once occupied by a glacier which filled it from the bottom to a point high above the present water-level, and being lavishly fed by the snows of the encompassing mountains, crawled slowly, like a mighty river, over the north rim of the basin, crushing and grinding the lower mountains that lay in its way, and it was only at the end of the ice period that this noble lake, at least in anything like its present form, came into existence. . . .

The destructive action of man in clearing away the forests has not as yet effected any very marked change in general views. Perhaps about 150,000,000 feet of lumber for the Comstock mines has thus far been cut from the lake shores. . . . It is estimated that the Tahoe basin still contains about 600,000,000 feet of lumber available for the mines.

In summer the woods resound with the outlandish noise of loggers and choppers and screaming mills; skiffs and steamboats skim the lovely blue water in work and play; and ever and anon as you thread the groves along shore you come upon groups of gay tourists sauntering about, gathering flowers, or resting luxuriously in the rosiny shade of the pines, some in easy picnic attire, others all ribbons and colors, glaring wildly amid the green leaves and frightening the wondering squirrels and birds. But winter brings rest. At sight of the first snowflake pleasure-seekers flee as from a plague, the ax leaves the woods, and the kind snow heals every scar.

FOUR

Visitors and Vexations

1880–1889

For Lake Tahoe, 1880 to 1889 was a time of joy and jeopardy. Tourism thrived. New hotels and resorts were constructed. Established holiday hideaways expanded, offering more and better activities and greater creature comforts to the ever-growing and endlessly delighted vacationing public. But dark clouds were on the horizon.

While expanding and generally welcomed, the tourist trade came under scrutiny. Was it growing too fast? Should it be regulated, and, if so, how much?

The leadership of the Washoe people continued their formal protests to government officials decrying the destruction of the forest and fisheries and the continuing encroachment of the Euro-Americans on Washoe traditional lands. Their appeals were in vain. After the passage of the General Allotment Act of 1887 (the so-called Dawes Act) unclaimed 160-acre parcels on formerly communal tribal lands were allotted to individual Washoe, but their petitions to secure land at Lake Tahoe were not granted. The Washoe people existed only on the periphery of the lake or as resort employees, loggers, or fishers. By the end of the decade, Washoe children were educated at the Stewart Indian School, a government boarding school in Carson City that officially opened in 1890. In a military-like setting, the students were subjected to what is known as forced assimilation, a policy that prohibited the children from speaking their Native language and practicing tribal customs. The Stewart Indian School depended on the unpaid labor of their students to keep it afloat.

Despite laws specially crafted to regulate and reign in the most harmful aspects of logging and commercial fishing, these economic engines continued to chug along with increasingly dire consequences.

The decade witnessed ongoing intensive logging, albeit slightly slowed by legislative directives. Huge strips of forestlands continued to be clear-cut, a process that scientific monographs and government documentation called "denudation." Sawdust dumps clogged waterways and spawning grounds.

Commercial fishing continued apace. Thousands of pounds of native and planted nonnative fish were routinely harvested and shipped to waiting markets. Concerns were growing that the Lake Tahoe fishery was being depleted by overfishing. Especially vulnerable were the lake's signature fish, the Lahontan cutthroat trout.

In 1883 the California Legislature responded to these spreading worries by authorizing the Lake Bigler Forestry Commission, which was charged with addressing the problems associated with logging, fishing, and unchecked tourist development. Among its many recommendations was to create a national park at Lake Tahoe, to be formed by transferring state, federal, and private lands to the State of California. The proposal was shelved, primarily due to the widespread conception that the land transfer would inordinately benefit the Central Pacific Rail Road. However, the idea of a Lake Tahoe National Park would be revisited several times in the next few years.

Utilization of Lake Tahoe Basin water remained of paramount interest. In 1887 the Nevada and Lake Tahoe Water and Manufacturing Company unsuccessfully championed a four-mile water diversion tunnel through the Carson Range from Lake Tahoe to the Carson Valley. In 1889 Francis G. Newlands, future member of the House of Representatives and United States senator from Nevada (whose Newlands Reclamation Act of 1902 created the Bureau of Reclamation) and son-in-law of former United States senator from Nevada William Sharon, included Lake Tahoe in his proposed network of Sierra Nevada reservoirs designed to serve and promote future economic development in Nevada.

As reported in the *Reno Evening Gazette* of October 7, 1889, Newlands's intentions were unambiguous. Francis G. Newlands asserted that in an "age of material progress," society would be negligent to shun the natural resources at its fingertips. He argued that "at the bottom of all this progress lies the question of power, the utilization of some form of nature inexpensively, to accomplish what the labor of many men would otherwise accomplish." Newlands concluded, "When this is accomplished, can you form any conception of the great wealth that can be produced by the proper utilization of water not only for irrigation, but for power."

Joining other pipelines already in use at Marlette Lake, a small lake turned into a logging and water reservoir on the rim of the Carson Range just east of Lake Tahoe, was a third pipe that delivered water to the mines and communities of the Comstock Lode.

At the end of the decade, John Wesley Powell, director of the U.S. Geological Survey, issued his *Eleventh Annual Report of the Director of the United States Geological Survey, Part 2—Irrigation: 1889-1890*. The report noted that his agency's efforts in the Lahontan Division (which included Lake Tahoe and surrounding regions) "consisted of surveys of outlets of Lake Tahoe and of storage sites and irrigation canals along the Truckee and Carson rivers" with the desirability of using these water sources "to irrigate the vast areas of desert land in the broad valleys of Nevada." Beyond the vision suggested by Powell, no subsequent actions occurred.

In a harbinger of modern fears, fires were an escalating worry, threatening timber resources, businesses, and lives. Wildfires had always been a feature of Sierra Nevada history, but, fueled by logging slash and often triggered due to the larger human presence, forest fires were regarded as a rising menace. By 1889 the *Sacramento Daily Union* ominously reported that "in this matter of forest fires in California, the day of disaster is already here."

By the 1880–1889 decade, the Gem of the Sierra was a splendid natural wonder in search of an identity. What was Lake Tahoe? Was it primarily a pleasure ground? Was it an essential and vital commercial resource? Was it an endangered ecosystem? Were all three tangled in a byzantine and uncertain coexistence?

Perhaps this quandary is best exemplified by two documents from 1883.

The first is the opening declaration of the February 1883 California Assembly resolution establishing the Lake Bigler Forestry Commission and condemning the ruin of the Lake Tahoe Basin forests:

> It should be the duty of the State to preserve from destruction, and reserve for the health, pleasure, and recreation of its citizens and tourists, the most noted, attractive, and available features of its natural scenery; and whereas, in the rapidly proceeding denudation of the forests on the shores of Lake Bigler the State is losing one of its most attractive features for tourists, and available, valuable, and pleasant resorts for residents.

That same year, the *Truckee Republican* of December 15, 1883, published a gushing tribute to E. J. Brickell, founder of the Truckee Lumber Company in 1867. It began:

> Among those who crossed the mountains with the first rails of the overland railroad, was a keen but quiet man, just coming into the prime of life, whose mission it was to be the leader in the development of the great timber interests. . . . The great forests that had been growing to perfection for hundreds of years, were now needed by the restless race that has the work of subduing the American continent to civilization, and men of nerve and brain and energy were in demand to gather it from the steep and rocky mountain sides and out of the dark and silent canyons, to build mills and turn the monarchs of the woods into lumber, ties and timber.

The testimonial concluded:

> Mr. Brickell [states that] the Truckee timber belts is far from being exhausted. He says that although millions and millions have been cut he can see to-day more timber [at his] mill with the present methods of working than he did when he set the first ax to felling trees.

That is perplexing.

The questions concerning Lake Tahoe's future were momentous. Acquiring the answers was a challenge.

≈≈≈

> How feeble seem all words; entrancing beauty and
> enrapturing grandeur, we land in a very garden of delight.
> —"The Quiet Hour," *Sacramento Daily Union*, August 21, 1880

While some might extol the economic potential of Lake Tahoe or marvel at the size of the lake's extraordinary trout or savor a gourmet meal at a top-notch lakeside resort, for most the premier attraction of Lake Tahoe was the majesty of the surroundings.

The startling color and clarity of the water, the snow-capped ridges embracing the lake, the natural perfume of the pines drifting on gentle zephyrs, and the awe-inspiring sunsets inspired writers of all stripes and skills to paroxysms of prose, both poetic and purple, for decades.

A common outlet for nineteenth-century authors were newspapers, the information superhighway of the era. In the last quarter of the century, the Sacramento Daily Union featured a column entitled the Quiet Hour, a grab bag of assorted remarks, rhymes, and riddles that were referred to as "tangles." Fans of the featured section were nicknamed "tanglers." A frequent contributor and a favorite of the tanglers was a young woman known only as Sibyl.

In this tangle from August 21, 1880, Sibyl recounts a recent visit to Lake Tahoe, a place she calls "a very garden of delight," the dazzling home of "sylvan deities."

A Summer Letter

Dear Quiet Hour:

Once more I am at dear old Forest Lodge enjoying a delightful summer near to the "heart of Nature" . . . far beyond, set like a jewel among the overgazing hights, gleam and glisten the blue waters of Lake Tahoe. In the magnitude of the scene our voices are silenced. Our road, like a winding staircase, descends the mountain; we pursue it, and when part way down encounter a snowdrift surrounded by moss-pinks and penstemons growing in tropical luxuriance. Nature seems indeed to blend her seasons here to make the landscape fair. . . . Lake Tahoe is very beautiful in the purple half light in which we behold it, for the sun has passed: far down the sky when we arrive. Every influence about the place is quiet and restful, and we are heartily sorry that we must limit our stay to two days. Fallen Leaf Lake is distant about three miles, and is reached by a delightful woodland road brightened all along its way by the wonderful snow-plant. . . . How smooth and clear and beautiful the waters of the lake. Like my own life they seemed to me—so very quiet. And all around the lofty flights arise, whose summits other footsteps have attained. But we must be content to glide in sweet tranquillity below. Let others toiling struggle on up, up the flights; they win what they achieve by weary hours. Ah, why not be content to sail forever here in dreamful ease. They tell me beautiful Lake, that you, too, grow weary of these narrow bounds, and moan in maddened restlessness and toss your waters high to fall again in tired spray. That you are treacherous, beautiful waters, and that in your still deeps many a warm heart has ceased to beat, and that you hold your victims for your very own, and taking them to the deepest depths, pin them there forever. That in your waters there is a mystery that none can solve. But it does seem to me, if dying were all over, it would be very sweet to sleep in your calm purity. Oh, dreamy happiness, to glide and muse and love the water. But, wafted on, we come at length to Emerald Bay. How feeble seem all words; entrancing beauty and enrapturing grandeur, we land in a very garden of delight. The home it might be of the sylvan deities. Their nectar the purling rill of cold crystal water which, through mosses and fern, threads the flower strewn velvety sward. Their ambrosia the life-giving perfumed air that sets the aspen leaves all aquiver above the moss grown rocky grottoes that may be their homes. But we hear a voice in the distance. It is the rush of waters, and now we'll climb, and all unheeding the brambly way we hurry on up, up, the flights, but still we are in the depths when we have reached the highest crag our footsteps dare. Most glorious reward for the toil of the upward way. . . . We see the last day-beam folded away in the garments of the night, and feel in real sadness that no longer for us will gleam the blue waters or arise the lofty, snow-crowned hights; and we bid them adieu as to a noble new-found friend. . . .

Sibyl.

≈≈≈

Nothing seemed improbable in the wonderful land of Washoe.

—Piscatorial Precepts, Pipedreams and Prejudice: Fishing at Lake Tahoe

Sport and commercial fishing in Lake Tahoe was a major component of the lake's economy and culture throughout the nineteenth century. The Washoe people caught the wide variety of available species as an essential facet of their resource-harvesting existence. From the 1860s onward, commercial fishing extracted thousands of pounds annually, and dozens of well-equipped vessels cruised the Gem of the Sierra. Widely advertised and world-renowned sport fishing for tourists and resort guests was a major Lake Tahoe amenity factor for decades.

*Not surprisingly, the importance of piscatorial pursuits led to breath-
less exaggeration, disbelief of remarkable fishing reports and exploits,
tall tales, downright lies, tutorials on technique, and periodic violence.*

*Following is a collection of reports on fishing at Lake Tahoe. Chron-
icled are the almost unbelievable clarity of the Lake Tahoe water, the
size of trout, the best time of day and the hot spots to fish, a scientific
report detailing Lake Tahoe angling tackle and methods, an account of
tension and potential violence between Washoe Native fishers and the
California Fish Commission, and two curious tales, the first explaining
why Lake Tahoe fish must eat stones and the second describing "trout
mining" in frozen Emerald Bay.*

William Brewer, *Up and Down California in 1860–1864*

[August 23, 1863] The purity of its waters, its great depth, its altitude,
and the clear sky all combine to give the lake a bright but intensely
blue color; it is bluer even than the Mediterranean, and nearly as picturesque as Lake Geneva in Switzerland. Its beautiful waters and the
rugged mountains rising around it, spotted with snow which has perhaps lain for centuries, form an enchanting picture. It lacks many of
the elements of beauty of the Swiss lakes; it lacks the grassy, green,
sloping hills, the white-walled towns, the castles with their stories and
histories, the chalets of the herders—in fact, it lacks *all* the elements
that give their peculiar charm to the Swiss scenery—its beauty is its
own, is truly Californian.

The lake abounds in the largest trout in the world, a species of speckled trout that often weighs over twenty pounds and sometimes as much
as *thirty pounds*! Smaller trout are abundant in the streams. An Indian
brought some into camp. I gave him fifty cents for two, and they made
us two good meals and were excellent fish.

Charles F. McGlashan, "Resources and Wonders of Tahoe," *Sacramento Daily Union*, May 29, 1875

The Fishing Interests

Are more extensive than might be supposed. Six varieties of trout are
found in the lake, and they are considered as being far superior in
delicacy of flavor to river trout. From twenty to twenty-five men are
constantly employed in fishing for market. Generally a trolling line is

used, and a fisherman's average day's work is from forty-five to sixty pounds. Fifteen cents per pound is the price received. Ben Coy is said to have made the biggest showing ever made on the lake. He caught one hundred and forty-eight pounds of trout in three hours. The largest fish ever drawn from the lake weighed twenty-nine pounds, and was sent to General Grant by Burton of the Island Ranch. In different seasons different hours of the day are best for fishing. Sometimes the trout bite best at midnight. The silver trout spawn in the lake, but other varieties run up into the little brooks. Indians at Taylor creek and Chinamen at Glenbrook, spear, seine and trap every fish that runs up to spawn. If the Indians slaughtered trout for their own use it would be all well enough, but they make a regular practice of selling to white men for market. Surely an Act should be passed by our Legislature prohibiting the wanton destruction of trout by Indians in the employ of white men.

"Trout Mining at Lake Tahoe," *San Francisco Daily Alta California*, January 10, 1878

Trout Mining at Lake Bigler

The following voracious narrative is from the *Carson Appeal*:

In the general freeze which has converted the lake into a sea of ice, Emerald Bay has been frozen solid. It is one vast ledge of ice from the surface of its transparent waters to the bottom. More than ever is that beautiful bay a gem of purest ray serene, crystallized as it is, and firm set within its own rock-bound shores. From some cause, best known to themselves, the fish, especially the trout, have fairly swarmed here. When the great and sudden freezing came, it imprisoned them by hundreds of tons all over the bay. There they are fixed, like a bee in a drop of amber. Of course the fisherman of the Rubicon and its neighborhood are reaping a rich and novel harvest. The present abundance of fish in the Carson market is due to this remarkable occurrence. Monk says that the bay presents a wonderful appearance. He says in all truthfulness that Sailor Jack and some associates have actually sunk a winze in the ice between the boat landing and Cap'n Dick's Island, and that by dint of tunnelling and stopping in the solid ice, they are actually mining out the imprisoned trout by the cart load. Hank says he has an interest in one of these extraordinary "claims," and that he has every reason to expect prompt and numerous dividends. The present state of the weather seems to guarantee a continuance of this strange species of mining for some days yet to come, if not, indeed, for the remainder of the Winter.

Report upon the Fishes Collected During the Years 1875, 1876, and 1877, in California and Nevada by Prof. David S. Jordan and H. W. Henshaw, United States Engineer Office, Geographical Surveys West of the 100th Meridian, Appendix K, June 30, 1878

This beautiful trout is universally known about Lake Tahoe as the "Silver Trout." . . . Its prevailing tint when freshly taken from the water is of a rather pure silvery-white, the sides showing traces of golden reflections. The black spots are larger, more irregularly shaped, and more numerous than in the "Black Trout," and on the back become aggregated into a broad black band. The belly is white, not smoky-brown, as in the other, and is marked with numerous small black spots. The color is variable to some extent in both species, and perhaps at other seasons the distinct colors of the two fish might not be maintained, although we have never seen specimens that appeared at all doubtful; hence we are inclined to attribute a greater degree of constancy to the respective markings of these two fishes, as they occur together in Lake Tahoe, than is usually to be found in the various species of the family. The Silver Trout is said to spawn in the gravel beds of the lake, and not to accompany the other species on its periodical journey up the Truckee. At Lake Tahoe, the capture of trout, as followed by the fishermen for market, is rather peculiar in that trolling supersedes all other methods. We had no opportunity to test them with the fly, but were told that it had been tried, with but poor success. On several occasions, the ordinary spoon bait was used, such as is employed successfully in the East with Pickerel, and which elsewhere in the West we have found to be fairly successful with trout, but here it proved of little value. The tackle which experience has shown to be the best, and which is in almost universal employ upon the lake, is very similar to the ordinary trolling apparatus used upon the East coast for Bluefish, and consists of an oblong-oval, flat piece of lead either run on to the shank of a good-sized hook or placed upon the line immediately above it. The hook is always baited with a fresh "Silver-sided Minnow," the bright lead serving merely to attract the attention of the fish to the bait. The wonderful transparency of the water renders the use of a long line, 150 feet or more, imperative, as the trout are too shy to be trolled in very near the boat. With the above simple equipment, the fisherman is ready for work, and in season it is only necessary to troll leisurely over the fishing-grounds upon a calm day, and good fishing is assured, as the trout are very numerous and eager for the bait. Nearly all the fish are caught between the green and blue water, the former color indicating the shallower parts, the blue the deep. The sharpness of definition of this dividing line is quite remarkable, deep water succeeding shallow with cliff-like abruptness.

It is during the spring months that the trout take the bait most eagerly, and great numbers are then caught. As summer comes on, they bite less readily, and during the late fall good catches are rarely made.

Besides the trolling method, still-fishing is sometimes resorted to, chiefly by visitors and amateurs.

"Field and Wood," *San Jose Mercury-News*, March 12, 1882

Fish That Eat Stones

It is a subject of remark among old residents of the Comstock that the Lake Tahoe trout are not now so much addicted to the swallowing of stones as in former times. In the early days it was not an unusual thing to find the bellies of trout stuffed with pebbles weighing from one to six ounces each. When our people found fault with this unprofitable stuffing the fishermen swore they had nothing to do with it and could not help it. They declared that it was the constant habit of Lake Tahoe trout to thus fill themselves up with stones. Their idea of the matter was that owing to the great altitude of the lake there was such a lack of density in the water that the fish would all float on top unless they took in a goodly ballast of stones. This explanation was accepted by credulous householders—for nothing seemed improbable in the wonderful land of Washoe, and for a long time was firmly believed by nearly everybody on the Comstock. In those days several tons of Tahoe pebbles must have been sold at from two to four bits per pound. —[Reprinted from the] *Virginia Nev. Enterprise*

Fish Commissioners

Extracts From Biennial Report Relative To Truckee

The following extract is from the *Report of the California Fish Commissioners* from the published journal of Deputy John P. Babcock.

[UNDER DATE OF JUNE 11, 1892]

From the mill we drove to Griff's Creek, a tributary of Lake Tahoe. [Secretary William] O'Neill had located an Indian fish trap on the creek several days before, but was in doubt as to his powers in the matter. We found the trap in place. It was a most ingenious contrivance for catching fish, made from woven green willows. The Indians who were working this engine of destruction for numberless spawn fish, were camped beside the creek. We ordered them to leave the lake and took out their trap. We worked over an hour and a half to get it out of the water. The Indians made no objections, as O'Neill told them that he was a Government man, and would put them in jail they did not leave.

≈≈≈

> She invoked the aid of her guardian spirit, and plunged
> into the water, which at once closed over her. The
> spirit appealed to having heard her prayer, preserved
> her life by transforming her into a beautiful fish.

—Mamie Anderson, "A Legend of Emerald Bay and the Origin of Tahoe Trout," *Sacramento Daily Union*, November 19, 1881

The literature of nineteenth-century Lake Tahoe is rife with stories of the celebrated, brilliantly hued trout that graced its waters.

Spying these creatures gliding a hundred feet under the surface in the crystal-clear waters was a sight that many visitors recalled for years afterward. The accounts of the extensive commercial fishing operations were excitedly described. The dimensions of individual fish and the magnitude of fisher's limits were itemized and acclaimed. Fishing contests were publicized with zeal.

Something that magnificent demanded a marvelous origin story. Mamie Anderson of Sacramento provided one on the pages of the November 19, 1881, issue of the Sacramento Daily Union *in an article entitled "A Legend of Emerald Bay and the Origin of Tahoe Trout."*

Anderson was inspired by a painting of Emerald Bay by Norton Bush "which called to mind," she wrote, "an old legend connected with the subject of the picture, which it is believed has never been in type." It is likely that Mamie Anderson massively embellished this timeworn tale.

The "Legend of Emerald Bay and the Origin of Tahoe Trout" is the fable of how the lake's trout were formed from blood droplets shed by a beautiful huntress who transformed into an even more beautiful fish.

Norton Bush, an artist of the Hudson Valley school of landscape painting, became popular for his interpretations of the Sierra Nevada, New England, and Central and South America. Lake Tahoe was a favorite subject. Bush's paintings were in the luminist style, which emphasized the effects of light on the landscape. Norton Bush's works were all the rage among the industrial barons of the era, purchased by such figures as the Big Four magnate Leland Stanford and Bonanza King James C. Flood.

Mamie Anderson writes this phrase: "The beautiful valley (now called the Sacramento), with its pure and limpid streams, was one vast garden spot (there were no 'slickens' in those days)." Slickens was the debris from hydraulic mining that was deposited in downstream watersheds, fouling rivers and often burying farmland.

A Legend of Emerald Bay and of the Origin of Tahoe Trout

On visiting the art exhibition of Norton Bush I observed a fine painting representing a scene on Emerald Bay, with cascades and summit peaks in the near background; also the little island so familiar to all sightseeing visitors, and which called to mind an old legend connected with the subject of the picture, which it is believed has never been in type, and which gives one version of the origin of Lake Tahoe trout.

Who does not love the romance, the ideals, the legends of the past? Life is as much made up of the ideals as of the realities. The ideals and legends of the past form the food which nourishes the imagination, guides the pencil of the artist and the pen of the poet, and upon which is founded our choicest literature and finest art. "Tis the very soul and life of poetry and art. From the fabulous realms brilliant, golden thoughts are culled and garnered into beautiful truths. They form the treasure-house of literature, the handmaid of poetry and art. Without them we would be like the lonely walls of a ruined temple bereft of its altars and shorn of its ivy clingings."

The scene of this painting, so goes the legend, centuries ago was the summer resort of a people of great culture and refinement, much greater than any that has succeeded. The women were possessed of great beauty; the men of great passions. The beautiful valley (now called the Sacramento), with its pure and limpid streams, was one vast garden spot (there were no "slickens" in those days), and was the home of a beautiful princess, who was a great lover of all field sports, and a daring huntress—in fact, a regular Diana. As was her custom, one summer, she betook herself (in those days ladies did not fear to travel alone) to the pleasant scenes of the "Mountain Water," as it was then called, to revel in her hunting sports. While engaged in this pursuit near the summit, just back of that part of the lake now called "Emerald Bay," she was accosted by a strange being, not of her race, who at once laid claim to her by right of discovery, and who attempted to possess himself of her, without the formality of asking her permission. Being powerless in such determined hands, she sought safety in flight. Springing from rock to rock, over crags and cascades they went, she bending every nerve to escape, and he to capture. The pursuit brought her at length to the edge of the lake, and rather than submit to capture, she invoked the aid of her guardian spirit, and plunged into the water, which at once closed over her. The spirit appealed to having heard her prayer, preserved her life by transforming her into a beautiful fish. Her pursuer was at the same instant metamorphosed into a monstrous eagle, and from his craggy hight kept constant watch over the place where she disappeared. After a time she, desiring a breath of air, sprang out of the water, as fish often do, when her watcher, always on the alert, with a sudden swoop fastened his talons in her sides, and spread his wings to bear her away. But before he arose more than a few feet above the surface of the water some invisible power struck him dead, and he fell with wings outspread, and was changed into earth and stone. The beautiful fish swam away, but carried with her the marks of the eagle's talons in her side, and from which drops of blood were shed into the water. These drops of blood at once assumed the form of fish, which had marks or spots just the game as those from which they issued. These spots ever after remained upon her finny tribe, and which in our day form the distinguishing marks for Tahoe trout.

The legend runs on that the island thus formed . . . rests upon two pillars (the eagle's legs); that beneath the surface of this island is a magnificent palace, studded with emeralds, and from which the water receives an emerald hue. Here the huntress assumes her personality, but secluded from mortal eyes, when she is not sporting in the waters in the form of a fish.

On any clear bright day near this island can now be seen deep in the water a large and beautiful trout, and which many sportsmen have endeavored to lure to the hook. But she shows her spotted and silvery sides, and when too closely pressed darts under the rocks of the island and disappears. It is said that this is the legendary huntress and the parent of all trout.

As the legend goes, at intervals of a great many years this beautiful huntress for a time assumes her maidenly form and wanders amid the hills and peaks around the lake, and has within the recollection of man been seen to sit, clothed in white, upon Summit Peak. Just before these events the hills and glens around Emerald Bay and Idlewild resound with strains of the sweetest music, softer and more enchanting than the Sirenic muse or the Æolian harp. During these periods the greatest prosperity and happiness abound throughout the whole land. They are also the harbingers of great events. This is only one of the many legends connected with these mountain lakes.

Mamie Anderson, Sacramento, November 16, 1881.

≈≈≈

My deliberate belief is that we went at a rate
that annihilated time and space.

—H. J. Ramsdell, "The Great Nevada Flume: A Perilous Ride," *Pacific Tourist: Adams and Bishop's Illustrated Trans-Continental Guide*, 1881.

Lumber from Lake Tahoe was a highly desired commodity, and demand surged in the 1870s and 1880s with increases in railroad construction and underground mining.

Railroad snow sheds alone required three hundred million board feet of lumber, with another twenty million needed annually for maintenance.

The Comstock Lode used more than seventy million board feet for mine shaft timbering in its silver and gold mines. The skyrocketing Comstock population needed millions more board feet every year for building homes, businesses, and fences. For example, Virginia City, Nevada, became a boomtown, as thousands of starry-eyed prospectors descended upon the desert community. Soon there were hotels, restaurants, shops, saloons, boarding houses, and even an opera house. All this mining and civic development required astonishing amounts of lumber. The solution was to harvest timber from the nearby Lake Tahoe Basin, about thirty miles away, and transport it to Virginia City,

Conveying cut timber to lumberyards, mills, and markets required an assortment of methods, including narrow-gauge railroads, wagons, drag roads, floating timber rafts called booms, and flumes. Arguably, the most spectacular were the flumes—V-shaped wooden troughs that used running water and gravity to move the lumber. At least ten flumes spread tentacles through the Lake Tahoe and Carson Valley areas.

One flume was known as the Bonanza V. Long dismantled and with evidence of its location nearly impossible to find, it remains fresh in memory as the site of one of the most dramatic and terrifying events in Lake Tahoe history.

The Bonanza V was the creation of the Pacific Wood, Lumber and Flume Company, a business providing lumber for the escalating needs of the Comstock Lode. Most notable among the company stockholders were James C. Flood, James G. Fair, John Mackay, and William S. O'Brien, all principal mine owners in the Comstock Lode region and known collectively as the Bonanza Kings or the Silver Kings. The Bonanza V was located about twenty miles north of Lake Tahoe and plummeted roughly fifteen miles eastward to Huffaker's Station, a stop on the Virginia and Truckee Railroad south of Reno.

The Bonanza V flume was constructed for the then colossal sum of nearly $300,000 (the equivalent of $8 million in 2023), but Flood estimated that the flume saved his company nearly $500,000 annually ($13.5 million in 2023's money) in transportation costs. The flume wove through the mountains on a trestle that ranged from twenty to seventy feet above the ground and dropped a total of 1,750 feet in elevation. Constructed in only ten weeks, the flume used two million feet of lumber and twenty-eight tons of nails. When finished, it moved approximately five hundred thousand feet of lumber per day.

In the 1870s one of America's most influential newspapers was the New-York Tribune. In 1875, reporter H. J. Ramsdell of the Tribune was invited by James C. Flood and James G. Fair to visit the Bonanza V flume; they then dared him to take a ride along its length. Ramsdell accepted the challenge, and two flume boats were summoned. In the first boat would be Ramsdell, James G. Fair, and a plucky company volunteer whom Ramsdell described as "a red-faced carpenter, who takes more kindly to whisky than his bench." The other vessel would hold James C. Flood and John Hereford, superintendent of the flume.

H. J. Ramsdell's account of the harrowing thirty-five-minute "perilous ride" follows.

The Great Nevada Flume

"A Perilous Ride" by H. J. Ramsdell of the *N.-Y. Tribune*

A 15 mile ride in a flume down the Sierra Nevada Mountains in 35 minutes, was not one of the things contemplated on my visit to Virginia City, and it is entirely within reason to say that I shall never make the trip again.

The flume cost, with its appurtenances, between $200,000 and $300,000. It was built by a company interested in the mines here, principally owners of the Consolidated Virginia, California, Hale & Norcross, Gould & Curry, Best & Belcher, and Utah Mines. The largest stockholders are J. C. Flood, James G. Fair, John Mackey, and W. S. O'Brien, who compose, without doubt, the wealthiest firm in the United States. . . .

A Ride in the Flume— . . . I found that Mr. Flood and Mr. Fair had arranged for a ride in the flume, and I was challenged to go with them. Indeed, the proposition was put in the form of a challenge—they dared me to go.

I thought that if men worth $25,000,000 or $30,000,000 apiece, could afford to risk their lives, I could afford to risk mine, which was not worth half as much.

So I accepted the challenge, and two boats were ordered. These were nothing more than pig-troughs, with one end knocked out. The "boat" is built, like the flume, V shaped, and fits into the flume. It is composed of three pieces of wood—two two-inch planks, 16 feet long, and an end board which is nailed about two and one-half feet across the top.

The forward end of the boat was left open, the rear end closed with a board—against which was to come the current of water to propel us. Two narrow boards were placed in the boat for seats, and everything was made ready. Mr. Fair and myself were to go in the first boat, and Mr. Flood and Mr. Hereford in the other.

Mr. Fair thought that we had better take a third man with us who knew something about the flume. There were probably 50 men from the mill standing in the vicinity waiting to see us off, and when it was proposed to take a third man, the question was asked of them if anybody was willing to go.

Only one man, a red-faced carpenter, who takes more kindly to whisky than his bench, volunteered to go. Finally, everything was arranged. Two or three stout men held the boat over the flume, and told us to jump into it the minute it touched the water, and to *"hang on to our hats."*

The signal of *"all ready"* was given, the boat was launched, and we jumped into it as best we could, which was not very well, and away we went like the wind.

One man who helped to launch the boat, fell into it just as the water struck it, but he scampered out on the trestle, and whether he was hurt or not, we could not wait to see.

The grade of the flume at the mill is very heavy, and the water rushes through it at railroad speed. The terrors of that hide can never be blotted from the memory of one of that party. To ride upon the cow-catcher of an engine down a steep grade is simply exhilarating, for you know there is a wide track, regularly laid upon a firm foundation, that there are wheels grooved and fitted to the track, that there are trusty men at the brakes, and better than all, you know that the power that impels the train can be rendered powerless in an instant by the driver's light touch upon his lever. But a flume has no element of safety. In the first place the grade can not be regulated as it can on a railroad; you can not go fast or slow at pleasure; you are wholly at the mercy of the water. You can not stop; you can not lessen your speed; you have nothing to hold to; you have only to sit still, shut your eyes, say your prayers, take all the water that comes—filling your boat, wetting your feet, drenching you like a plunge through the surf,—and wait for eternity. It is all there is to hope for after you are launched in a flume-boat. I can not give the reader a better idea of a flume ride than to compare it to riding down an old fashioned eave-trough at an angle of 45°, hanging in midair without support of roof or house, and thus shot a distance of 15 miles.

At the start, we went at the rate of about 23 miles an hour, which is a little less than the average speed of a railroad train. The reader can have no idea of the speed we made, until he compares it to a railroad. The average time we made was 30 miles per hour—a mile in two minutes for the entire distance. This is greater than the average running time of railroads.

Incidents of the Ride,—The red-faced carpenter sat in front of our boat on the bottom, as best he could. Mr. Fair sat on a seat behind him, and I sat behind Mr. Fair in the stern, and was of great service to him in keeping the water, which broke over the end-board, from his back.

There was a great deal of water also shipped in the bows of the hog-trough, and I know Mr. Fair's broad shoulders kept me from many a wetting in that memorable trip.

At the heaviest grade the water came in so furiously in front, that it was impossible to see where we were going, or what was ahead of us; but, when the grade was light, and we were going at a three or four-minute pace, the vision was very delightful, although it was terrible.

In this ride, which fails me to describe, I was perched up in a boat no wider than a chair, some-times 20 feet high in the air, and with the ever varying altitude of the flume, often 70 feet high. When the water would enable me to look ahead, I would see this trestle here and there for miles, so small and narrow, and apparently so fragile, that I could only compare it to a chalk-mark, upon which, high in the air, I was running at a rate unknown upon railroads.

One circumstance during the trip did more to show me the terrible rapidity with which we dashed through the flume, than anything else. We had been rushing down at a pretty lively rate of speed, when the boat suddenly struck something in the bow—a nail, or lodged stick of wood, which ought not to have been there. What was the result? The red-faced carpenter was sent whirling into the flume, 10 feet ahead. Fair was precipitated on his face, and I found a soft lodgment on Fair's back.

It seemed to me that in a second's time. Fair, himself a powerful man, had the carpenter by the scruff of the neck, and had pulled him into the boat. I did not know that, at this time, Fair had his fingers crushed between the boat and the flume.

But we sped along; minutes seemed hours. It seemed an hour before we arrived at the worst place in the flume, and yet Hereford tells me it was less than 10 minutes. The flume at the point alluded to must have very near 45° inclination.

In looking out before we reached it, I thought the only way to get to the bottom was to fall. How our boat kept in the track is more than I know. The wind, the steamboat, the railroad never went so fast. I have been where the wind blew at the rate of 80 miles an hour, and yet my breath was not taken away. In the flume, in the bad places, it seemed as if I would suffocate.

The first bad place that we reached, and if I remember right, it was the worst, I got close against Fair. I did not know that I would survive the journey, but I wanted to see how fast we were going. So I lay close to him and placed my head between his shoulders. The water was coming into his face, like the breakers of the ocean. When we went slow, the breakers came in on my back, but when the heavy grades were reached, the breakers were in front. In one case Fair shielded me, and in the other, I shielded Fair.

In this particularly bad place I allude to, my desire was to form some judgment of the speed we were making. If the truth must be spoken, I was really scared almost out of reason; but if I was on the way to eternity, I wanted to know exactly how fast I went; so I huddled close to Fair, and turned my eyes toward the hills. Every object I placed my eye on was gone, before I could clearly see what it was. Mountains passed like visions and shadows. It was with difficulty that I could get my breath. I felt that I did not weigh a hundred pounds, although I knew, in the sharpness of intellect which one has at such a moment, that the scales turned at two hundred.

Mr. Flood and Mr. Hereford, although they started several minutes later than we, were close upon us. They were not so heavily loaded, and they had the full sweep of the water, while we had it rather at second hand. Their boat finally struck ours with a terrible crash.

Mr. Flood was thrown upon his face, and the waters flowed over him, leaving not a dry thread upon him. What became of Hereford I do not know, except that when he reached the terminus of the flume, he was as wet as any of us.

This only remains to be said. We made the entire distance in less time than a railroad train would ordinarily make, and a portion of the time we went faster than a railroad train ever went.

Fair said we went at least a mile a minute. Flood said we went at the rate of 100 miles an hour, and my deliberate belief is that we went at a rate that annihilated time and space. We were a wet lot when we reached the terminus of the flume. Flood said he would not make the trip again, for the whole Consolidated Virginia Mine.

Fair said that he should never again place himself on an equality with timber and wood, and Hereford said he was sorry that he ever built the flume. As for myself, I told the millionaire that I had accepted my last challenge. When we left our boats we were more dead than alive.

We had yet 16 miles to drive to Virginia City. How we reached home, the reader will never know. . . . The next day, neither Flood nor Fair were able to leave their bed. For myself, I had only strength enough left to say, *"I have had enough of flumes."*

≈≈≈

Lake Tahoe is the great sanitarium of the Pacific coast.

—JCH, "The Baldwin," *Pacific Rural Press,* June 3, 1882

As the 1880s began, more and more attention was paid to the tourist trade at Lake Tahoe. During the early years of the decade, lumber operations continued at an unrelenting pace, but their environmental impact was facing challenges and possible government restrictions. Commercial fishing was still big business, but alarms were raised that the fisheries were approaching depletion. But tourism was booming, and observers increasingly focused on the effects of the mushrooming service economy and the quality of tourist amenities.

On June 3, 1882, the Pacific Rural Press *published an article entitled "The Baldwin," a puff piece primarily concentrating on the Baldwin Hotel in San Francisco but also commenting on the luxurious Tallac Point House, one of the finest at Lake Tahoe. Both San Francisco's Baldwin Hotel and the Lake Tahoe southwest shore Tallac Resort were owned and operated by Elias Jackson Baldwin, also known near and far as "Lucky Baldwin." Baldwin was a roguish wheeler-dealer, but the article generously described him as "enterprising and public-spirited."*

The newspaper correspondent (identified only as "JCH"), itemized the cost, the ambience, nearby excursions, the changeable weather, and the "feast of mountains for such as hail from level lands" of the Tallac

Resort. He concluded with a claim that could easily appear in any
present-day travel brochure: [Lake Tahoe] "possesses climate, scenery
and means of health-giving pleasure to the careworn and debilitated,
far ahead of any other place of resort."

The Tallac House

The attention of excursionists and tourists is called to the Tallac house, which has lately been thoroughly renovated, improved and furnished. This fine summer resort is beautifully located on the southern and sheltered side of Lake Tahoe, near Emerald Bay Soda Springs Fallen Leaf and Cascade lakes, and amid magnificent scenery, shady groves, grassy meadow. Broad verandas encircle the house; Chinese lanterns adorn the groves; swings, croquet, lawn tennis and archery grounds; with fine drives through the valleys; good trout fishing, horses, carriages, boats and fishing implements at the command of guests. The table will be first-class in every respect. Billiard tables, piano, dance hall, and, in fact, everything possible for the pleasure and comfort of patrons will be found at the Tallac house. This well-known resort is now open. Fare from San Francisco via Truckee, is $16.50 [$500 in 2023].

Lake Tahoe

This lake is 1,700 ft. deep, is on a line between California and Nevada, is ice-cold and crystalline clearness. Although hundreds of millions of gallons flow off through the Truckee river every day, the supply is ever kept up by melting snow and great subterranean springs. Its fine beaches and shore groves of pine make it the most picturesque and attractive lake in the world. While calm it is one of the loveliest sights conceivable—serenely beautiful—but during mountain storms its glassy bosom is lashed into whip crested billows, which dash in fury on its pebbly shore. To understand its beauties one must go there and spend some time. The route from San Francisco is via C.P.R.R., to Truckee, 259 miles, stage 14 miles. Passengers coming from the East and desiring to visit the lake should leave the C.P.R.R—at Reno, then via V.-R.R. to Carson City, and thence by Benton's stage 18 miles, to Glenbrook, on the eastern shore of the lake from which a steamer runs to the Tallac house, at the southern end of the lake, to a fine hotel with magnificent surroundings. This house is owned by Mr. E. J. Baldwin, of the famed Baldwin hotel.

Tahoe trout, fresh from the cold waters of the lake are served at every meal and the visitor will find ample facilities in the way of boats and tackle to try his hand at the enticing sport of capturing the fish himself. It is in the form of a parallelogram, lying northeast and southwest, partly in Nevada and partly in California. At a distance of three miles from shore its depth is from 1,000 ft. to 1,200 ft. The greatest depth yet found is 1,800 ft. The water is so transparent that trout and other objects can be seen at the bottom, where the depth is from 80 ft. to 100 ft. Owing to the rarity of the atmosphere the water has little buoyancy. In order to swim in the lake one must be very industrious. Nothing is ever seen floating on the lake but boats or rafts of logs in transit. Stray logs, driftwood, and even shingles soon sink. The bodies of persons drowned in the lake never rise—are never seen again.

This celebrated lake is about 25 miles long by from 10 to 14 miles wide, and it forms a miniature inland sea. Its elevation above the sea 6,700 ft., and the mountains which surround are covered with snow for eight months out of the twelve; its water never freezes, but remains about the same temperature throughout the year.

Grand old mountains stand about the lake like sentinels. Here is a feast of mountains for such as hail from level lands. On all sides they tower—mountains that are pine-clad and mountains that are but stupendous piles of rugged granite. It is a region of granite. To the west rise mountains cold and stern, covered with snow, while on the north and east all mountains clothed in groves of pine, fir and spruce. The entire distance around the lake is 144 miles.

Lake Tahoe is the great sanitarium of the Pacific coast. It possesses climate, scenery and means of health-giving pleasure to the careworn and debilitated, far ahead of any other place of resort. The business man is bound to forget his business while here. The scenery is too grand, the air too quieting and dreamy to allow business cares to absorb the attention.

≈≈≈

All nature seems glad in the unison of two holy young lovers.

—"A Lake Tahoe Romance," *Santa Barbara*
Morning Press, September 12, 1882

While lyrical reverie might be the goal of visiting nineteenth-century authors and artists steeped in Romanticism, for some Lake Tahoe offered an even better attraction—good, old-fashioned romance. As the lake's popularity as a tourist destination grew in the 1880s, Lake Tahoe became a preferred venue not only for vacations and retreats, but also for celebrations. A Lake Tahoe wedding was particularly appealing, and a wedding on a boat in the middle of the lake was even more desirable.

In this article from the Santa Barbara Morning Press *of September 12, 1882, correspondent and father of the bride G. W. Chandler Jr. recounted the marriage of his daughter Lizzie ("well known to the society of Santa Barbara") to William E. Fisher of San Francisco. The ceremony would occur on the steamer* Governor Stanford *just after the boat crossed the state line between California and Nevada, a moment heralded by a short blast on the vessel's whistle.*

A Lake Tahoe Romance

A Marriage in High Life (Altitude About 6,000 feet)

The following account of the wedding of Miss Lizzie Chandler, formerly well known to the society of Santa Barbara . . . :

Sunday morning, the 27th, your correspondent was aroused from his couch of pine boughs and grass at an unusually early hour. With a sleepy yawn and prolonged stretch he sits up and contemplates the scene before him. The first rays of the morning sun illumine the East. The grand old pines tower above him stately and majestic, casting long, weird shadows. Through the opening of the forest he catches glimpses of the lovely blue lake, its coloring so softened and mild, its waters so placid and quiet, that it rests the eye and brain to gaze upon it. The bustle in the surrounding camps recalls his half awakened senses, and it suddenly dawns upon him that

SOMETHING MORE THAN ORDINARY

Is on the tapis. [*On the tapis* means "up for consideration" or "on the table."] He bounces up, takes a hasty wash, scrapes the coals of the camp fire together, puts on the coffee and potatoes, and then sings out to the camp that "the morn is up—the lark is soaring." A drowsy voice replies that it might be a good idea to "let her soar." In half an hour we are all seated around the breakfast table, and trout, quail and beans disappear in a manner that can only be appreciated by campers. Breakfast jokes are not quite as frequent as usual this morning, as we are all a little serious, knowing that when we gather around the table again, one of our young ladies will no longer be a Miss. The steamer *Gov. Stanford* had been chartered for the occasion, and is now lying at the Tallac House wharf, with forty or more friends (our neighbor campers) and music aboard waiting to receive us. We all file on board. The music strikes up, the whistle shrieks, the engineer's bell jingles, and we glide swiftly out on the

DEEP BLUE WATERS.

Presently we stop at McKinney's and take the Rev. Mr. Eastman of Austin, aboard. Now we steer boldly out for the center of the lake, and soon the whistle of the steamer tells us we have crossed the State line, and are in Nevada. The passengers all form in a semi-circle on the upper deck with the music in the center. "I am waiting, my darling, for thee," rendered by a trio consisting of Mr. and Mrs. Meder and Mr. Flanders, and then, as a wedding march is played, the bridal party emerge from the cabin and are received by the Rev. Mr. Eastman—first the bride, Miss Lizzie Chandler, a Cincinnati belle, supported on the arm of your correspondent, upon whom devolves the paternal duty of giving the bride away; next, Miss Katie Kinkead, the bosom friend of the bride, accompanied by Thomas K. Stewart, who are to assume the respective parts of

BRIDESMAID AND GROOMSMAN;

and last the groom, Mr. Will. E. Fisher of San Francisco, tenderly supported by Miss Emma Gibbs. . . . In a few moments the impressive ceremony of the Episcopal church has been performed: the solemn vows have been exchanged; the wedding ring given; the happy pair have been made man and wife, and congratulations are in order.

Truly, a romance has occurred to us that will ever be vividly recalled by each of our little party, and mark a bright and happy episode in our lives. The sky is clear and cloudless, the water of the lake without a ripple, the grand old forests stare calmly at us from every side, and all nature seems glad in the unison of two holy young lovers. May their voyage in life, so joyously begun, be ever prosperous and happy.

G. W. C., Jr.

≈≈≈

I can only express myself in exclamations.

—Caroline Nichols Churchill, *Over the Purple Hills,*
or Sketches from Travel in California, 1883

If you ever wondered for whom the phrase "a force of nature" could best
be applied, Caroline Nichols Churchill would be a prime candidate.

Churchill was an editor, publisher, author, and influential advocate
for women's rights in the American West. She also wrote two well-regarded
travel narratives of California and the West in the last quarter of the
nineteenth century.

Caroline Nichols Churchill was born in Canada in 1833 and emigrated
to the United States in 1846. Widowed at age twenty-nine in 1862, she
suffered a second blow when diagnosed with tuberculosis. As were many
TB patients in those days, Churchill was advised to seek a drier climate.
Choosing California, she journeyed westward in 1869. The Golden State
restored her health and spirits, and a reinvigorated Caroline Churchill
plunged into state politics. Incensed by a California bill that would
punish and regulate "immoral women," Churchill worked incessantly to
defeat the legislation. She was particularly outraged that women could
be held accountable for certain immoral activities under the proposed
law, while men would not be held liable for the same behavior.

The experience made Caroline Churchill acutely aware of the inequities
faced by women in the West. Now relocated to Denver, Colorado, Caroline
Churchill emerged as a leading feminist voice in the American West.
She published an influential newspaper—the Colorado Antelope, *later*
renamed the Queen Bee—*which championed a wide range of reforms,*
including alcohol prohibition, equal education for women, financial
support for women with dependent children, and voting rights. In 1893,
partly due to her efforts, women earned the right to vote in Colorado.

Caroline Churchill also wrote and published two very entertaining
narratives of travels in the American West. In 1874, Little Sheaves,
a collection of letters describing her trips throughout California and
Nevada from 1870 to 1873, was issued. Over the Purple Hills, or Sketches
from Travel in California (1883) *presented an account of Churchill's*
rail journeys from San Francisco to Lake Tahoe and from Visalia to
Placerville, California, in 1874.

The following selection from Over the Purple Hills, or Sketches from Travel in California *presents Churchill's impressions of, as she wrote, the lake that "lies near heaven"—Lake Tahoe.*

Now for the first time I walk out upon the wharf to take a look at the matchless waters of Lake Tahoe. I can only express myself in exclamations. The water is so clear that one can see to the depth of fifty feet any object that is visible at that distance in the open air. When at a distance from the lake I had not been much impressed with its superiority over other bodies of water. To be sure the green, purple, blue and white lines were rather wonderful; but one must get acquainted with this delightful sheet of water to appreciate it. The lake is thirty-six miles in length and fifteen in width; lies partly in the Golden and partly in the Silver State; is literally cradled in the Sierra Nevada mountains, six thousand four hundred feet above the level of the sea. All along the northern shore there are springs of boiling hot water coining to the surface, containing lime, magnesia, sulphur. The hot baths are delightful, the water possessing just the requisite properties for cleansing both the cuticle and all kinds of clothing. One comes from the bath as white and pure as a new kid glove. Notwithstanding these hot springs, which can be seen boiling up between sheets of melted lava, the body of the lake water is extremely cold. No animal life exists except that which is indigent to northern latitudes. There are plenty of trout, whitefish and salmon trout, I am told. The trout do not stroll about alone, but are always seen in shoals. A finny community of these graceful fishes is one of the most beautiful sights associated with these transparent waters. The water is so clear from foreign substance, so cold and void of insect life, that it is a wonder how the fishes manage to subsist. No vegetation is seen growing in any part of this lake, the bottom being melted lava or rocks. Dead fishes are occasionally seen lying upon their backs, showing no signs of decay. . . .

There have been thirteen human lives lost upon this water within a few years; not a body has ever been recovered. It is supposed that, the water being so cold, no gasses form, and the bodies are preserved, never rising to the surface. Upon this lake there is a beautiful little steamer, of sixty-four tons burden, drawing about three feet of water. This boat wears the brand of the Central Pacific Railroad, as nearly everything does upon the Pacific coast, being called the *Governor Stanford*. At eight o'clock every morning this steamer leaves Hot Spring wharf for Tahoe City and all the points of interest upon the lake. . . .

From Hot Springs to Tahoe City the distance is nearly ten miles, and is a most enchanting voyage. The water is so clear that it is impossible to detect the surface except by the ripples made by the steamer, or in case some foreign substance should chance to be borne along on the surface; and leaning over the side of the steamer gave one the impression of being propelled through the air. The boat was not heavily loaded, and seemed to glide upon the surface like a bird. The agitation caused by the movement of the boat made a most charming picture, giving the steamer the appearance of being trimmed with white and pearl-gray lace upon a deep blue satin background, thickly spangled with silver buttons. The water is blue as indigo where it is over a hundred feet deep, and green as a piece of beautiful green silk where it is only fifty and seventy-five feet. Where the green and blue waters join a line of the most delicate purple is the result; and the reason the beautiful tints are so fine and distinct is because of the water being so perfectly pure. No person can conceive or imagine the perfection of color and its wonderful beauty without first beholding it. There are places which are known as beyond the soundings, where the water is so deep that exquisite blue and violet is turned to a blue-black, and is called the black waters. Where the water is fifty feet deep we are shown the coral beds, so called from their resemblance to coral, but really beds of pumice stone, which have been for ages subject to the action of volcanic fires, and at last settled down, been overcome by another element, become the bed of a lake which is decidedly cool; and when earth's changes shall drain Tahoe of its crystal waters, it will leave something such a valley as Yosemite, minus, however, the grand rocky formation of that valley. The shadow of the smoke coming from the steamer could be seen at the depth of fifty feet as plainly as if it had fallen upon a board walk.

Thus far I have been so enchanted with the waters of this lake that I have entirely overlooked the surroundings, almost forgotten that it had any; but it lies in a fairy land, being enclosed in an unbroken chain of hills covered with brown and fringed with mountain pines. The distance around the lake is about one hundred miles; but at intervals all along the shores are public houses, giving accommodations to the tourist in a variety of locations. There are stage lines, post-offices and telegraph lines in all directions. Beautiful women and children, in, gay dresses, are seen playing croquet, swinging, and participating in all manner of outdoor games, fishing and hunting pebbles, for there are no little shells to be gathered on these shores. . . .

In our steamboat route we pass a place known as Emerald Bay. Here, in one view, the blue water, the violet and the most exquisite green, all come before the sight in rotation. It seemed to me that the waters of this bay, and the hills around must be peopled with spirits, fairies, or some unearthly beings. One realizes that this lake lies near heaven; it is the only way to satisfy the imagination in regard to its unearthly colors and indescribable beauty. . . . There is a bluff rising perpendicular from the water's edge three or four hundred feet, and the water is said to be a hundred feet deep at its base. Crossing over from Emerald Bay to this bluff is termed spanning the Rubicon. Just around one point there is standing a rough stone image, which a little stretch of the imagination will convert into a grizzly sitting on his haunches, with paws drooping. . . . Here the whistle of the steamer was sounded so that the passengers might listen to the echo. Further on we were shown a cave, a singularly conspicuous formation, standing with its entrance very properly toward the lake. It stands alone at the foot of the hills, upon the bank, as if for the convenience of water; is a mass, I should think, seventy-five or a hundred feet in height, having the general outline of an old-fashioned mud oven; the entrance is shaped like the mouth of an oven and is said to lead to a room thirty feet deep. Some of the gods may have done their baking in this locality while planning the design for Tahoe and experimenting upon its exquisite colors. At Glenbrook, a lumbering point, the steamer ties up for the night. Here we fully realize that this beautiful lake can be desecrated by practical purposes. . . . There is a rumor to the effect that the railroad company intend some day to tunnel the mountain at this point to save the vast yearly expenditure for snow sheds. If this tunneling is ever accomplished, it will be an easy matter to conduct the waters of Lake Tahoe to the cities of Sacramento, San Jose, and San Francisco, furnishing them with the best water in the world. Then an extra pipe could be laid from the Hot Springs, thus giving them water for cleansing purposes that if properly used would cleanse the dirty pool of politics. Sacramento would have occasion to rejoice.

≈≈≈

> The fact that the bodies of the drowned do
> not rise to the surface cannot be accounted for by
> ascribing marvelous properties to its waters.
>
> —John LeConte, "Physical Studies of Lake Tahoe,
> Part One," *Overland Monthly*, November 1883

Lake Tahoe does not freeze in winter. Drowned bodies never resurface at Lake Tahoe. These contentions were two of the most persistent observations about the physical qualities of Lake Tahoe water throughout the nineteenth century. But were they true?

In 1883 Professor John LeConte of the University of California, Berkeley, provided answers. In three articles for the Overland Monthly *entitled "Physical Studies of Lake Tahoe," LeConte detailed his findings. His studies had enormous credibility, as Professor LeConte had conducted the first limnological (i.e., relating to the study of the physics, chemistry, geology, and biology of lakes and other inland waters) examination of Lake Tahoe in 1873.*

The series "Physical Studies of Lake Tahoe" considered many aspects of Lake Tahoe, such as depth, drainage, water temperature, and transparency and presented long passages contemplating the colors of the lake's water and the rhythmical oscillations of the lake level, called seiches.

But the "facts" that the primary expanse of Lake Tahoe does not freeze (although shallow stretches along the shoreline and, occasionally, Emerald Bay do freeze) and drowned bodies are never seen again was what fascinated the public and were repeated by and intrigued visitors and newspaper correspondents for decades. In the following excerpt from "Physical Studies of Lake Tahoe—I," John LeConte offered scientific explanations for both phenomena.

Born in Georgia in 1818, John LeConte was a professor of physics at the University of California, Berkeley, from 1869 to 1891 and served as president of the university in 1869–1870 and again from 1875 to 1881. His younger brother, Joseph, was a professor of geology at UC Berkeley from 1869 until his death in 1901. In 1924 the two wings of the physics building on the Berkeley campus were collectively named LeConte Hall in recognition of the contributions of the LeConte brothers to the university.

However, the LeContes were also unreconstructed Southerners, fought for the Confederacy, owned a plantation that enslaved two hundred people, and openly expressed venomous white supremacist views. In

2020 the university condemned their racist philosophies and stripped the LeConte name from the physics building. Today, the old LeConte Hall is known generically as Physics North and Physics South.

Why the Water Does Not Freeze in Winter—Residents on the shores of Lake Tahoe testify that, with the exception of shallow and detached portions, the water of the lake never freezes in the coldest winters. During the winter months, the temperature of atmosphere about this lake must fall as low, probably, as 0° Fah. (−17.78° Cent.). . . . As it is evident that during the winter season the temperature of the air must frequently remain for days, and perhaps weeks, far below the freezing-point of water, the fact that the water of the lake does not congeal has been regarded as an anomalous phenomenon. Some persons imagine that this may be due to the existence of subaqueous hot springs in the bed of the lake—an opinion which may seem to be fortified by the fact that hot springs do occur at the northern extremity of the lake. But there is no evidence that the temperature of any considerable body of water in the lake is sensibly increased by such springs. Even in the immediate vicinity of the hot springs . . . , the supply of warm water is so limited that it exercises no appreciable influence on the temperature of that portion of the lake. This is further corroborated by the fact that no local fogs hang over this or any other portion of the lake during winter, which would most certainly be the case if any considerable body of hot water found its way into the lake.

The true explanation of the phenomenon may, doubtless, be found in the high specific heat of water, the great depth of the lake, and in the agitation of its waters by the strong winds of winter. In relation to the influence of depth, it is sufficient to remark that, before the conditions preceding congelation can obtain, the whole mass of water . . . must be cooled down to 4° Cent.; for this must occur before the vertical circulation is arrested and the colder water floats on the surface. In consequence of the great specific heat of water, to cool such a mass of the liquid through an average temperature of 8° Cent, requires a long time, and the cold weather is over before it is accomplished. In the shallower portions, the surface of the water may reach the temperature of congelation, but the agitations due to the action of strong winds soon breaks up the thin pellicle of ice, which is quickly melted by the heat generated by the mechanical action of the waves. Nevertheless, in shallow and detached portions of the lake, which are sheltered from the action of winds and waves—as in Emerald Bay—ice several inches in thickness is sometimes formed. . . .

Why Bodies of the Drowned Do Not Rise.—A number of persons have been drowned in Lake Tahoe—some fourteen between 1860 and 1874 and it is the uniform testimony of the residents, that in no case, where the accident occurred in deep water, were the bodies ever recovered. This striking fact has caused wonder-seekers to propound the most extraordinary theories to account for it. Thus one of them says, "The water of the lake is purity itself, but on account of the highly rarefied state of the air it is not very buoyant, and swimmers find some little fatigue; or, in other words, they are compelled to keep swimming all the time they are in the water; and objects which float easily in other water sink here like lead." Again he says, "Not a thing ever floats on the surface of this lake, save and except the boats which ply upon it."

It is scarcely necessary to remark that it is impossible that the diminution of atmospheric pressure, due to an elevation of 6,250 feet (1,905 meters) above the sea-level, could sensibly affect the density of the water. In fact, the coefficient of compressibility of this liquid is so small that the withdrawal of the above-indicated amount of pressure (about one-fifth of an atmosphere) would not lower its density more than one one-hundred-thousandth part! The truth is, that the specific gravity of the water of this lake is not lower than that of any other fresh water of equal purity and corresponding temperature. It is not less buoyant nor more difficult to swim in than any other fresh water; and consequently the fact that the bodies of the drowned do not rise to the surface cannot be accounted for by ascribing marvelous properties to its waters.

The distribution of temperature with depth affords a natural and satisfactory explanation of this phenomenon, and renders entirely superfluous any assumption of extraordinary lightness in the water. The true reason why the bodies of the drowned do not rise to the surface is evidently owing to the fact that when they sink into water which is only 4° Cent. (7.2° Fah.) above the freezing temperature, the gases usually generated by decomposition are not produced in the intestines; in other words, at this low temperature the bodies do not become inflated, and therefore do not rise to the surface. The same phenomenon would doubtless occur in any other body of fresh water under similar physical conditions.

Like all things wild and shy, it must be
approached slowly and with patience.

—John Vance Cheney, "A Day at Lake Tahoe," *Lippincott's,* August 1883

There was always one constant at Lake Tahoe throughout the nine-teenth century—writers struggled to adequately convey the splendor of the Gem of the Sierra. Mostly they failed in the quest. Occasionally a wordsmith would nearly grasp the brass ring. On rare occasions, someone would briefly rise to summit. But as sure as night follows day, they never stopped trying to find the right words, the right feeling, to describe Lake Tahoe.

One sterling attempt was made by poet and essayist John Vance Cheney in the August 1883 edition of the monthly magazine Lippincott's. *Cheney's article was entitled "A Day at Lake Tahoe" and ostensibly reported on a short steamer cruise skirting the western shore of the lake. But it was more than that. It was John Vance Cheney's word rainbow of his Lake Tahoe experience—a love letter to an emotional, surprising, transcendent moment. For Cheney, Lake Tahoe is not just a lake, it is the quintessence of a spirit, an untamable and largely unknowable essence exhibited in a kaleidoscope of color and mystery.*

Born in 1848 in New York, John Vance Cheney abandoned law practice and moved to California, where he taught music and worked as a postal clerk. Cheney ascended to the position of librarian of the Free Public Library of San Francisco, opened the library system's first branches, and hosted the first Pacific Coast Conference of the American Library Association in 1891.

Cheney was a frequent contributor to many of the literary magazines of the era, including Lippincott's, The Century, Atlantic Monthly, *and* Harper's Monthly. *Upon his death in 1922, John Vance Cheney's collected works were published, filling eight volumes.*

For nature pure and simple, for chaste beauty and native grandeur, one will hesitate before naming the rival of Lake Tahoe. This singularly impressive sheet of water, one of the highest in the world, gains an indescribable but easily-perceived charm by its remoteness, its high, serene, crystal isolation. Its lights and shades, its moods and passions, are changing, rapid, and free as the way of the wind.

A true child of nature, it varies ever, from hour to hour enchanting with new and strange fascination. The thousand voices of the lofty Sierra call to it, and it answers; all the colors of the rainbow gather upon it, receiving in their turn affectionate recognition. Man has meddled with it little more than with the sky; the primeval spell is upon it, the hush, the solitude of the old gods. The breath of powers invisible, awful, rouse it to the sublimity of untamable energy; again, hush it into deepest slumber. Night and day it is guarded, seemingly, by wonder-working forces known to man only through the uncertain medium of the imagination. The traveler who looks upon Lake Tahoe for a few hours only learns little of its rich variety. Like all things wild and shy, it must be approached slowly and with patience.

[As we looked] into the water below, the immediate shock of surprise cannot be well described. Every pebble at the bottom showed as distinctly as if held in the open hand. We had all seen clear water before, but, as a severe but unscholarly sufferer once said of his rheumatism, "never such as *these*." The day being perfect, no breeze stirring, and the Lake without a ripple, the gravelly bottom continued visible when we had steamed out to a point where the water reached a depth of eighty feet. . . .

We were not wholly enchanted until, gliding past many a snowy peak, we suddenly changed course and put into Emerald Bay. This little bay, or rather lake in itself, about three miles in length, is the gem of the Tahoe scenery. Through its narrow entrance, formed by perpendicular cliffs some two thousand feet high, we moved on toward an island of rock and a succession of flashing waterfalls beyond.

For a time the dazzling mountain-crests and glistening gorges absorbed attention. So high, white, silent! We longed to be upon the loftiest one, from the top of which can be seen thirteen charming little mountain-lakes, midair jewels. . . .

But not even the crystal summit ridges delighted us as did the changing waters. . . . Following immediately upon the transparency preserved to a depth of some eighty feet, a blur passed over the surface. This changed by imperceptible degrees to a light green. The green, again, speedily deepened, shading into a light blue; and finally, in deepest water (where the Lake is all but fathomless), the color becomes so densely blue that we could not believe our eyes. Indigo itself was outdone. Description fails; the blue deep of Tahoe must be seen to be appreciated.

≈≈≈

The water is as pure as any in the world—
because it is unbottled direct from heaven.

—"Lake Tahoe," *Pacific Rural Press*, May 17, 1884

Aside from the plethora of utilitarian guidebooks, nineteenth century Lake Tahoe travel narratives of individuals or newspaper correspondents were usually presented in tones befitting the grand traditions of Romanticism, but, occasionally, a correspondent would address the nuts-and-bolts of visiting the lake.

In the May 17, 1884, edition of the Pacific Rural Press, *a missive from a reporter for the* San Francisco Bulletin *offered details about a Lake Tahoe sojourn. The author noted the substantial expense of traveling to the Gem of the Sierra, including train and stagecoach fares. Once at the lake, the cost of steamer excursions and boat rentals were itemized. The writer tendered assorted options for accommodations and their variable rates. Spotty mail service is lamented. Weather warnings are issued, including the ominous admonition "Don't move or go on the lake in your boat when there is even a single cloud in the sky." The reporter advocated visiting Lake Tahoe in winter rather than the summer: "Lake Tahoe in summer is not, in peace and beauty, nearly equal to Lake Tahoe in Winter." After all, he concluded, "a snow-storm at Tahoe is most enjoyable."*

Lake Tahoe

A writer for the [San Francisco] *Bulletin* gives the following detailed information about visiting Lake Tahoe and vicinity:

It was announced in a telegram from Truckee, published about three months ago and evidently unauthorized, that round-trip tickets would this year be issued from this city to Lake Tahoe and return at a greatly reduced price, but inquiry at the railroad offices here does not fully verify the above statement. There is to be quite a reduction, it is true, but not such a large one as was promised in the unauthorized dispatch referred to. Last year the round-trip ticket was $25. This year it will be $20. To the bulk of tourists, especially to heads of families, Lake Tahoe and the Sierras will be a region beyond their purses and visits. This is greatly to be regretted. When residents of the city leave here on a summer vacation they should go, not to the coast range or the plains, but to the mountains, the change there being radical to all of the senses, and therefore far more likely to be thoroughly beneficial to the health. The Lake Tahoe region is the most accessible high mountain region to which tourists can go. Leaving the city at 3 p. m., the tourist reaches Truckee at 4:40 the next morning. A stage ride of two hours through the Truckee canyon and by the beautiful Truckee river takes him to the lake at Tahoe City. At that point the steamer (a new and fine one now being completed, we believe, by Todman & Co.) will be found ready to make the round trip of about two-thirds of the lake, viz.: to McKinney's (Yanks, now Baldwin's), Rowland's (Lake valley), Glenbrook, sometimes including the hot springs, and thus back to Tahoe City. The water trip on the steamer takes in a run on the lake of about 42 miles. The steamer trip occupies about 5 hours, including detentions at stopping places.

Camping

The Lake Tahoe region is unsurpassed anywhere for camping purposes. A boat—a stogy, flat-bottomed but safe, solid and easily rowed by one, can be had at McKinney's, probably for about $1 a day. It will carry four or five persons and all their baggage, blankets, kettles, pots and even the pans in which the solid, stomach-depressing and body-sinking camping bread is to be mixed; for when camping, no one of experience expects bread of any other pattern or make than that which sits heavy on the soul and stomach. But the spirits and senses cannot be kept down at Tahoe by the solidity of camping bread. The air is light, pure and balmy. The water is as pure as any in the world—because it is unbottled direct from heaven, on the clear granite of the mountains, and is by the sun melted direct into tinkling rills and pure, ice-cold streams. It is so soft that to wash in it is like bathing in oil. Dry pine and fir-wood for camping fires is to be found everywhere. The campers with a boat can move when they like, one word of caution alone being necessary: Don't move or go on the lake in your boat when there is even a single cloud in the sky. Clouds, however light and fleecy, mean wind, and the lake is dangerous in wind. The west side of the lake is much the safest, because the best sheltered from prevailing winds. Campers should send all their provisions and baggage solidly packed as slow freight to Tahoe City a week ahead of them, making particular inquiry at Truckee on the way in, to make sure that the baggage has already been sent in to the lake.

The Hotels and Their Charges

Camping is not a necessity, however, on any score of economy. Board at McKinney's, Rowland's at Lake valley, and Glenbrook, in most comfortable and home-like mountain houses, can be had at $10 to $12 per week, while much lower prices are made for children. At Tahoe City the Grand Central, at the Tallac House (formerly Yanks) and at the Hot Springs Hotel, which are more fashionable and stylish, the rates are from $2 to $3 per day. Boats, to guests who can do their own rowing, are free at the Tahoe City Hotel and at McKinney's, and probably at the other hotels also. Formerly, at Tahoe City, one of the heaviest items of expense was the cost of hiring boats. Mr. Bayley, of the Grand Central, Tahoe City, has for years kept that house. He treats tourists not as prey, but as friends, whom he expects to see every year. Mr. McKinney, and his partner, Mr. Honsucker, are two old Californians—relics of the early mining days—hunters, trappers, and moat genial and whole-souled Californians. The hotel at Glenbrook, furthest from the lake, is neat, clean and comfortable. The house at the Rubicon Soda springs, nine miles west of McKinney's, will be open as usual. It is a most comfortable and utterly secluded mountain home, in the very heart of the Sierras. It is set in granite and crystal lakes, away from the world and well up toward heaven, the elevation being some 8,000 feet, we believe.

Only about one person in ten, even of old residents and tourists, has been to Lake Tahoe. This is due to the cost of the trip. A twenty dollar trip will never attract, because the expense is too great for the majority of the tourists. When the round trip is reduced to $10 or $12, twenty persons will visit Tahoe where one now does. We are not in the councils of the railroad company, and do not therefore know whether a $10 or $12 rate to Tahoe can be made or not; but, if such a rate is among the possibilities, the Tahoe trip would, with its aid, become the trip to the Sierra, because, leaving the city at 3 p.m., the tourist can the next day at 9 or 10 a.m. be at a lake 6,400 feet above the sea, 20 miles long, 12 miles broad and 1,640 feet deep at the deepest point—deep almost as an ocean, blue as the Pacific or Atlantic, 1,000 miles from shore, clear as crystal, very cold, and yet surrounded mostly by deep woods despite the vandalic wood-chopper and accursed saw mills—a Sans Souci, a home of peace, where silence and lonely contemplation dwell; where even yet, "God hath his solitudes, unpeopled yet save by the peaceful and beautiful life of bird, pine tree, deer and mountain flower." But Lake Tahoe in summer is not, in peace and beauty, nearly equal to

Lake Tahoe in Winter.

The silence then is almost painful in clear weather, when snow is on the ground, the "Sabbath of the Woods" is continuous. The writer visited Tahoe in February last, going out and coming in on snow-shoes. . . . The weather in February last was perfect and the sky like steel. The trees in the Truckee canyon stood out with a clear-out, fern-like individual expression, only to be noted in snow time. But a snow-storm at Tahoe is most enjoyable, "When heavenly gales are blowing with peace upon their wings." The offer of a premium of $500 a year would probably cause the road from Truckee to Tahoe to be kept open each winter, and perfect sleighing in high mountains would then be within fourteen hours time of the city. Loud and long complaints have been made this winter because the mails were not as before, sent three times a week from Truckee to Tahoe City on snow-shoes. They went by Carson last winter, the supposition being that that road would be kept open for sleighs. But the contractor did nothing in that direction, and therefore the mails were like angel visits, few and far between, or like the payment of old debts, genuine surprises. Every resident of the lake was either complaining or cursing about the double isolation from the world he was thus subjected to.

≈≈≈

In the rapidly proceeding denudation of the forests
on the shores of Lake Bigler the State is losing one
of its most attractive features for tourists.

—*Report of the Lake Bigler Forestry Commission
to Governor George Stoneman*, 1884

It became impossible to look away. Since the onset of large-scale logging in the Lake Tahoe Basin in the early 1870s, concerns were raised about timber industry practices and the denudation of forestlands around Lake Tahoe. However, these qualms were largely overlooked, as the lumber industry provided a critical shard in the mosaic of the booming railroad and mining economies of the region. That changed in the early 1880s as the environmental impact of the logging juggernaut could no longer be ignored.

In 1883, during the administration of California governor George Stoneman, a three-member Lake Bigler Forestry Commission was appointed to study the problem. The chair of the commission was James V. Coleman, a member of the California Assembly (D-San Mateo). Coleman had introduced Assembly Resolution, No. 31, earlier in 1883 "to inquire into and report a plan for the Preservation of the Forests on the California Shore of Lake Bigler." By this time most called the lake Lake Tahoe, but Lake Bigler was the officially recognized name of the lake and would remain so until 1945.

John V. Coleman's resolution condemned "the rapidly proceeding denudation of the forests on the shores of Lake Bigler" and urged the California State Legislature to seriously consider "any desirable plan . . . whereby the natural beauty of the California shore of Lake Bigler can be saved from the threatened total defacement, and the wooded shores be preserved to the people forever, for their benefit, health, and pleasure." Control of almost all the California forestlands in the Lake Tahoe domain were split between two powerful entities—the Central Pacific Rail Road and the federal government. There was also acreage set aside for schools and a handful of private holdings on the lakeshore.

Charged with drafting a blueprint, the Lake Bigler Forestry Commission issued its report in 1884. Disappointed with the response of California, which, the report caustically noted, "has remained in apparent unconsciousness of the threatened danger from the criminal waste of her magnificent forest wealth," the Lake Bigler Forestry Commission focused on a more receptive United States Congress.

The commission recommended that Congress exchange the Central Pacific's lands for property of equivalent value outside the Lake Tahoe Basin and then deed all federal lands to the State of California "for the purpose of forever holding and preserving it as a State park, in connection with and for the sake of preserving Lake Bigler."

Most of the Forestry Commission's recommendations came to naught. The California legislature opposed the plan as too favorable to the rail-road. There were also controversies over the alleged mismanagement of the Yosemite Valley State Park, and many legislators did not want to compound an already existing problem by establishing another large state park. However, the concept of a Lake Tahoe State (or National) Park would be revisited several times in the next decade.

One recommendation of the commission was adopted. On March 3, 1885, the California Legislature passed "An Act to Create a State Board of Forestry, and to Provide for the Expenses Thereof." The California State Board of Forestry was the first such state agency in the United States. The board was short-lived, however. The act was repealed in 1893. It was not until 1905 that a new State Board of Forestry was authorized.

In the following excerpts, John V. Coleman's original 1883 California Assembly Resolution calling for the appointment of a commission to formulate a plan to address logging practices at Lake Tahoe is presented, as are selected passages from the 1884 Lake Bigler Forestry Commission report to Governor George Stoneman.

Assembly Concurrent Resolution, No. 31 [1883]

Introduced by Mr. Coleman, February 6, 1883

Assembly Concurrent Resolution, relative to the appointment of a Commission to inquire into and report a plan for the Preservation of the Forests on the California Shore of Lake Bigler.

Resolved by the Legislature of the State of California, the Assembly and Senate concurring, as follows:

WHEREAS, it should be the duty of the State to preserve from destruction, and reserve for the health, pleasure, and recreation of its citizens and tourists, the most noted, attractive, and available features of its natural scenery; and whereas, in the rapidly proceeding denudation of the forests on the shores of Lake Bigler the State is losing one of its most attractive features for tourists, and available, valuable, and pleasant resorts for residents; and whereas, it is right and expedient that the Legislature of this state should be informed whether any desirable plan can be adopted whereby the natural beauty of the California shore of Lake Bigler can be saved from the threatened total defacement, and the wooded shores be preserved to the people forever, for their benefit, health, and pleasure; therefore, be it—

Resolved, That the Governor of this State be directed to appoint a Commission of three citizens of this state, who shall inquire into the feasibility of such plan, and report to the Governor before the meeting of the next Legislature, the result of their inquiry, with any and all suggestions and recommendations their investigations may suggest; provided, that the members of such Commission shall serve without pay, or any remuneration whatever, nor incur against the State any expense whatever, except for the salary of one Secretary, such salary not to exceed in the aggregate three thousand dollars during the term of the Commission, and that the existence of the Commission shall cease from and after the date of its report to the Governor.

Resolved, That the Governor be directed to inform the Governor of the State of Nevada of the passage of these resolutions.

Report [1884]

To his Excellency GOVERNOR STONEMAN: . . .

The preservation of this lovely gem in California's coronet is urged, first, as a fitting beginning in the direction of forestry legislation; second, because it is the duty of the State to keep for its people's enjoyment this perfect resort; and, third, because such an attraction as Lake Bigler brings thousands of desirable visitors within the State, to the State's profit and renown. It seems as if it need only be stated that unless speedy measures are taken Lake Bigler's hills will be first robbed of their forests, which add so much to the beauty of the lake, and next will be deprived of the rain and snow and springs, which make the lake itself. . . . Already much of the Nevada shore of the lake has been denuded of forests. Fortunately, the greater line of the lake is in California, where, as yet, the work of destruction in the forests has not progressed so far as to either destroy the beauty of the scenes, or deprive the lake of its water supply. . . .

We feel that there is no need of emphasizing in this report to any greater extent the advantages of preserving the forests about the California shores of Lake Bigler. It would be a valuable step in the direction of intelligent forestry legislation; it would preserve for the citizens of this State forever one of the most beautiful pieces of natural scenery in the world; it would preserve one of the State's greatest attractions to visitors from abroad, and it would be the first check in what must soon be a system of checks set up by the State to regulate the destruction of forests within its borders. The plan which we have developed from place to place in this report may be summarized as follows:

We suggest that the Legislature of this State request our Representatives in Congress to introduce a bill in Congress authorizing the granting of lieu lands to the Central Pacific Railroad (or the persons holding their lands), in exchange for lands in place in an area designated, such lieu lands to be of equal value and similar character as . . . the land in place as practicable, such request to emphasize the desire of the Legislature that such lieu land shall not exceed in value, nor be of superior quality in any respect, to the land in place; that the Legislature requests our Representatives in Congress to introduce a bill, following the passage of the above, for the transfer to this State, for the purpose of a public park, of all Government land in an area designated; that the land now held by this State in the area designated be withdrawn from sale and made part of such public park.

We also recommend that the Legislature create a permanent State Forestry Commission, with power and authority to act in all such matters as will aid the work of preserving the forests on the shores of Lake Bigler; preventing the unlawful cutting of timber in all parts of the State; encouraging the replanting of land denuded of redwoods; encouraging the planting of new land in suitable forest trees; collecting useful information concerning the adaptability of different forest trees to the different climates and soils of the State, and the special value and uses of different timber which shall be found adaptable to the State; the best mode of planting, caring for, thinning, and general treatment of growing timber trees; and the free dissemination of all such information to the citizens of the State, together with all such information concerning the profit, healthfulness, and other advantages of forest culture as will have a tendency to induce a general and intelligent pursuit of such industry.

To your Commissioners, who have made a long and close study of this most important subject of forestry as it affects the welfare of this State, it appears to be a most unfortunate omission on the part of the Legislature that such a permanent Commission as we have recommended has not already been created. While this State has remained in apparent unconsciousness of the threatened danger from the criminal waste of her magnificent forest wealth, the Government at Washington has already been startled into a consideration of the subject.

In the Report on Forestry submitted to Congress in 1882, by the Commissioner of Agriculture, the writer of the report, Franklin B. Hough, says:

We believe that the time has now come when important portions of the heavily timbered lands still owned by the Government upon the Pacific Coast, and especially those occupied by the native redwood (Sequoia sempervirens), might be at once withdrawn from entry and permanently devoted to the production and maintenance of timber.

These grand supplies of timber are now, and have been since the first settlement of the country, undergoing a rapid waste; and the lumbering operations in these forests have been carried on in the most reckless and improvident manner, without yielding any revenue what-ever to the Government or any adequate benefit to the country. In short, they have been plundered and destroyed, with scarcely a semblance of restraint, until a time can be foreseen when they will be exhausted altogether, and we shall be left wholly destitute of those inestimably valuable resources which, under judicious management, might be maintained for a long period. It is well known that the natural limits of the redwood are of relatively small extent, not reaching far inland, and being limited to the western slope of the Coast Range within the State of California. To the casual observer these supplies may appear inexhaustible, but there is nothing more fallacious or more dangerous than this imperfect conception of the limit of supply, in the midst of local abundance, and without allowance for the enormous demand or the vast exhaustion. There are also large areas from which the timber has been cut away that are now lying waste, in which every condition favorable to a new plantation exists in full degree.

The redwood shows an unusual tendency to reproduction, and when we consider the relatively small district within which all the conditions essential to its prosperity exist, and the remarkable result to which they may lead, we cannot but regard these localities as peculiarly valuable for timber culture, and this still more from the fact that from their broken surface they are worth little for any other use. . . .

We therefore submit our plans and recommendations to your thoughtful attention, confident that our efforts will be but a second to the endeavor you will feel a pride in making toward reserving the forests on the California shores of Lake Bigler for a State park, and toward beneficial forestry legislation for the whole State. In this hope and expectation this report is respectfully submitted.

JAMES V. COLEMAN, Chairman.

SANDS W. FORMAN.

CHARLES M. CHASE, Commissioners.

E. W. TOWNSEND, Secretary.

≈≈

It is absurd to say that the deposit of sawdust in
our river does not deteriorate its quality.

—*Report of the California Assembly Committee on Fish and Game*, 1887

The 1884 Lake Bigler Forestry Commission report and its aftermath opened the gates for additional and more intense reconsideration of Lake Tahoe Basin lumber industry practices.

In 1887 both the California Assembly and California Senate Committees on Fish and Game held hearings on the "depositing" of sawdust in the Truckee River by California residents. Depositing was a very understated term for the wholesale dumping of sawdust into the river by timber interests. The people of Nevada were understandably enraged, particularly those downstream in Reno. They depended upon the Truckee River for drinking water, irrigation, and fishing. According to the citizens of the Silver State, sawdust clogged the watersheds, destroyed fish habitat, made irrigation nearly impossible, ruined farmland, and contaminated potable river water.

In February 1887, at the request of the Nevada State Legislature, a joint meeting of the California Committees on Fish and Game was held in Truckee to hear the testimony of Nevada residents. The chair of the Assembly committee was George Williams (R-Humboldt) who reported to Assembly Speaker William H. Jordan (R-Alameda) in the following letter:

Mr. Speaker:

Your Committee on Fish and Game, to whom was referred the memorial from the Legislature of the State of Nevada, relative to the depositing of sawdust in the Truckee river by residents of the State of California, respectfully submit the following report: That in conjunction with the Senate Committee they visited Truckee and Reno. At Truckee they were met by a delegation from the Nevada Legislature. A joint meeting was held, Senator [Albert F.] Jones [D-Butte] of this State presiding.

Three reasons were submitted to your Committee why the further depositing of sawdust in the river should be stopped, viz:

First—Its presence in the river tends to destroy trout and food fish.

Second—It is conveyed by the waters of the river through its entire length, and through ditches and canals used for irrigation purposes upon valuable farming and grazing lands, and spreading over the surface thereof, tends to render them almost valueless and unavailable for agricultural purposes.

Third—It renders the waters of the river unfit for drinking and domestic purposes, particularly in the summer months, and sickness and death has resulted to the people of Nevada from its use.

At Truckee testimony was taken principally upon the amount and character of the sawdust deposited in the river, and its injury to the fish.

The testimony showed that forty million feet of lumber was cut annually, in the cutting of which is produced about seven million feet of sawdust, which passes into the river.

Above the mills, on the river, and up as far as Lake Tahoe, an abundance of fish are found, while below they are scarce.

It was developed in the testimony taken that the most serious cause of complaint was the injury to the health of the people of

Reno and vicinity, caused from the use of the waters of the Truckee river, which is their principal source of supply for domestic purposes.

At the urgent invitation of the Nevada delegation your Committee visited Reno for the purpose of hearing the statements of the leading physicians and prominent citizens of that place.

Upon our arrival a meeting was immediately called, and addresses were made as follows:

At this point in George Williams' letter, he provided excerpts of testimony from many prominent figures in Reno and Western Nevada, including lawyers, physicians, the United States surveyor-general of Nevada, and the attorney general of the State of Nevada. Three of these testimony passages are presented here:

Dr. Lewis, a graduate of Long Island (N. Y.) Medical College, said:

In the first years of my practice here, there was little or no and fever. It has become more frequent every year, When the disease first commenced to afflict our people, we laid the trouble to other causes, but we have been forced to the conclusion that the water rendered impure from the sawdust is the main cause of disease.

C. C. [Christopher Columbus] Powning, United States Surveyor-General of Nevada, said:

We ask that a few mill men be prevented from contaminating the main and largest river of Nevada. We have repeatedly urged and petitioned the California Legislature to take some action, and they have as yet failed to notice our petitions. In the bed of the river from Tahoe to Truckee there is no sawdust, but from Truckee to Reno and to Pyramid Lake there is a continual deposit from one to three feet of sawdust. We ask that the matter be not delayed longer.

Attorney-General [John K.] Alexander of Nevada, said:

This is a friendly conference. We meet to abate, if possible, the trouble between Nevada and California on a friendly basis. The question is whether four or five men running mills on the Truckee river can impair the health of the people of Nevada? Will not the people of California require these men to use their property as not to interfere with the neighbors of your State. Because these mill men claim that it is convenient for them to deposit the sawdust in the river, will you acknowledge that as an excuse or reason why they can render our water impure? We ask that the Truckee river shall be allowed to run unimpaired from its source to its mouth, and we wish you to acknowledge that the water of this river is as much ours as yours.

Your Committee herewith present a bill amending Section six hundred and thirty-five of the Penal Code, making it a misdemeanor to deposit sawdust in any of the waters of the State, and recommend its passage.

We also recommend that the State Board of Health make investigation into the effect caused by the deposit of sawdust in, the Truckee river upon the health of the people of the State of Nevada.

GEO. WILLIAMS, Chairman.

≈≈≈

In this matter of forest fires in California, the day of disaster is already here. Witnesses fresh from the Lake Tahoe region inform us that almost that entire section is a scene of desolation.
—"Mountain Vandalism," *Sacramento Daily Union*, July 27, 1889

Forest fires were underreported in the nineteenth-century Lake Tahoe Basin. Surprisingly, while considerable analysis was forthcoming about destructive lumber-industry operations and the callous dumping of sawdust in the Truckee River, relatively little commentary about forest fires occurred. Structure fires were reported, brownish-red forest-fire smoke hovering over the lake was noted, and the occasional forest-fire-related adventure might be recounted, such as Mark Twain's story of his retreat from his timber camp conflagration in his 1872 book Roughing It, *but there were comparatively few articles about actual forest fires in the region.*

For years, influential journals of the era, such as the Daily Alta California *and the* Sacramento Daily Union, *attempted to rouse public ire about the immediate damage and devastating aftermath of forest fires, but they were frustrated by the seeming lack of concern and coordinated response. With the growing emphasis on the impacts of denudation of*

Lake Tahoe forests by timber interests, newspaper editorials exhibited
greater urgency as the decade of the 1880s ended.

In "Mountain Vandalism" an editorial from the July 27, 1889, edition
of the Sacramento Daily Union, *the newspaper ominously advised, "In*
this matter of forest fires in California, the day of disaster is already
here." The apparent purpose of the article was not only to impugn greedy
sheepherders or negligent campers (the mountain vandals of the title)
for allegedly sparking a "raging" fire near Emerald Bay but also to once
again spur public action to address forest fire threats. The editors list
the results of inadequately responding to fires, such as rapid erosion,
the exodus of game, the ruin of timber resources, desecration of scenery,
and the loss of millions of dollars in lumber and tourism revenue.

Mountain Vandalism

The [*Sacramento Daily Union*] has for many years labored to arouse the
people to a due sense of the great danger that resides in the denuding
of the mountain. Several other journals have done equal service in that
direction, but it has seemed that the public at large has not that sensibility on the subject that should distinguish a people so enlightened as
ours. It requires some great calamity to fully arouse the American public
to action upon questions of vital interests of this character. They may be
told times without number that if certain practices are persisted in there
will result certain ills, but they appear to be content with the present,
and to provide for the evil day when it comes. In this matter of forest
fires in California, the day of disaster is already here. Witnesses fresh
from the Lake Tahoe region inform us that almost that entire section
is a scene of desolation, on account of the destruction by forest fires of
the wooded raiment of the noble slopes of the Sierras. At the head of
Emerald bay last week, a fire was raging of many miles extent, destroying the finest park of tree growth in all that region. The conflagration
was the result of the cupidity of sheep-herders, or of the carelessness of
campers. Most likely the sheep men are chargeable with most blame,
since it is to their interest to have the hills cleared of timber in order
to enlarge the grazing area. Yet it is as certain as that night comes after
departing day, that the destruction of the timber will induce floods in
one season and drouths in another; greatly raise the heat in summer and
correspondingly lower it in winter; deprive the soil of its ability to retain
moisture and feed the streams gradually, and will cause the erosion of

the slopes under the fall of rain to go on a hundred-fold more rapidly than under normal conditions. The game is driven out, valuable timber supplies destroyed, the finest scenery in the State reduced to a spectacle of desolation, and millions of value eliminated from the prosperity of the State. If the people were quick to the importance of this subject, they would have a small army of foresters in the hills and mountains seizing upon the vandals chargeable with the outrages refered [*sic*] to, and bringing them to such swift punishment as would make these incendiaries flee from the bounds of the State in terror.

≈≈≈

It would have been well years ago had the General Government
reserved the slopes leading to this lake as a permanent pleasure
ground, to be regulated for the benefit of all the people.
—George M. Wheeler, *Report upon United States Geographical
Surveys West of the One Hundredth Meridian*, Volume One, 1889

Our geographical knowledge of the nineteenth-century American West can largely be attributed to the efforts of one man—George Wheeler. From 1868 to 1880, Wheeler was responsible for more than fifteen geographical expeditions, forty-one volumes of observations, over a dozen atlases, more than 150 maps, and countless surveys, both large and small. George Wheeler filled in numerous gaps for a region that had never been accurately charted.

Born in Massachusetts in 1842, George Montague Wheeler graduated from West Point in 1866. Initially, Wheeler was posted to surveying duty in California and the Southwest. In 1868–1869, he was engaged in surveys in Colorado, Nevada, Utah, and Arizona. During these missions, Wheeler was the first to apply the term Colorado Plateau to the area. In 1875 he published a report of his findings, entitled Preliminary Report upon a Reconnaissance through Southern and Southeastern Nevada, Made in 1869.

In 1871 George Wheeler was ordered to lead an expedition to eastern Nevada and Arizona. Its primary function was to prepare accurate maps and to comment on Native American cultures and available natural resources. At the completion of the expedition, Wheeler and his corps had surveyed 72,250 square miles. In 1872 Wheeler issued a report on the journey entitled Preliminary Report Concerning Explorations and Surveys Principally in Nevada and Arizona.

Also in 1872 George Wheeler proposed mapping the entire west past the 100° meridian. His plan approved and dubbed The United States Geographical Surveys West of the One Hundredth Meridian, *the survey would last through 1879. At any one time, more than fifty officers and units were in the field. By 1875 the enterprise had grown to the point where it was split into two divisions, the California and the Colorado sections. Fourteen expeditions were undertaken under Wheeler's command.*

Reports of the missions would be published in forty-one separate volumes and in the comprehensive Report upon United States Geographical Surveys West of the One Hundredth Meridian. *This latter report would appear between 1875 and 1889 in ten volumes featuring 164 maps. The goal of the surveys was to provide a "reasonably accurate" map of 1.5 million square miles at a cost of approximately $2 million.*

Primarily because privately financed surveys, such as those led by Ferdinand Hayden and John Wesley Powell, were accomplishing the same result, Congress slashed funding for the project and dismantled Wheeler's organization in 1879.

In the years that followed, Wheeler produced more than twenty additional volumes and articles on his western endeavors. In 1888 Wheeler retired due to poor health with the rank of major. George Wheeler died in 1905 at the age of eighty-two.

In this selection from Report upon United States Geographical Surveys West of the One Hundredth Meridian, *volume 1, 1889, George Wheeler considers the Lake Tahoe Region. He comments on the beauty of the lake and the wholesale stripping of timber from the surrounding ridges, and Wheeler suggests that the federal government should revisit the idea of turning at least a portion of the Lake Tahoe Basin into a government-protected and -administered "permanent pleasure ground." While this report was originally submitted in 1879, it would not be officially published until 1889.*

Letter of Transmittal

United States Engineer Office, Geographical Surveys West of the One Hundredth Meridian, Washington DC, June 1, 1879

GENERAL: I have the honor to forward herewith manuscript of Volume I, the last of the quarto reports of this office, the publication of which is authorized by acts approved June 23, 1874, and February 15, 1875.

This affords a pleasing opportunity once for all to express my thanks to the large number of assistants, officers, civilians, and others whose genuine enthusiasm for their various tasks has alone made possible the systematic production of so great an amount of geographic, geologic, and other scientific material.

The aid extended by the supply branches of the War Department has added materially to the augmentation of results.

Very respectfully, your obedient servant,
GEO. M. WHEELER, Captain of Engineers, In charge.
Brig. Gen. H. G. Wright, Chief of Engineers, United States Army, Washington, D. C.

NOTE.—This report, brought substantially to a close in June, 1879, was not presented for publication until 1887, from press of other duties and subsequent prolonged illness. . . .

Lake Tahoe Region

One of the crowning beauties of the Northern Sierra Nevada (the whole range being justly celebrated for its massive grandeur) is the Lake Tahoe region, the lake itself having been aptly termed "the gem of the Sierras." It is the reservoir of the waters of the upper Truckee River, and several minor streams, having a single outlet, the main Truckee.

The water is of the deepest colored and most perfect blue, scintillant from its own purity, changing to aqua marine, as seen from its banks, with a depth in the center reaching at one measured point over 1,600 feet.

One of the most beautiful points on its shore is on the Nevada side, at Glenbrook, immediately opposite Tahoe on the Truckee, a location more readily accessible from the Central Pacific Railroad. The most lovely spot is at the southern end, near Tallac Point, from which the peak of that name is reached by a wide trail at a distance of approximately 10.4 miles.

This peak, rising high above the surrounding foothills (9,715 feet), commands a landscape at once unique and comprehensive and equalled by few of the many wonderful mountain views of our western region.

At its foot lies Fallen Leaf Lake (lovely within itself) having an outlet into Tahoe. A perfect view of all the main body of Tahoe is spread before one, the horizon on every hand is mountain-crowned, the massive Sierra Nevada peaks—Freels, Monument, Job's, and Job's Sister (all over 10,000 feet)—lying to the south and east, with others still higher in the distant horizon. The most remarkable feature of all is in the number of lakes (large and small) to be seen within the horizon's circumference. In addition to those named (Tahoe and Fallen Leaf), there may be seen Washoe, Martell, Echo, Cascade, Gillmore, and Grass lakes, sixteen small ponds or lakelets in the Devil's Basin (nearly all visible from the peak), and eight others (all small) without names.

These little mountain lakes (belonging to the Truckee and American River basins) are mostly fringed by forests of evergreens, pine, fir, and hemlock. Sadly enough, on the eastern shores of Tahoe, and part of the southern, the flanks are being stripped for timber, to be swallowed in the Comstock mines. There seems to be no method of arresting this spoliation. It would have been well years ago had the General Government reserved the slopes leading to this lake as a permanent pleasure ground, to be regulated for the benefit of all the people, as well as a specially beautiful spot for rest and recreation for travelers from all lands.

The boundary between California and Nevada traverses it longitudinally, two counties (Placer and El Dorado) abutting on the California side, and three in Nevada (Washoe, Ormsby, and Douglas). As Lake Luzerne of Switzerland is sometimes known as the "Lake of the Four Cantons," so might lovely Tahoe be called the "Lake of the Five Counties."

≈≈≈

On a small island in Lake Tahoe dwelt the fairy princess
Snowray. . . . A garland of musk-blooms was her banner,
and round it thousands of elves and fairies gathered at her
call, and she was as good as she was noble and fair.

—Margaret Davis Burton, "The Fairy's Isle in Emerald
Bay," *Pacific Rural Press*, September 21, 1889

As the decade of the 1880s concluded, a few subjects dominated the day-to-day Lake Tahoe realm: the noticeable growth of tourism, apprehensions over logging practices, and the apparent precipitous depletion of the fisheries. However, regardless of the topical issues, one timeless aspect of Lake Tahoe was always present—the enchantment offered to the careworn traveler and seekers of beauty by the Gem of the Sierra.

On at least one occasion, this endless appeal became fantasy. In the September 21, 1889, issue of the Pacific Rural Press, in a department called the Young Folk's Column, the children's fable "The Fairy's Isle in Emerald Bay" appeared. Labeled "A Story Founded on Fact," it is a fantasy of a fairy princess named Snowray who resided on Fannette Island in Emerald Bay with her retinue of elves and fairies. The tale chronicles her encounters with Captain Dick, a bedraggled visitor to Lake Tahoe, and a tramp who burns down a house at Emerald Bay.

The captain was "gloomy and reckless and spent most of his time indulging his bad disposition" and carried a demon on his back who "took all of the captain's money, and health, and time, and gave him nothing but bad advice, and sickness, and rags in return." Captain Dick was based on a real person—retired British sea captain Richard Barter, who lived and worked as the sole caretaker of Ben Holladay's house at Emerald Bay for twelve years. Barter was often alone at the house and became known as the "Hermit of Lake Tahoe." Barter excavated a stone crypt for himself on Fannette Island, but it is unoccupied to this day. Captain Dick Barter drowned in Lake Tahoe, and his body was never found.

In the story, a tramp burns down "Ben Holladay's beautiful house at the head of Emerald bay." This element of the story was based in fact as well. Ben Holladay was the founder and owner of the Overland Stage, which made the stagecoach magnate very wealthy. Holladay loved Lake Tahoe, and he built the first private estate on the lake in 1863—a two-story, five-room villa he dubbed "The Cottage." In 1879 the estate was occupied by what the historical record identified as a "tramp" who would subsequently torch The Cottage.

However, nowhere in the Lake Tahoe historical chronology is found a factual reference to a fairy princess named Snowray who lived at Emerald Bay and who "sat upon the rim of a rainbow and talked with the Snow King."

The author of "The Fairy's Isle in Emerald Bay" was Margaret Davis

Burton, who was best known for her 1886 authorized biography of Mary Ann Bickerdyke, entitled The Woman Who Battled for the Boys in Blue: Mother Bickerdyke; Her Life and Labors for the Relief of Our Soldiers. Sketches of Battle Scenes and Incidents of the Sanitary Service. *During the Civil War, Mary Ann Bickerdyke traveled with the Union Army for four years. She participated in nineteen battles, assisted in amputations, brewed barrels of coffee, cooked for the soldiers, and offered comfort to the wounded and dying. Bickerdyke was so beloved that she earned the nickname "Mother of the Union."*

The Fairy's Isle in Emerald Bay

A Story Founded on Fact

[Written for the *Rural Press* by Margaret Davis Burton]

On a small island in Lake Tahoe dwelt the fairy princess Snowray. Her hair, which rippled in flossy masses to her feet, was fair and golden as the edges of the snow-peaks when the sun rises behind them. Like the glancing blue waters of the lake were her deep, clear eyes, and her cheeks were pink and white as wild roses on the island's rocky shores. A garland of musk-blooms was her banner, and round it thousands of elves and fairies gathered at her call, and she was as good as she was noble and fair.

She danced about in the shadowy crevices of the rocks, brightening them up like sunshine, and every flowery dingle and grassy niche where she tripped so gaily shone ever after as if the star-beams had got tangled in with the buds and leaves.

When mortals came to dwell on the lakeshore she often sent her ministers, who were called advisers, to visit them in secret. Just at sunset, when long rays of crimson shot between the mountains, these noble servants would hasten across the water upon the sunbeam bridges, running with all their might so as to gain the shore before the beams should fade away. Tallac, a lively town on the shore near Emerald bay, was their favorite resort. The reports they brought to the Princess interested her deeply, yet they disagreed with all that she had yet learned of mortals.

One of them, a man called Captain Dick, had come boldly to her island and built a cottage. He was gloomy and reckless and spent most of his time indulging his bad disposition. Never did he notice the flowers or listen to the joyous thrush-like birds, but instead he made a queer little tomb and marked it with a cross, so that when he should be found dead some day the people might lay him in it, and there he would always sleep lonely and gloomy as he had chosen to live.

He had but one friend, and this was a demon whom he carried on his back, as Sindbad the Sailor did the Old Man of the Sea. Often the demon curled up in Captain Dick's pocket, or rode on his head. He took all of the captain's money, and health, and time, and gave him nothing but bad advice, and sickness, and rags in return. Besides, he was a hideous-looking creature, yet he flattered until he seemed a friend, and then he bit like a serpent.

Princess Snowray was distressed because these vile companions lived upon her island, for they alone marred its loveliness, yet she endured them with patience, until one morning the whole place was thrown into excitement by a great smoke and fire on the lake shore. It was kindled, so the fairy messengers learned, by a tramp who had slept all night in Ben Holladay's beautiful house at the head of Emerald bay, which extends inland some three miles. After resting all night in the elegant dwelling, the tramp burnt it down as a mark of his carelessness, or bad temper, and then sneaked away.

Snowray, who stood shading her eyes with her hands so that she could see the gold and purple flames shoot up through the smoke that veiled the green hills, became disgusted with what she had seen of mortals.

"They must be a hopeless race," she said, "wicked and worthless, and I am going myself to see if this is not true; and if it is, mark you," she added, holding up her finger in warning, "I can easily induce the Snow King to freeze them all out this winter, and I shall do so without hesitation."

Two sprites brought her a cloak of moss velvet and a simple forget-me-not flower for her travelling bonnet. An elf took honeysuckle flask of dew so that she might not be thirsty on the lake, and the retinue of elves and fays carried her upon the back of a large dragon-fly, with two pairs of long, lacy wings, which bore them all over the water faster than sails, while a golden bumble-bee went ahead as pilot.

He took them in a bee-line to the first house, the villa near Tallac, where they were welcomed with a splendid concert, given by some mocking-birds in the orchard. The Princess and her party rested upon a spray of blossoms, ate a lunch of honey, which was spread in flower-cups.

After a nap the Princess called for her court robe of mauve velvet, with its lavender satin train and ruby jewels. Last of all was placed upon her head her tallest diamond crown, and all looked grand and imposing as a princess should. Then calling her attendants and her most important advisers, three blustering bumble-bees in uniforms of gold and black velvet, they flew off to the villa. Although unexpected, they found no difficulty in gaining admittance, for one of the dining-room windows was open, and they flew in and settled upon a banquet that graced the dining-table.

Snowray thought the glass vase was ice and the table-cover snow, but her advisers soon explained these things and many others which seemed just as curious to her. In answer to a silver bell, the family came in to dine.

"O mamma! see what a lot of butterflies and bees have come in to our flowers," exclaimed a merry boy, bounding up to the table and bending over the vase.

"Now, Artie, stop, please do," said Cara, his sister. "It'll be such fun to watch them while we eat. They are prettier than the flowers."

"What a lovely butterfly," remarked the children's mother. "See, my dears, it has a tiny spot of silver upon its head, and gems of red upon its wings, which are so finely shaded. It is a beauty."

"Say, mamma, can't we keep it in the birdcage, covered with mosquito net?" asked Cara.

The advisers were alarmed at this hint of imprisoning the Princess, and they prepared to hurry her away, but were again reassured when the lady answered, "No, my child, it is scarcely worth while to keep a full-grown butterfly." Then her husband, a kind-looking man, who had seated himself and was unfolding his napkin, added: "If you can find a caterpillar or a chrysalis in the willows, where they are likely to exist, it will be very interesting to keep it in the cage, well supplied with willow leaves, and watch it change into a bright-winged creature like that."

"Oh, let's try it," said Artie.

"Yes, and right away," answered Cara.

When the dessert was brought in the lady said: "Down in the logger's cabin both of the children are very sick with a fever, and don't you think, my dears, that we can give our dessert to them this evening? We will all have had plenty when you have finished drinking your glasses of milk, and we our tea, and it will be pleasant walking down to the canyon in the cool of the day."

"What a kind, charitable lady," remarked the Princess, shaking out her wings airily as she settled herself in the heart of a pink. She beckoned to a fay with her fan and whispered something to him; then he flew to the lady and placed upon her finger the gift he carried—a beautiful diamond. This was a charmed jewel, which would make the wearer always beloved and blessed for her goodness.

The Princess and her train accompanied the family down the long slopes to the logger's cabin, and heard the sick children's cry of delight for the sweet, ripe berries and delicate custards which were so kindly given.

After the guests had left the fairies settled upon a rose vine that climbed up by the door which stood partly open. The logger's wife was weary and worn by taking care of the sick children. She hastened to get supper, for her husband would soon be home. The potatoes were boiling in the kettle, the bacon was sliced in the spider ready to fry, and she stood cutting bread at the table when some one knocked at the door. She looked up and saw a poor tramp with bleared eyes and tattered clothes.

"Say mam, I've been out'er work for three weeks, an' I ha'n't got a cent; an' I'm awful hungry. Can't yer jest give a poor feller a bite—a piece o' bread, or anything handy?" he finished, hat in hand, and looking forward hungrily.

The woman hesitated. There was only enough cooked for the family supper. Besides, there was very little food in the cabin, and when they had sickness at home they could hardly supply their wants.

"He's a bad, dissipated-looking creature, any way," thought she, "and I'm sure a steady, industrious man like my husband ought not to go hungry for such as he;" and she looked at him again. "He is certainly miserable and starved, poor wretch. Well, there cannot be any harm in giving him my own supper;" so she gave him her slice of bacon, her portion of bread, some of her potatoes, and an old yeast powder can full of milk.

"Much obliged, mam, God bless you," said the tramp, taking the eatables gratefully and hurrying away. That evening the logger came home very tired, and his wife after spreading the meal, made an excuse to wait upon the children, so that he would not notice how scant her own meal was.

"Noble, tender-hearted woman," exclaimed the Princess, admiringly, and she sent a fairy to give the logger's wife a pearl that would make her always happy; and that she might be so now, the Princess sprinkled a healing dew upon the foreheads of the children, which made them fall asleep and wake up well. Princess Snowray and her whole train were hurrying back to the isle when they overtook the tramp. As he was stumbling along munching his bread and bacon, an unfledged wild bird dropped from a branch overhead and fell at his feet.

"Poor thing!" exclaimed the tramp, noticing his little helpless wings and piteous chirps. "Yet you are richer than I, since God has provided for you all you need," and he put the trembling bird back into its nest again.

"Well, there is something good even in this wretched tramp," said the Princess in surprise; "hasten and give him my gift," and the fay put in his pocket a little purse that would make its owner industrious to fill it with honestly earned coins.

The next morning, though the lake was without a ripple, they could see by the white squalls gathering in the north that the Snow King intended to make them a visit. While they were skimming over the water in the sunshine it began to dimple with a few splashes of rain. Then the white squalls flew down, rippling the lake with ten thousand pearls. But the dark battalions of the storm grew impatient and opened fire. Deep thunder peals shook the tall peaks of the mountains, and boomed through the glacier-plowed gorges, while lightning flashed from cloud to cloud and split the pine shafts with their random bolts. The Snow King then pelted the lake with hail; great frozen drops as big as bullets that hissed as they fell into the water, and sent up spurts of spray, until the whole lake seemed a wonderful fountain of flashing, silvery jets.

In the meantime Snowray and her train sat upon the rim of a rainbow and talked with the Snow King. The Princess was so pleased with what she had seen of the mortals near Tallac that she told him about them, and never once thought of poor Captain Dick and his demon.

"Very true, very true, Princess Snowray, some of those mortals are good," said the king, stroking his frosty beard in deep thought, and he pulled out of his overcoat pocket two more rainbows and hung them over the lake to show that the storm was ended.

At evening the Princess took a walk on her own little green isle to see what flowers needed care after their pelting, and as she sat binding up some broken buttercup stalks, near the water's edge, who should call upon her in the most unusual way, too, but Captain Dick's demon. He came bobbing along the shore in his new glass house and crying, "Hurry up, Miss Princess, and pick me out of this or you will lose a subject who can warm folks up on a cold night and make them jolly any time."

"Ha! ha!" laughed a cool water-sprite, who was stretching out her graceful white arms slowly to catch him at her leisure. Then she nodded to the Princess.

"This demon has drowned your poor Captain Dick, gracious Snowray," she remarked. "The poor man was rowing along over the lake when this deceitful demon jumped upon his head and demanded a lively song. He grew faint and dizzy, still the demon never thought of letting him rest or of giving him time to look about and see the thunder-storm which was gathering; so when the Snow King came blustering down the boat turned over and both fell into our forbidden domain."

"Ha! ha!" laughed the water-sprite, as she caught up the struggling demon, "we'll not let you go even if you did send us Captain Dick," and she poured him out of his glass house into the water where he drowned, and then smashed the glass upon the rocks. The water-sprite waved a gentle farewell to the Princess and floated away, winding gleefully about her shoulders the carmine scarf which the setting sun was trailing along the water.

Since that eventful summer afternoon no mortal has ever dwelt upon the isle, and the Princess Snowray, who still reigns there, has twined the lonely cross with a vine crowned with starry white blossoms, which is a sign that no demon shall ever again inhabit her peaceful domain.

Pleasures and Protection

1890–1900

Lake Tahoe's fin de siècle was a decade of recreation and reckoning. By 1900, tourism was the dominant economic activity, as timber production waned. Additional lodgings and attractions were constructed or upgraded. More and more, Emerald Bay was a desirable excursion as a small resort opened in the cove. Widespread advertising enticed a growing cadre of mostly affluent vacationers. Visitors were motivated by relaxation and reverence. As the historian John Sears noted in his excellent 1989 book *Sacred Places: American Tourist Attractions in the Nineteenth Century*,

> People visited famed natural sites as if they were shrines, where solemn reflection and adoration were the prescribed responses. In this regard, Tahoe was no exception. Nineteenth century tourists came to the Lake to experience its restorative powers, to see its sights, and to be spiritually uplifted amidst its well-known beauties.

Resort proprietors were spiritually uplifted by their profits.

Ease of access improved. Roads had modernized appreciably over the preceding decades. But overland travel was still dicey, as it was not until 1935 that a road completely circled Lake Tahoe. New routes were established, such as in 1891 with the first permanent passable road linking Reno to Lake Tahoe via the Mount Rose Highway. Many steamers plied the waters, ushering visitors to resorts, to fishing camps, or just to sightsee.

By 1898 large-scale logging ended in the Lake Tahoe Basin. In the previous thirty-years, two-thirds of the lake's marketable timber had been removed, with 60 percent of the Lake Tahoe watershed clear-cut. And, from the logging perspective, the remaining Lake Tahoe Basin lands were barren, magnificent but useless granite knobs, or inaccessible. With many fewer trees to harvest, the timber industry moved to more abundant and profitable locales elsewhere. By the end of the decade, the Carson Tahoe Lumber and Flume Company abandoned wood camps and closed its Glenbrook mills. Some logging infrastructure transitioned to other uses. For example, in 1898 the Lake Tahoe Railway logging line between Truckee and Tahoe City was repurposed as a tourist line operated by the Lake Tahoe Railway and Transportation Company.

Legislation to protect the Lake Tahoe watersheds from abusive logging practices were passed or enhanced, such as an 1894 law that reinforced prohibitions on sawdust dumping in streams and lakes. Through the 1890s, organizations, such as the Sierra Club, lobbied to designate a protected area—a forest reserve—for Lake Tahoe timberlands, under the guidance and administration of the federal government. However, this proposal was far from universally supported. Creating a forest reserve, critics argued, would reduce regional property taxes, violate the grazing rights of sheepherders, restrict the cultivation of private farms, and threaten jobs and investments. A typical complaint was lodged by the *Placer Herald* on March 19, 1898, which dismissed the forest-reserve concept as the elitist plaything of a "sporting organization in San Francisco"—namely, the Sierra Club—whose "members . . . have no interest in [Lake Tahoe] and simply desire to have this vast body of land set aside as a game preserve for hunting and recreative purposes."

In 1899 thirty-eight thousand acres of basin forestlands were established as the Lake Tahoe Forest Reserve, by decree of President William McKinley. This reserve, under the administration of the Department of the Interior, allowed the "wise use" of the timber, waters, and forage resources for public benefit but would not permit the damaging practices utilized by private timber interests in the past. In 1905 the forest reserves were transferred to the Department of the Agriculture, when the Bureau of Forestry became the U.S. Forest Service. In 1907 the forest reserves were renamed *national forests*. Today, Forest Service lands comprise 78 percent of the Lake Tahoe Basin.

Efforts promoting a Lake Tahoe National Park continued through the 1890–1899 decade, culminating in unsuccessful attempts to establish a park in 1900, 1912, and 1918.

Commercial and sport fishing endured, but the available fish were less and less native. The Lake Tahoe native fishery was always remarkably diverse, featuring Lahontan cutthroat trout, mountain whitefish, tui chub, Lahontan redside, speckled dace, Tahoe sucker, and Paiute sculpin. However, overfishing led to a rapid decline in native fish, particularly the prized Lahontan cutthroat trout. The California and Nevada Fish and Game Departments created an even larger school of market and game fish by introducing nonnative species such as rainbow trout, brown trout, mackinaw (or lake trout), brook trout, golden trout and kokanee salmon. At the turn of the twentieth century, eighty commercial fishing vessels operated on the waters of Lake Tahoe.

Animal grazing in the Sierra Nevada ridges and valleys ringing Lake Tahoe remained common and controversial. In 1900 George Bishop Sudworth wrote the study "The Stanislaus and Lake Tahoe Forest Reserves and Adjacent Territory" for the *Annual Reports of the Department of Interior, 21st Annual Report of the U. S. Geological Survey*. In his monograph, Sudworth addressed the impacts of sheep and cattle grazing on the Lake Tahoe biosphere at the end of the nineteenth century. He noted that these grazing herds had stripped the forest of practically all grasses and other herbaceous plants: "The forest floor is clean. The writer can attest the inconvenience of this total lack of grass forage, for in traveling over nearly 3,000,000 acres not a single day's feed for saddle and pack animals was secured on the open range." Grazing and trampling hindered tree regeneration. Needing more grazing land, sheepherders routinely eliminated downed trees by setting fires. Sudworth reported, "No less than seventeen such fires of this kind were found on the trail of one band of sheep, covering a distance of 10 miles." This likely was a factor in statistics that indicate that near today's D. L. Bliss State Park, Sugar Pine Point State Park, and Emerald Bay State Park on the California side of Lake Tahoe, fires were more frequent in the 1890–1899 era than at any other time. Coupled with extensive logging, the impact on the Lake Tahoe ecosystem from animal grazing was substantial.

As the decade ended and the new century beckoned, it was time to assess the journey of nineteenth-century Lake Tahoe. In the half-century since the arrival of Euro-Americans, Lake Tahoe had seen many changes and confronted myriad complicated and thorny issues. In the 1860s the Lake Tahoe terms of engagement were the encroachment of the Euro-American society on the traditional lands of the Washoe people; rapid economic growth; resource exploitation; political controversies; unregulated consumption versus conservation versus preservation; and the struggle to define the direction of Lake Tahoe's future. More than four decades later, while progress had occurred, the themes persevered—all remained part of the ongoing Lake Tahoe challenge.

Thankfully, one aspect of Lake Tahoe never changed, never could change, never should change, and that was the enduring vision, the eternal sunrise, of the breathtaking Gem of the Sierra itself.

In 1900 the posthumous memoirs of David Augustus Shaw were published as *Eldorado; or, California as Seen by a Pioneer* Shaw, a native of New York, came to California in 1850. *Eldorado* recounted his first impressions of his adopted home. His captivating description of Lake Tahoe from fifty years earlier resonated when published in 1900, and it would have rung true had it been written a thousand years ago, a hundred years ago, or yesterday. David Augustus Shaw wrote,

> Lake Tahoe . . . is the queen of the Sierras, whose frowning granite walls upon the one side and rich foliage upon the other, have been the theme of romantic poets and enthusiastic tourists. . . . The soul catches that sweet inspiration which calmly draws us into communion with the harmony of nature and a contemplation of a better land as we stand upon the silvery shores of Lake Tahoe, while amidst a stillness sublime and awful the rays of the morning sun, like ribbons of gold dart through the dense forest, streaking with amber and golden sheen the dark blue waters through whose transparent depths the landscape is mirrored below, God's fountain in the wilderness to beautify his footstool and invigorate all his creatures that partake of its crystal waters.

It was a love affair at first sight. We know the feeling.

≈≈

> We were followed for a time by a monstrous trout which
> must have weighed fully twenty-five or thirty pounds.
> —Henry Theophilus Finck, *The Pacific Coast Scenic Tour,*
> *from Southern California to Alaska, the Canadian Pacific*
> *Railway, Yellowstone Park and the Grand Cañon,* 1890

By the 1890s, Lake Tahoe was no longer as rustic as in past decades. But it still had the capacity to dazzle.

The landscape that awaited the tourist was very different from that of earlier years—the ridges and watersheds had been denuded of trees, resorts ringed the lake, steamers skimmed the surface, and communities had transitioned from ephemeral Comstock Lode or logging boomtowns to established settlements. But the beauty of the lake and the attendant outdoor pursuits were still an enticement.

Lake Tahoe was certainly a magnet for Henry Theophilus Finck, the music and culture critic for the New York Evening Post *and its sister journal* The Nation *from 1881 to 1924. In 1887 Finck undertook a Pacific Coast scenic tour with an extensive looping itinerary, including Los Angeles, San Francisco, Portland, Seattle, Alaska, Canada, Yellowstone, and the Grand Canyon. In California he made lengthy stops at Yosemite and Lake Tahoe. In 1890 Finck's observations were collected in a book entitled* The Pacific Coast Scenic Tour, from Southern California to Alaska, the Canadian Pacific Railway, Yellowstone Park and the Grand Cañon. *His reflections were wide-ranging, and he often remarked on a menagerie of local critters, such as ostriches, gophers, rabbits, wild goats, rattlesnakes, and crawfish.*

In this excerpt, Henry Theophilus Finck notes that Lake Tahoe "tourists anxious to see a wild animal in its native haunts will have no great difficulty in gratifying their curiosity." He then chronicles immediate encounters with mosquitoes, butterflies, a cinnamon bear (probably a black bear), a mountain lion, and "monstrous" trout.

Tallac's is the largest of the hotels on Tahoe, but not large enough to indicate that San Franciscans come here in vast crowds during the season. The reason is obvious. Though scenically incomparable, Tahoe is not in midsummer as cool a place as San Francisco, which, during July and August, is the coolest place on the Pacific Coast. Were Tahoe within eleven hours' ride of sultry New York, there would be a score or two of hotels on its bank in place of half-a-dozen. Residents say it was Eastern tourists who made Tahoe the resort it is now. Tallac's is si'uated in the midst of a primitive mountain wilderness, and tourists anxious to see a wild animal in its native haunts will have no great difficulty in gratifying their curiosity. One day I set out to climb part way up the mountain which begins to rise about a mile or so behind the hotel. I followed a cow-path, but it soon was lost in a swamp which is fed by snow-water brooks, and which I had some difficulty in crossing.

Beyond the swamp, on beginning to climb the mountain, I soon found myself in the midst of thousands of manzanita bushes, which presented a curious spectacle. The branches were bowed down by heavy snow, which formed a continuous layer over them thick enough apparently to walk on. But appearances were deceptive; for as soon as I came into contact with the bushes, the snow slipped off, the liberated branches flapped against my face, and I was surprised to find them covered with blossoms. To add to the contrast, several butterflies were flitting about in the warm sunlight. It takes California for such odd mixtures of the seasons,—snow-fed swamps haunted by mosquitoes, flowering bushes bowed down by snow, under a blue sky, and visited by butterflies.

The finishing touch was given by a large cinnamon bear, who suddenly hove in sight only a few hundred yards below me. As these bears are considered quite as vicious and aggressive, at certain times, as grizzlies, and having no means of defence except an olive walking-stick, I concluded not to molest the poor beast, but edged off quietly to the left, unseen, and made my way back through the trackless jungle of the swamp. In the evening I met two ladies who had been out alone in the afternoon for a walk, and had seen "a large yellowish animal with a slender body and a long tail." They changed color on hearing that it was undoubtedly a California lion, and made a vow never again to go into the woods alone. A small boy who is attached to the hotel as a guide for brook-trouting parties told us his bear story, which had a somewhat more dramatic climax than mine. He went fishing alone one day, and having found a good place, he tied his horse to a tree, and started up the creek. Suddenly he heard a crackling and whining noise near him, and at the same moment a cinnamon bear thrust her head through the brush. A small tree being close at hand, the boy climbed out of reach just as the bear arrived at its foot. She was in a dangerous mood because she had her two cubs with her; but it was to the cubs that the boy owed his release; for after a moment they became impatient and moved away, and the old bear followed them. As soon as they were out of sight, he slid down the tree, ran for his horse, and thus survived to tell the tale.

The same boy assured me that he had seen trout caught in the lake weighing twenty-two, twenty-four, and twenty-nine and three-quarters pounds respectively. This being both a fish story and a California story, seemed a tough combination; but in the morning he took me out in a boat to fish, and as luck would have it, we were followed for a time by a monstrous trout which must have weighed fully twenty-five or thirty pounds. He would not take the bait, however, and such monsters are not often caught, the average catch being from one to three pounds. I caught three in a couple of hours, weighing together about four pounds, and that seemed to be considered a good catch at the hotel for that season. Fishing luck at Tahoe varies greatly with the season, the time of day, and the knowledge and skill of the fisherman. The best place to throw the line is just where the water becomes so deep that the bottom is no longer visible. Row slowly all the time, and let out a very long line, with a very bright silver spoon, to attract the game. The bright spoon seemed to be of prime importance; for I had one and caught three fish, while the boy, who had a dull spoon, did not get a bite.

≈≈≈

The waters are also drunk for liver and kidney diseases,
chronic constipation and cutaneous affections.

—Winslow Anderson, *Mineral Springs and
Health Resorts of California*, 1890

Lake Tahoe had a cure for what ails you, said many. Beyond the psychic value of refreshing one's spirit at the Gem of the Sierra, the health and medicinal benefits of the lake's rarefied air, translucent water, and hot and cold mineral springs were regularly promoted throughout the nineteenth century.

But, perhaps, the most ballyhooed were the supposed health-giving properties of Lake Tahoe's mineral springs. Several dozen hot and cold springs were at the lake, and establishments catering to those seeking their rewards became common. There were assorted venues, including Dr. George Bourne's Hygienic Health Resort in Carnelian Bay and Campbell's Hot Springs, later Brockway Hot Springs (on the north shore); Deer Park Springs (west of Tahoe City); Rubicon Springs and Moana Villa, near Tahoma (on the west shore); and several more.

These hot and cold springs ventures were part sanitoria, part bathhouse, and part tourist retreat—some were quite luxurious, while a few prided themselves on their rustic appeal. Throughout the era, the proprietors would have wholeheartedly ascribed to the sentiments offered by George Wharton James in his 1914 book California: Romantic &

Beautiful: *"The invalid or neurasthenic, the physically overworked or mentally overtaxed, who are benefited by baths in natural hot springs find at [Lake Tahoe] that rest, care and natural stimulation that will restore them to health." Whether the springs provided actual physical and psychological improvement can be debated, but it is beyond question that many visitors and patrons believed the waters of Lake Tahoe had healing powers. Sometimes, however, the benefits came with a caveat, such as the backhanded compliment paid to the waters of Campbell's Hot Springs by the Nevada* Daily State Register *on May 26, 1871: "When cool the water is pleasant to drink, having a faint taste of gunpowder."*

In 1890 Dr. Winslow Anderson, a San Francisco surgeon and editor of the Pacific Medical Journal, *released his book* Mineral Springs and Health Resorts of California, *a guidebook and summary of the attributes found at the state's heath resorts. Anderson's assessments carried immense credibility not only because he was a prominent physician but also because, after the book's publication, Dr. Anderson was president of the College of Physicians in San Francisco and a member of the California State Board of Health and the California Board of Medical Examiners.*

In this excerpt, Dr. Winslow Anderson evaluates Carnelian Hot Springs.

Lake Tahoe or Carnelian Hot Springs

"O, lovely lake, while life remains,
Will thy enchantment hold my heart!
And song rehearse in willing strains,
Lake of the hills! how fair thou art!"

These hot and cold mineral springs are located on Carnelian Bay, at the northern end of Lake Tahoe, in Placer County. They form part of the attractions of this famous inland sea. They are reached by railroad to Truckee, and then by stage over a good mountain road for about two and a half hours' drive.

The scenery is grand. The Truckee River is crossed and recrossed. Mountain sides and heights are scaled. Fertile valleys, grazed by immense herds of cattle, are traversed. Forests of beautiful pines and cedar rear themselves at intervals. Humming sawmills fill the air with life, and wild, romantic views, greet one at every turn. The appointments of the resort are most complete in every detail. There are about fifty boiling and cold springs on the lake shore. They are well kept and cared for. Excellent bathing facilities have recently been erected, where cold and hot sulphur baths, tub and plunge, can be taken. There are also steam baths, and the resort has become very popular. The baths are used with success by the rheumatic and gouty. The waters are also drunk for liver and kidney diseases, chronic constipation and cutaneous affections.

The waters are sulphurous and saline, and a few are carbonated. They contain:

Sodium Chloride.
Calcium Sulphate.
Magnesium Sulphate.
Silica.
Organic Matter.
Free Sulphureted Hydrogen Gas.

The elevation is 6,250 feet. Bronchitis, asthma and consumption do well among the pines at this place. There are splendid facilities for camping, hunting and fishing.

≈≈≈

Tahoe, you are a very witch for loveliness,
and show as many moods!

—Alfred Lambourne, *Bits of Descriptive Prose* ,1891

There was something about Lake Tahoe that compelled thoughts of the eternal. The Gem of the Sierra was subject to myriad interpretations and depictions over the decades. The lake was considered from a cornucopia of perspectives, including economic worth, exploitable resources, environmental protection, psychological enrichment, artistic merit, and the violation of Native sovereignty. But for some the theme was the probability of a heavenly connection between Lake Tahoe and cosmic immortality.

In 1891 Alfred Lambourne pondered this idea in his book Bits of Descriptive Prose. *Lambourne reckoned that a place as magnificent as Lake Tahoe must be part of a grand plan—an intriguing fusion of the secular and the spiritual. There must be a reason why at Lake Tahoe the sky, the water, the flora, and the fauna are "eternal yet evanescent—playmates of Time and the elements."*

Alfred Lambourne was born in England in 1850. When Lambourne was a young child, his family migrated to the United States before, in the 1860s, joining the Mormon migration to the Utah Territory. Encouraged by his parents, Lambourne honed his artistic skills and become well-known as an interpreter of American West landscapes though sketches and painting. In 1871 Alfred Lambourne accompanied Mormon patriarch Brigham Young on an exploration of Zion Canyon and produced the first known sketches of the majestic multicolored canyon. In later life Lambourne turned to the pen and wrote fourteen books, one of which was Bits of Descriptive Prose, *a collection of essays on flowers, streams, dawn, autumn, rain, midnight, art galleries, and Lake Tahoe.*

In this excerpt, Alfred Lambourne describes the tranquil voyage of a sailboat on Lake Tahoe, but the journey might as well have been about cruising the galaxy on a star. Lambourne refers to "Koh-i-noor." The Koh-i-noor Diamond is one of the largest cut diamonds in the world, weighing 106 carats, and is part of the Crown Jewels of the United Kingdom.

Across Lake Tahoe

Never was there a day more like unto those which might have hung over the fabled "Islands of the Blessed," than was that day; and Tahoe, you are a very witch for loveliness, and show as many moods! Always the same hills around thee, always the same dark forests of pine and fir, and always the same great clusters of peaks along the horizon. But how the seasons and the great sun play with them, so that though the same, they seem never the same; eternal yet evanescent—playmates with Time and the Elements.

Yellow rose the September sun, yellow over the eastern hills; yellow it climbed into the sky; and even at noonday it was tinged with a yellow hue, faint indeed, but enough to make it seem as if a vast Koh-i-noor illumed the sky. A violet haze enshrouded the hills all day; the broad, luminous surface of the lake was pale, pale blue, blurred across with a still paler tint of aquamarine, a league lovely indeed to behold.

The boat was all gaily adorned. Upon its sail were emblazoned the arms of the Bohemians; from its mast-head floated white and gold ribbons; the mast itself was entwined with hop vines; whilst along the boat's side festoons of evergreens hung, and at the prow was a great bunch of ferns—the broad branching, graceful aspidium—around the edge of the poop-deck were bunches of golden-rod, circled at the base with the purple-green leaves of the monardella.

It was a fair evening, as might have been expected. The pensive hues of twilight soon supplanted the fiery colors of sunset. Beyond the dense, dark mass of wood which clothed the Eagle Cliff, the mountains long retained their Alpen-gild. Sailor Jack pulled the boat up under the shadows of the giant promontories and all could hear the fretting of a mountain torrent as it came down from the snows above. A slight breeze then puffed out the sail and sent the boat gliding noiselessly past the dusky woods. Two or three stars suddenly popped out; among the pine branches sounded the cicada's piercing trill.

Why do the water and the twilight always provoke the spirit of song? No sooner are the shadows fallen, than we are tempted to sing. Whatever be our feelings, then we long to pour them forth in melody. Be they sad, pensive or gay, we can restrain them no longer, but must tell them all to the waters and the first of the stars.

≈≈≈

It was found that Cave Rock, which was over 300 feet above
the level of the lake, had toppled over into the lake.

—"Swept by a Huge Wave," *Sacramento*
Morning Union, November 28, 1893

Sometimes the reports from Lake Tahoe were simply bizarre, such as the 1893 account of a tremendously destructive "tidal wave" that struck Cave Rock and Glenbrook on the eastern edge of the lake.

Swept by a Huge Wave

Commotion on Lake Tahoe Due to the Fall of Cave Rock

Carson (Nev.), November 25.—The citizens of Glenbrook, Lake Tahoe, were startled yesterday morning by an awful roaring which made the earth tremble. Immediately a huge wave forty or fifty feet high was seen coming around the point to the left of Glenbrook. The wall of water came rolling into that place with great velocity over the wharf, up into the store and wetting the front of the Lakeshore House. When the wave receded it was found a great deal of damage had been done to the goods in the store, the butcher shop had been lifted off its foundation, and the wharf was badly damaged. Jellerson's saloon was almost a wreck, and that part of the wharf around the store and saloon was covered with debris. A large log was driven through the rear of the saloon, and one end now rests on the billiard table.

The steamers *Meteor* and *Emerald*, moored in the breakwater near the mill, were thrown against the wharf with such force as to completely knock it out, also knocking over the boathouse where Mr. Bliss keeps private boats. The mill being high and well enclosed suffered little damage, though the lower part was flooded.

When the water calmed the *Meteor*, which being iron, only suffered the loss of her smokestack and pilot house, got up steam and started to locate the cause of the wave.

It was found that Cave Rock, which was over 300 feet above the level of the lake, had toppled over into the lake. The water had been undermining it at the base for years, and it is probable that its fall is dire to the action of the waves. Nothing remains but an unsightly hole in the mountain.

The only damage inflicted at Baldwin's Tallac was the flooding of the clubhouse and tennis court. At Emerald bay only a small portion of the wave got in and only some small pleasure boats suffered. At Bellevue the boathouse was floated off the wharf.

At McKinney's the dance hall was twisted from the piles and lies close to the clubhouse, the stairs of which were swept away and the windows broken.

The stock of liquors is a total loss.

The old snag where so many fish have been caught is now on shore. The wave had spread out a good deal when it got around to Tahoe City, and beyond causing the steamer *Tod Goodwin* to pull up a couple of piles did no harm. The only damage done on the other side was to small boats. No fatalities were reported. By this catastrophe one of the main points of interest on the lake is lost forever.

"Brief Local Items," *Sacramento Morning
Union*, December 2, 1893

In the hinterlands of Lake Tahoe, this story was broadly circulated and believed—for about a week. In the December 2, 1893, edition of the

Sacramento Morning Union, *one item in the Brief Local Items section revealed the origin of the tidal-wave story. In its entirety, the item read,* "The Truckee Republican *says the yarn telegraphed from Carson about Cave Rock falling and creating a tidal wave on Lake Tahoe was a huge joke, of which Sam Davis was the author."*

≈≈≈

It is probable that [Lake Tahoe] will never be selected as a place of continued residence by any considerable number of families.

—Israel C. Russell, *Lakes of North America: A Reading Lesson for Students of Geography and Geology,* 1895

Sometimes experts make mistakes.

In 1895, Israel C. Russell, the preeminent chronicler of lakes, rivers, volcanoes, and glaciers in North America, published a primer entitled Lakes of North America: A Reading Lesson for Students of Geography and Geology. *In this student reader, Russell outlined the geography, geology, and scientific studies related to the lakes of the continent. Naturally, Israel C. Russell included Lake Tahoe. His abstract mentioned all the defining characteristics of the lake, including the remarkably transparent water, that the main body of the lake does not freeze in winter, and that Lake Tahoe is one of the deepest lakes in the world.*

Many of these observations had already been made years earlier by other scientists, such as John LeConte. However, Russell's representation of the Gem of the Sierra is best remembered for his conclusion that it was unlikely that Lake Tahoe would ever sustain a permanent year-round population.

Israel C. Russell was wrong. Today, many proudly call Lake Tahoe their home. According to the 2020 census, the full-time residents of the Lake Tahoe Basin number approximately fifty-four thousand. During the summer tourist season, the overall population can increase by as much as three hundred thousand daily.

Israel Cook Russell was an American geologist and geographer in the latter half of the nineteenth century. Born, raised, and educated in New York, Russell traveled throughout the world as a United States government employee. In 1874 he was sent to New Zealand to track the transit of Venus. In 1878 Russell was a geologist on the United States survey west of the one hundredth meridian. As a member of the United States Geological Survey (USGS), he worked at Mono Lake in California and served on an expedition to Alaska that surveyed a portion of Alaska's eastern boundary. In 1890 Israel Russell was credited with the first-known sighting of Mount Logan, the tallest mountain in Canada. In 1892 Russell became a professor of geology at the University of Michigan, where he remained until his untimely death in 1906 at age fifty-three. At the time, Israel C. Russell was president of the Geological Society of America.

LAKE TAHOE.—This "gem of the Sierra" is situated at an elevation of 6200 feet above the sea and is enclosed in all directions by rugged, forest-covered mountain slopes which rise from two to over four thousand feet above its surface. Its expanse is unbroken by islands and has an area of between 192 to 195 square miles. Its diameter from north to south is 21.6 miles and from east to west 12 miles.

On looking down on Lake Tahoe from the surrounding pine-covered heights, one beholds a vast plain of the most wonderful blue that can be imagined. Near shore, where the bottom is of white sand, the waters have an emerald tint, but are so clear that objects far beneath the surface may be readily distinguished. Farther lakeward, the tints change by insensible gradation until the water is a deep blue, unrivaled even by the color of the ocean in its deepest and most remote parts. On calm summer days, the sky with its drifting cloud banks and the rugged mountains with their bare and usually snow-covered summits, are mirrored in the placid waters with such wonderful distinctness and such accuracy of detail, that one is at a loss to tell where the real ends and the duplicate begins. While floating on the lake in a boat, the transparency of the water gives the sensation that one is suspended in mid air, as every detail on the bottom, fathoms below, is clearly discernible. . . .

The only instance in this country in which waters have been found to be more transparent is in the great limestone-water springs of Florida.

Soundings made in Lake Tahoe by [John] LeConte . . . gave a maximum depth of 1645 feet, but a more detailed survey may possibly discover still more profound depths. Those measurements show that the lake, with the exception of Crater lake, Oregon, is the deepest inland waterbody in America yet sounded, and exceeds the depth of any of the lakes of Switzerland, but is not so deep as lakes Maggiore and Como on the south side of the Alps.

The temperature observations made in Lake tahoe . . . furnish an illustration of the fact that deep lakes, even when situated at a high elevation and subject to low winter temperatures, do not freeze. The surface waters are cooled in winter and descend, while warmer waters from below rise and take their place, thus establishing a circulation, but the body of water is so great that its entire mass never becomes cooled sufficiently during the comparatively short winters to check the upward circulation and allow ice to form. . . .

Lake Tahoe is situated at such an altitude that its shores are bleak and inhospitable during a number of months each year. For this reason it is probable that it will never be selected as a place of continued residence by any considerable number of families, but during the summer, when the adjacent valleys are parched by desert heat, the air in the lake-filled valley is cool and bracing; it then furnishes a charming retreat for the dwellers of the cities of the Pacific coast, as well as for more distant wanderers. As a place for summer rest and recreation it is second to none of the popular resorts of the United States or Canada. . . .

A careful investigation of the various problems [at Lake Tahoe] would form a thesis of unusual interest. Will not some student or some class of students in our universities tell the world what the mountains and streams in this fascinating region are doing, explain how the present conditions came into existence, and point out the results towards which they are tending?

≈≈≈

If we could look into her mind, we should find her chief incentive
to be love of her tribe, its past, its laws, its myths, and its sorceries.

—Mrs. C. Amy Cohn, "Arts and Crafts of the Nevada Indians,"
Biennial Report of the Nevada Historical Society, 1909

As the nineteenth century ended, the Washoe people of Lake Tahoe had become virtually invisible. In the previous decades, their tribal homeland had been overwhelmed by the influx of Euro-American trespassers; their sovereignty had been usurped; their formal protests to federal, state, and local government officials were habitually dismissed or ignored; their petitions for land rights at Lake Tahoe were not granted; and their children were educated at government schools practicing forced assimilation.

Washoe people lived on the lake margins and mostly labored as resort employees, loggers, and fishers. Their only widespread visibility was as artists, particularly basket weavers.

The best-known of these Washoe basket weavers was Dat-So-La-Lee. Born around 1829 in the Carson Valley, her Washoe name was Dabuda. In 1888 she married Washoe arrow craftsman Charlie Keyser and adopted the name Louisa Keyser. In the mid-1890s, Louisa was given the nickname Dat-So-La-Lee. There are disputes as to the origin and meaning of Dat-So-La-Lee, but the name may have been the result of a commercial promotion by her patrons.

The patrons were Abram and Amy Cohn. Abram "Abe" Cohn owned the Emporium Company, a men's clothing store, in Carson City, Nevada. In 1895 he purchased several of Louisa Keyser's willow-wrapped bottles and became aware of her beautiful woven baskets.

She primarily wove degikup baskets, a design with a small circular base extending upward and outward until reversing to a small opening at the top that mirrors the size of the base. Her baskets were not totally unique, as she was inspired by similar woven baskets from Pomo and Miwok artists, but most of her design elements were distinctive and singular. In the summer, the Cohns and Dat-So-La-Lee lived and worked at Lake Tahoe near Tahoe Tavern in Tahoe City.

The Cohns became Dat-So-La-Lee's business managers and greatest promoters. Dat-So-La-Lee worked for the Cohns for thirty years and produced at least 120 documented baskets. Dat-So-La-Lee and Amy Cohn traveled to many arts-and-crafts exhibits. And the Cohns served as Dat-So-La-Lee's press agents.

Amy Cohn concocted an elaborate biography of Dat-So-La-Lee that was heavy on attention-grabbing details but deficient on facts. In an excellent and skillfully researched essay entitled "Louisa Keyser and the Cohns: Mythmaking and Basket Making in the American West," University of British Columbia art historian Marvin Cohodas concluded, "In promoting baskets woven by Louisa Keyser, . . . the Cohns obscured all factual information on Louisa's life with a barrage of exaggerations and falsifications. . . . After subjecting all these sources to detailed analysis, I am left to conclude that almost nothing the Cohns said was true." However, the publicity was effective, and Dat-So-La-Lee's baskets sold well and today are highly prized.

The story of Dabuda/Dat-So-La-Lee/Louisa Keyser sadly conforms *with the historical chronicle of the Washoe people at Lake Tahoe. Her work was admired for its skill, craftmanship, and expression of Washoe values, but her authenticity, her identity, was concealed. It was the same pattern for the nineteenth century Washoe people—appreciation for their ancient culture but their hidden end-of-the-century reality.*

In 1909 the Biennial Report of the Nevada Historical Society *published an article by Amy Cohn entitled "Arts and Crafts of the Nevada Indians." In the excerpt that follows, Cohn presents her version of the history of Nevadan Indigenous basket weaving and her partly hagiographic and partly unbecoming portrait of Dat-So-La-Lee.*

Arts and Crafts of the Nevada Indians

The arts and crafts of the Nevada Indians were few, but in them they gained the greatest degree of perfection attainable in handicraft. If these Indians had been permitted to progress naturally toward civilization, they would have excelled in every aboriginal handicraft, with the abundant stores of stone, clay, and malleable metals at their command in prolific Nevada.

The males essayed only to fashion the finest bows, perfect arrows, nets, traps, snares, and wove the softest rabbit-skin blankets and robes.

The art of basketry was perfected among our Indians over three hundred years ago. All industry leads to fine art. Basket-weaving commenced at the lowest point of industry, necessity, and passed beyond all art criticism. The utilitarian basket has some beauty to us, but an exalted specimen of this handicraft is the product of the natural inspiration, skill, and discrimination of its creator. The Shoshone Indians of our State made beautiful bottle-neck or vase-shaped baskets for ceremonial and mortuary uses. The Paiute women never gained a great degree of fineness, but they wove ingenious and graceful double-pyramidal shaped water-baskets or bottles which they covered or smeared with fragrant pine pitch, and these they traded with the Shoshones and Washoes for their fine basketry. The Washoe women were noted among all the Western Indian tribes for their fine baskets.

A weaver was compelled to be historian, botanist, astronomer, mystic, religieuse, and reader-at-law. She must be a botanist to know when and where to gather the materials to make her weaving threads; an historian to embody in her work the facts of history, as the Washoes had no photographs, stone-carvings or skin-painting to record and transmit the history of their tribes—they did it only by word of mouth and in their weaving; a mystic to be able to exemplify their legends; a religieuse to know how to shape the basket used in their ceremonies. She must also be well versed in her tribal laws in order to keep strictly to the designs and symbols which she as a member of her family would be permitted to use, since patterns or designs were heirlooms or family crests, and the deviations or variations were worked out by the weaver to express the thought or intention she aimed to portray. All of these were interwoven in her productions governed by the laws of her people, with earnestness of purpose and faithfulness; her genius, inspired by nature, prompted her delicate, artistic fingers to portray the long-planned, well-thought-out subject for which she had no sketch or model. As their laws forbade them to copy or duplicate, when each basket was finished it was an original and unique gem of perfect art. . . .

It is a question if one could find any two baskets alike in any tribe. I can safely assert that this is never the case among the Washoes.

Let no one say we are enthusiastic over little things. It is no little thing to be thus brought near to nature, and to be able to penetrate to the inner life of our predecessors in the possession of the soil we now occupy. Advancing civilization should not forget the dying civilization of the aborigines, but should see in these baskets the evidences of an age when every article created by the hand of man had an artistic quality, when every housewife, by the labor of her own hands, made everything that could minister to use and comfort "from the cradle to the grave" shaping them with such expression of natural art-feeling and unspoiled thought that the products of her skill have become priceless treasures in private collections and public museums.

It is to the prospector who came to Washoe in search of gold that we owe the preservation of the remnants of this art, for in the 50's the Paiutes were bent upon exterminating the Washoes, who, upon the advent of white settlers, came under their protection.

The famous "Dat-So-La-Lee," the last of the old-school Washoe basket-weavers, dwells in Carson City, the historic Capital of the "Battle-Born State." This Washoe woman will be remembered in our history for her masterpieces of aboriginal American art. She is over seventy years of age, is gross and ungainly in figure, with dark copper colored skin, straight black hair, artistically proportioned hands, and scintillating black eyes. "Dat-So-La-Lee" is of erratic temper, but docile to friends and generous to her people. She keeps her art still untainted, producing the most perfect and beautiful "day-gee-coops" or sacred ceremonial baskets. The design or symbolic ornamentation embodied in each stitch commemorates some fact in her past or portrays some of her poetic dreams. If we could look into her mind, we should find her chief incentive to be love of her tribe, its past, its laws, its myths, and its sorceries. These are her guiding motives.

In the springtime "Dat-So-La-Lee" trudges over the hills and mountains to dig the well-developed roots of the bracken (*Pteridium Aquilinum*) from the inner stock of which she makes her black thread. And when she has traversed any section in such search the possibilities of that region are exhausted. In the summer, when the redbud (*Cercis Occidentalis*) is in its prime, red and lustrous, the bark, of which she makes her red thread, is gathered through many days of hard work and careful selection. Then again in the fall when all the sap has receded, she gathers the long straight boughs of the willow (*Salix*) for her white weaving threads and foundation sticks. The thread is taken from between the bark and the pith. After each long trudge she sits on the ground and with her teeth and finger-nails, assisted by an old knife or a fragment of broken glass in lieu of the ancient scraper of flint or obsidian, she prepares her materials for use. When prepared to her satisfaction, she rolls each variety of strands into balls or reels tied up securely and stores them away to be cured and seasoned for her next year's work. At all times she uses materials prepared the preceding year. . . .

As the days pass her fingers are cut and sorely wounded to the bone, her eyes are strained and dim, and her back aches. A year slips by, and the achievement is—a perfect masterpiece of art.

For these baskets we claim every attribute of art—motive, use, symmetry, meaning, coloring, and, most wonderful of all, such perspective as we have not found or heard of in the productions of any other aboriginal artist.

≈≈≈

I do not see but that civilization is complete . . . as I see no difference in their manners from those of white children.

—Report of School at Carson, Nev. Indian Industrial
School, Carson City, Nev., August 20, 1897

The policy was years in the making. In 1890, the children of the Washoe, Paiute, and Shoshone people surrounding Lake Tahoe were required to attend a new government-operated boarding school in Carson City, Nevada. In its history, the school went by various names—the Carson Indian Industrial School, the Carson Indian Training School, the Carson Indian School, the Stewart Institute, and Stewart Indian School. The school received federal funding due to the efforts of United States Senator William M. Stewart of Nevada, and the school was ultimately named in his honor.

The genesis of the Indian boarding school had begun years earlier, however. Beginning in 1879, off-reservation boarding schools were established throughout the United States, ultimately numbering twenty-seven in total. The reasoning behind these institutions was to "assimilate" and "civilize" Indigenous children. Richard Henry Pratt, who founded the first and most famous boarding school in Carlisle, Pennsylvania, argued that the schools were essential to the survival of the Native people and were a humanitarian obligation. The policy was summarized by a quote attributed to Pratt—"Kill the Indian; save the man."

Those who experienced life in the boarding schools did not consider them humanitarian. The schools functioned under a uniform set of rules and regulations designed to separate Native children from their families, denigrate their culture, and foster integration of the Indigenous population into the governing Anglo-American society. Boarding school advocates and administrators predicted that strong and steady pressure on the Native children would yield assimilation in a generation.

At the Stewart Indian School, the children were compelled to submit to rules enforced by physical and emotional malevolence. Corporal punishment was common. Predatory sexual abuse by at least one administrator has been chronicled. Boarding school students were removed from their families, often without warning, and delivered to schools usually far from their homes. Upon arrival at the school, the children were forbidden from using their Native language, a particular hardship on those youngsters who did not speak English. Students had to wear European-style, Western clothing and were required to alter their appearance and their behavior to seem more white and middle class. The Indigenous children were indoctrinated that their heritage was backward and semicivilized and incompatible with the "progress" they were expected to make in the larger, white-dominated society. Students spent about half the school day on literary development and the remainder of the day on industrial and domestic education. Funding shortfalls were bridged by the involuntary labor of the students. Runaways were frequent, and, when returned to the school, they were severely punished.

The impact on the Indigenous families and their children was harrowing. As historian Samantha M. Williams notes in her excellent 2022 book Assimilation, Resilience and Survival: A History of the Stewart Indian School, 1890–2020, "This traumatic process taught children to disavow their heritage, shattered bonds within Native communities, and fundamentally damaged familial relationships among generations of Indigenous peoples."

Annually, the superintendents of the boarding schools were required to report to the Commissioner of Indian Affairs in Washington DC on the status of their institution and their successes in promoting "advancement" of their Native charges. The reports usually offered recommendations for improvement and a forecast of future developments.

Following is a portion of the 1897 report of Eugene Mead, superintendent of the Carson Indian Industrial School. Mead ran the boarding school from 1894 to 1899. Mead's report pats himself on the back for the organization of the school band, which he claimed rendered the problem of runaways to be "entirely overcome." The report also included some cringeworthy descriptions of his students, such as the following:

> "When they have their stomachs full they are the most contented and serene beings in existence."
> "[The students talk in] an Indian lingo intelligible to no one—not even themselves."
> "The girls . . . are inclined to engage in games and practices of a lower order than white children would engage in."
> "That miserable practice of pupils sitting about in idle knots discussing idle nothings, and always, too, in the Indian language."

In 2010 Justin Zuniga, a member of the Reno-Sparks Indian Colony (whose members are Washoe, Paiute, and Shoshone), wrote a thesis about the Stewart Indian School while a student at the University of Nevada, Reno. His research unearthed a document that indicated that Eugene Mead was guilty of sex crimes at the Stewart Indian School. An October 3, 1898, report from a federal Indian agent stated, "Superintendent Mead has admitted to being criminally intimate with pupils." When *confronted, Mead "became violently enraged and abusive. Five minutes after this outburst, he broke down, and wept like a child. This exhibition of temper as well as other matters which are brought to my attention fully convinces me that Superintendent Mead is wholly unqualified mentally, morally, and physically to conduct a school of this kind."*

There is no evidence that Eugene Mead was punished for his offenses or that his departure from the Stewart Indian School was related to the incidents.

REPORT OF SCHOOL AT CARSON, NEV.

INDIAN INDUSTRIAL SCHOOL,

Carson City, Nev., August 20, 1897.

SIR: I have the honor to submit herewith the annual report of this school for the fiscal year 1897.

School.—On the 1st day of July, 1894, I took charge of this school, and up to that time it had been the custom to permit the pupils to go to their homes during the vacation period; but as no possible good resulted, or can result from this practice, they have been retained at the school excepting in 1895, when a part of them were allowed to visit their homes. Within the present vacation a small number were permitted to go, but they were the children, for the most part, of such parents as would not allow their children to enter school unless they were allowed this privilege. We have, however, kept our average up very well, and at the present writing 126 are enrolled.

The year just passed is the most interesting in the history of the school. It is comparatively a new school, having been established in the year 1890, and the Indians in this locality little understood the real object for which it was intended, but supposed it was to be a place where their children were to have nothing to do, plenty to wear and plenty to eat, with the latter commodity the most prominent; for when they have their stomachs full they are the most contented and serene beings in existence. Therefore, to see their children put to work was very distasteful to them, and as a result runaways were quite frequent up to the beginning of the year just passed; but this has been entirely overcome through various causes, one of which is the establishment of a band, of which I shall speak under a special caption.

There has been a steady advancement in the literary department, and a very noticeable improvement in the use of the language. Their enunciation is greatly improved, and by introducing the kindergarten and adopting such methods and literature in the higher grades as are suited to them, are now heard in their plays simple songs and talks instead of an Indian lingo intelligible to no one—not even themselves. In their work, plays, and games, I do not see but that civilization is complete— complete as far as the children are concerned, but outside influences tend to retrograde—as I see no difference in their manners from those of white children, excepting in the girls, who are inclined to engage in games and practices of a lower order than white children would engage in.

The advancement made in music the past year is very commendable, due to more enthusiasm thrown into the work by the teachers in charge of this department. The pupils have been taught to read music, and thus brought to under-stand something of its principles. They have been, therefore, more interested in it, as in this way they see an object beyond simply singing songs to fill in the time commonly dubbed the study hour.

Our school for the past year has been awake as a result of a little enthusiasm thrown into the work by a few of the employees. A little enthusiasm by the employees means a considerable among the pupils. I have noticed that our pupils work better, play ball harder, and are continually engaged in some healthful play when not otherwise engaged. That miserable practice of pupils sitting about in idle knots discussing idle nothings, and always, too, in the Indian language, has been very conspicuous by its absence.

At the close of the school there was an exhibit in our large kindergarten room of samples of work selected throughout the year. There was no especial attempt made to produce samples for this purpose, but such were selected from the regular class work as represented taste, skill, etc., in their manufacture. The work compared with that of previous exhibits showed plainly the advancement made both among boys and girls. The exhibit from the culinary department, made, of course, especially for this purpose from a knowledge the girls had gained from a regular course of instruction, was very fine and did them much credit.

Band.—For the two years preceding the present one I represented to your office repeatedly the benefits, in my judgment, that would arise from the establishment of a band in our school, and finally, at the close of the past year, through your efforts instruments were allowed us and an able disciplinarian and band instructor sent us in the person of Mr. Edwin Schanandore, an Oneida Indian. At the opening of the school in September he commenced the instruction of 21 of our boys, and at the present they make a very creditable showing considering the short time they have been practicing. I was not disappointed in the effect this band would have on our pupils, and not only on them but on their parents and friends as well. Such was the effect on the general moral tone and the contentment of our pupils that we have not a single runaway recorded for the year; and to illustrate the impression made upon the Indians—the parents and relatives of our pupils—on Memorial Day in Carson I presume there were between 400 and 500 Indians present to view them in the procession as they marched to the cemetery headed by our band, and not only this, but it has done more to create a favorable impression among the people here in behalf of our pupils than any other feature of our school. People have frequently remarked to me that they were surprised at the showing these Indian boys have made and that they had no idea that they had the ability to accomplish such results.

Attendance.—The average attendance for the year is 126. We have an appropriation for 125 pupils, and could easily have maintained an average of 150 had we the room for them; but as it is our dormitories are now crowded, and it is impossible to carry a much larger number. The total enrollment for the year is 154; the highest average for any quarter 131, and the lowest 116.

Industries. . . . Our girls pursue a regular course of instruction in all the domestic departments, and many of them can now enter white families and do very creditable work, and especially is this true of the larger ones in the sewing room. . . .

Conclusion.—I wish to thank your office for the kind consideration extended during the past year, and at all times.

Very respectfully,

EUGENE MEAD, Superintendent.

> Soon the monster appeared, slowly making his way in
> the direction where I was hidden in the tree-top.
>
> —Isaac C. Coggin, "The Unpleasant Serpent Coggin Declares He
> Saw at Lake Tahoe," *San Francisco Call*, November 21, 1897

What did Isaac C. Coggin see while perched atop a pine tree overlooking Lake Tahoe?

On November 21, 1897, Isaac C. Coggin, a well-known and respected figure in San Francisco society and manager of the Golden Gate Park Concert Band, related a curious story in the San Francisco Call. *Coggin described his 1865 encounter with a "monster" at Lake Tahoe.*

In 1865 Isaac Coggin was a young man toiling as an agricultural laborer at Lake Tahoe. On his day off, Coggin decided to hunt along the shores of Lake Tahoe with his favorite dog. As they hiked the edge of the lake, suddenly, the dog sniffed, stopped, turned his head in fear, and began running—away, very fast.

Isaac soon discovered why his dog had bolted, as Coggin heard thunderous rumblings from the ridge above. Alarmed, Coggin climbed a tree for safety and to get a better view. What Coggin claimed happened next is recounted in the following article: "The Unpleasant Serpent Coggin Declares He Saw at Lake Tahoe."

Isaac C. Coggin was named manager of San Francisco's Golden Gate Park Concert Band in 1883. The band had been formed in 1882 with civilian musicians and band members of the Second Artillery Regiment of the California National Guard. After Coggin was appointed, the Golden Gate Park Band expanded to thirty members—all thirty members, including the National Guard troops, were members of the Musician's Protective Union. The band was so popular that several new bandstands were constructed for its use over the years. In 1900 bandstand construction culminated in the erection of The Temple of Music, the still-standing, magnificent outdoor bandshell in the heart of Golden Gate Park.

On July 4, 1889, this unusual amalgam of civilian and military musicians led to an incident that resulted in band manager and conductor Isaac C. Coggin being court-martialed. On the Fourth of July, the Golden Gate Park Band, now numbering seventy-five performers, was to play and parade for the celebrations. However, the Musician's Protective Union had a falling out with the organizing committee that had hired nonunion bands. The union announced that member musicians would not play on the Fourth. However, since the band was also the Second Regiment Band of the California National Guard, the musicians were ordered to play by their regimental commander. Most refused. As their leader, Isaac C. Coggin was charged with fomenting a mutiny. Coggin was the only one charged. Besides being court-martialed, he was fined $50 in gold and dishonorably discharged from service in the National Guard. While he was dismissed from the Second Regiment Band, Isaac C. Coggin remained as business manager of the Golden Gate Park Band until his death in 1903.

But, in 1865, court-martial was far in the future as Isaac cowered on a tree branch as a massive serpent descended toward the deep blue waters of Lake Tahoe—allegedly.

The Unpleasant Serpent Coggin
Declares He Saw at Lake Tahoe

The following is related by a well-known citizen of San Francisco, [I. C. Coggin], manager of the [Golden Gate] Park band. It is presented unaccompanied by affidavits, and may be accepted as truth by anybody who chooses to believe it.

The story of a sea serpent comes from so many sources and from people of undoubted veracity that it cannot be doubted that there is living in the Atlantic Ocean a serpent of monstrous size, but it remains for California, with its remains of gigantic monsters scattered all over its surface and where animal life attained its greatest perfection, to have a serpent now living within its borders much larger than any described by so many witnesses.

It was my fortune to be one of the earliest settlers on the west shore of Lake Tahoe—from June, 1861, to 1869. I located a meadow and was engaged in cutting wild hay for the market on the Placerville road. In the fall of 1865, in the month of November, I took my gun and, accompanied by a very intelligent setter dog, started out for a hunt for grouse along the shore and in the creek bottoms emptying into the lake.

My attention was called to a very curious state of things happening around me. First, a flock of quail and other birds were flying out of the canyon, uttering cries of alarm; next came some rabbits and coyotes, and soon three deer came running at full speed; last of all, an old bear with one cub came along. All passed close to me, not seeming to notice me, and all running at their best.

All this did not occupy much time, and I began to wonder what was up. My dog kept looking up the canyon and was evidently alarmed, and I began to feel shaky myself. All at once the dog set up a howl and started for home, eight miles away, running as fast as dog could run, and going under the cabin staid there two days and nights and no amount of coaxing could get him to come out sooner, and never after would the dog go in the direction of the lake. I began to feel that some unknown danger was near, and looking about me, saw a spruce tree with very thick limbs, standing near a very large pine. I climbed up about sixty feet from the ground and began to look up the canyon. I had not long to wait. I heard a sound as if the dead limbs of trees, willows and alders that grew in the canyon were being broken and crushed. Soon the monster appeared, slowly making his way in the direction where I was hidden in the tree-top, and passed on to the lake within fifty feet of where I was, and as his snakeship got by, and I partly recovered from my fright, I began to look him over and to estimate his immense size. After his head had passed my tree about seventy feet, he halted and reared his head in the air fifty feet or more, and I was thankful that the large pine hid me from his sight, and I dared to breathe again as he lowered his head to the ground and moved on.

His monstrous head was about fourteen feet wide, and the large eyes seemed to be about eight inches in diameter, and shining jet black, and seemed to project more than half his size from the head. The neck was about ten feet, and the body in the largest portion must have been twenty feet in diameter. I had a chance to measure his length, for when he halted his tail reached a fallen tree, and I afterward measured the distance from the tree where I was hidden to the fallen tree and it measured 510 feet, and as seventy or eighty feet had passed me, it made his length about 600 feet. The skin was black on the back, turning to a reddish yellow on the side and belly, and must have been very hard and tough, as small trees two and three inches in diameter were crushed and broken without any effect on his tough hide. Even bowlders of 500 or 600 pounds weight lying on the surface of the ground were pushed out of the way. His snakeship slowly made his way to the lake, glided in and swam toward the foot.

This serpent has been seen by several of the old settlers at the lake since that time, but it was generally agreed that it would be useless to tell the world the story, knowing that it would not be believed. I will give a few names of the early settlers that have seen his snakeship at different times since I first saw him. William Pomin, now living in San Francisco; John McKinney, Ben McCoy and Bill McMasters, all at that time living on Sugar Pine Point; Homer Burton, now living in Sacramento; Captain Howland of the old steamer *Governor Blaisdell*, Tony and Burk, fishermen living near Friday's station; Rube Saxton, now at the Lake, and several others could be named.

I know many will doubt this story, but sooner or later his snakeship will be seen by so many that all doubt will be removed. I was induced to write this description by reading an article in *The Call* of last Sunday, stating that there was a living mastodon in Alaska and that it had been seen by the natives. Believing that I have seen a more wonderful sight and, as in time my story is sure to be verified, I venture to give this to the public.

I. C. Coggin.

≈≈≈

We regard the road as one of the most important in the State.

—"Lake Tahoe Wagon Road," *Sacramento Daily Union*, June 25, 1897

By the end of the nineteenth century, one of the principal elements that fueled Lake Tahoe's growth was disintegrating.

The Lake Tahoe Wagon Road, linking Placerville with the Washoe-Comstock Lode region, was the major midcentury funnel of people, supplies, and societal transformation to Lake Tahoe and beyond. During its heyday, from the onset of the Comstock Lode silver rush in 1859 through the 1870s, the Lake Tahoe Wagon Road often witnessed nose-to-tail wagon trains and thousands of eager pedestrians surging to the beckoning riches of the Washoe region. Tales abounded of travelers being warned not to withdraw from the snaking caravan as regaining your spot in line was problematic—accounts indicated it could take several hours or even a full day before an opportunity to rejoin the throng was possible. In one three-month period in 1866, more than six thousand pilgrims on foot, three thousand stagecoach passengers, and more than twelve thousand pack animals, horse and mule teams, and cattle passed through Lake Tahoe's south shore along the Wagon Road.

The road was dirt, occasionally partitioned into toll roads, and the quality of the route was excellent. It was well maintained and featured many way stations spaced at convenient intervals. This is not surprising, given the significance and profitability of the wagon road.

However, once the rush subsided and the transcontinental railroad was completed in 1869, the Lake Tahoe Wagon Road remained a vital link to Lake Tahoe and the Washoe, but it was less well traveled, and the incentive to maintain the road diminished. By the 1890s, the Wagon Road was in disrepair.

In 1897 the California State Highway Department, headed by Marsden Manson, inspected the Lake Tahoe Wagon Road and made Recommendations as to How It Should Be Improved. The report was published in the June 25, 1897, edition of the Sacramento Daily Union and is excerpted here.

The report reaffirmed the importance of the road as one of the few linking California and Nevada. The Highway Department also tellingly noted, "This road above all others in California is destined to be the line of travel for pleasure seekers who seek the cool and refreshing summer climate of the Sierra Nevada Mountains."

While advocates for Interstate 80 might quibble over the statement "This road above all others," no doubt the California Highway Department correctly assessed that the Lake Tahoe Wagon Road would be an important conduit to Lake Tahoe and the Sierra Nevada. Today, most of the old Lake Tahoe Wagon Road route constitutes Highway 50. On weekends and holidays, this heavily traveled corridor sometimes descends into gridlock, echoing the old days of endless, slow-moving wagon trains.

Lake Tahoe Wagon Road

Recommendations as to How It Should Be Improved

Result of the Inspection Made by Members of the State Highway Department

The following report was yesterday made by M. Manson, President of the State Highway Department, to Marco Varozza, Commissioner of the Lake Tahoe wagon road running eastward from Placerville. It will be read with interest by residents of El Dorado and all others accustomed to travel over that old-time highway. The report reads:

Marco Varozza, Commissioner of Lake Tahoe Wagon Road—Sir: On June 3d, this department received a letter directed to his excellency, James H. Budd, Governor of the State, requesting that some engineer be detailed to examine the Lake Tahoe Wagon Road and report upon the condition of the same, and "recommend such suggestions as the premises may require." This letter was duly referred to this department and in compliance with the same, Commissioners Ashe and Price were detailed to make the necessary examination and report, Commissioner Manson being engaged in the examination of road work elsewhere. From their investigations we are able to report as follows:

Leaving Placerville on June 10th they proceeded to drive over the road from its point of beginning to the line between the States of California and Nevada. The road is 58 miles in length, traversing for the greater portion of its route the mountain sides adjacent to the south fork of the American River to the Summit of the Sierra Nevada Mountains, thence descending into Lake Valley, at the southern extremity of Lake Tahoe, and thence through Lake Valley to the State line.

The State of California having assumed control of this important road, we deem it necessary to state concisely its former as well as its present condition. The road is known as the old emigrant road, which, through various changes from the original rough emigrant trail, has passed to toll roads and finally has become a State highway. When the road was operated under the toll road franchise system it was known and properly so, as a model wagon road. The toll franchises passed to the county of El Dorado and thence to the State through the operation of an Act approved March 26, 1895 (Statutes 1895, page 119).

Under the toll road system the road bed was broad, averaging in width from sixteen to twenty feet, and in some places wider, located on a true grade, varying with the conditions of the country, but in a few cases excessive. The road bed during the summer season was generally well sprinkled, making this one of the most attractive drives in the State of California.

In the interim of time from the abandonment of the toll road system to the present time, very little labor has been expended in the preservation of the width of the road bed, consequently the mountain sides have by process of natural wash filled a portion of the road bed with earth and rocks thus forcing the wagon track to the outside limit of the grade, making the roadway a single truck road. The side drains or ditches are completely obliterated by the deposit of this material. All bridges were originally constructed of wood resting on wood foundations. Some of these are still in a fair state of preservation, while others have decayed and must be rebuilt. The crossings of canyons and ravines were originally filled with logs and earth. These logs have decayed and the earth has been washed down the slopes of the canyons, leaving the log piles devoid of their covering, and the road impassable. These damages have been temporarily repaired from time to time so as to permit of the passage of vehicles.

The ditches, having been filled with earth and rocks, are no longer useful, and the result is that all storm waters attack the roadbed, causing deep washouts and material damage to it. To overcome this difficulty the various road tenders have adopted the plan of employing what are called "turnouts," consisting of a ridge across the roadway, thus directing the water from the roadbed.

The question of preventing the rain or snow water from running on the roadbed is of vital importance to the life of all mountain roads. Hence, the road tender has adopted the cheapest system to overcome the difficulty. If these turnouts could be removed during the summer and maintained during the winter season, they would do an inestimable amount of good. On the contrary, however, they are permitted to remain during the season of maximum travel and are very annoying to those who pass over the road.

The plan above described is not, in our opinion, the proper procedure. We would recommend that as soon as the necessary funds can be obtained, the roadbed be graded so as to give a transverse grade or gentle slope to the hill or ditch of only sufficient fall to cause all water to flow into the side ditch; that a ditch be constructed along the hillside of the grade of sufficient width and depth to meet the requirements of the flow of water and that under drains be placed at such intervals as the occasion may demand, conducting the water from the ditch to the opposite side of the road. These under drains may be made of terra-cotta pipe or of stone, as the circumstances will best subserve economy.

Where the roadbed rests upon a stone foundation, the drains should be cut into the stone and so covered that no earth can drop into the drain. The drain pipes should be given such grade as to discharge freely any sand or material that it may be desirous of passing through them. The outlets of the drains should be so protected as to do no damage to the road bed by washing the slope below the same. No water should be permitted to flow past the under drains, and each drain pipe should be proportioned to carry all the water safely from the roadbed. We are convinced that should this plan be adopted the great damage wrought by storms would be a thing of the past and the extra expense of initiating the system would soon be returned by a reduction in the cost of maintenance.

The deplorable condition of ravine crossings and foundations for bridges has forced us to the conclusion that all of this character of structures should when rebuilt be constructed in stone work. An abundant supply of stone is adjacent to the site of nearly every culvert, bridge and ravine crossing. This stone should be broken and laid in dry wall and fill upon a solid foundation. The length of the bridges can be materially shortened by a proper system of rock work which will serve as a lasting foundation for rock work to rest upon.

We recognize the fact that masonry would be the best material with which to construct culverts, bridges and ravine crossings, but the appropriation at hand will not justify the undertaking of this work at the present time. Fifty-eight miles of road with no less than sixty bridges, culverts and ravine crossings to repair and at the same time keep the roadbed open to travel is no small task, and we cannot expect to accomplish more than is absolutely necessary to be done with the appropriation made for this purpose by the last Legislature. . . .

We regard the road as one of the most important in the State and one that deserves the exercise of the very best of skill in good road building. This road above all others in California is destined to be the line of travel for pleasure seekers who seek the cool and refreshing summer climate of the Sierra Nevada Mountains. Its course is replete with scenery from its beginning to its terminus. It traverses a country noted for its small valleys and verdant pastures, where many of our thrifty stock raisers drive their herds to feed during the summer months. It is the connecting highway over which must pass the inhabitants of the one State to the other who travel by wagon or other vehicles. It is a road over which the bicyclist may pass without fear of excessive grades, and possessing all these important functions, we therefore regard it as of sufficient importance to justify the State in its maintenance.

≈≈≈

The reservation hereby established shall be known as
The Lake Tahoe Forest Reserve.

—William McKinley, twenty-fifth president of the United States,
1897–1901, "Proclamation 437—Establishing the Lake Tahoe
Forest Reserve in the State of California," April 13, 1899

In 1899, Lake Tahoe forestlands entered a new phase.

Although complaints were largely dismissed or ignored, there had been concerted efforts to mitigate the impact of destructive logging practices stretching over decades. This forest crusade was regularly coupled with actions by individuals and groups seeking government protection for Lake Tahoe scenic values. Often, these were lonely voices crying in the wilderness.

In 1884 the Lake Bigler Forestry Commission recommended that the California Legislature establish a Lake Tahoe State Park to protect forestlands, but nothing came of that proposal. In the 1890s some progress was made. Legislation was passed to regulate some logging practices, such as the dumping of sawdust into the Truckee River. But antilogging advocates felt this was not enough. Some organizations, such as the Sierra Club, called for the designation of a federally protected area—a so-called forest reserve—to administer the Lake Tahoe timberlands.

However, a federal forest reserve was controversial. Establishing a forest reserve, opponents argued, would open a can of worms regarding private property, water, and commercial rights and jeopardize jobs and investments.

On April 13, 1899, President William McKinley issued Presidential Proclamation 437, establishing the Lake Tahoe Forest Reserve, which placed thirty-eight thousand acres of Lake Tahoe Basin forests under federal protection.

By the President of the United States of America

A Proclamation

Whereas, it is provided by section twenty-four of the act of Congress, approved March third, eighteen hundred and ninety-one, entitled, "An act to repeal timber-culture laws, and for other purposes," "That the President of the United States may, from time to time, set apart and reserve, in any State or Territory having public land bearing forests, in any part of the public lands wholly or in part covered with timber or undergrowth, whether of commercial value or not, as public reservations, and the President shall, by public proclamation, declare the establishment of such reservations and the limits thereof;"

And whereas, the public lands in the State of California, within the limits hereinafter described, are in part covered with timber, and it appears that the public good would be promoted by setting apart and reserving said lands as a public reservation;

Now, therefore, I, William McKinley, President of the United States, by virtue of the power in me vested by section twenty-four of the aforesaid act of Congress, do hereby make known and proclaim that there is hereby reserved from entry or settlement and set apart as a Public Reservation all those certain tracts, pieces or parcels of land lying and being situate in the State of California and particularly described as follows, to wit:

Townships eleven (11), twelve (12) and thirteen (13) North, Range sixteen (16) East, Mount Diablo Base and Meridian, California; Townships eleven (11), twelve (12) and thirteen (13) North, Range seventeen (17) East; and so much of Township eleven (11) North, Range eighteen (18) East, as lies west of the summit of the Sierra Nevada Range of mountains in El Dorado County, California.

Excepting from the force and effect of this proclamation all lands which may have been, prior to the date hereof, embraced in any legal entry or covered by any lawful filing duly of record in the proper United States Land Office, or upon which any valid settlement has been made pursuant to law, and the statutory period within which to make entry or filing of record has not expired; Provided, that this exception shall not continue to apply to any particular tract of land unless the entryman, settler or claimant continues to comply with the law under which the entry, filing or settlement was made.

Warning is hereby expressly given to all persons not to make settlement upon the tract of land reserved by this proclamation.

The reservation hereby established shall be known as The Lake Tahoe Forest Reserve.

In witness whereof, I have hereunto set my hand and caused the seal of the United States to be affixed.

Done at the city of Washington this 13th day of April, in the year of our Lord one thousand eight hundred and ninety-nine, and of the Independence of the United States the one hundred and twenty-third.

WILLIAM MCKINLEY

By the President:

JOHN HAY,

Secretary of State.

≈≈≈

Little steamers furrow this transparent lake, much
as a diamond cuts a smooth expanse of glass.

—John L. Stoddard, *Scenic America, the Beauties
of the Western Hemisphere,* 1899

By the end of the nineteenth century, Lake Tahoe had been a well-known locale for decades, but a mechanical contraption raised awareness of the lake even further. The device was the stereopticon, or magic lantern. Essentially a slide projector, the stereopticon was conceived in the mid-nineteenth century. This gadget added photographic projections to the very popular nineteenth-century entertainment of informational lectures. And a pioneering practitioner of magic lantern lectures was John L. Stoddard, who is considered the most influential developer of the travelogue.

John Lawson Stoddard was born in 1850 to a wealthy Boston family. As a young man he traveled the world, snapping hundreds of photographs. In 1879 Stoddard began presenting public lectures on his sojourns and used the stereopticon to illustrate his lectures with his own photographs. The lectures were immediately well regarded and became trendy. Stoddard continued to travel and gather new material, which he also published in a series of best-selling books and widely anticipated newspaper installments.

By the 1890s Stoddard was famous and a multimillionaire. His lectures sold out quickly. For more than a decade in New York City, Stoddard would annually schedule dozens of sold-out presentations.

In 1897 John L. Stoddard was even invited to lecture before the United States Congress. In F. Scott Fitzgerald's 1925 novel The Great Gatsby, *the published collection of Stoddard's lectures is used a library prop by the enigmatic millionaire Jay Gatsby to demonstrate his supposed refined literary sensibility.*

One of Stoddard's books was printed and reprinted many times: Scenic America: The Beauties of the Western Hemisphere. *The book included a description and photograph of Lake Tahoe. Stoddard's description is presented in this selection.*

John L. Stoddard was celebrated, but he was also controversial. During World War I, he sided with Germany and the Central Powers over the Allies. Stoddard supported the establishment of Israel as a Jewish homeland and nation, a provocative stance during the early twentieth century.

What was not controversial was Stoddard's appreciation of Lake Tahoe, which, thanks to John L. Stoddard, was now available to millions of new Gem of the Sierra enthusiasts around the world.

LAKE TAHOE, CALIFORNIA.—Set like a sapphire in a circle of resplendent pearls and opals, lies what is probably the most remarkable and beautiful sheet of water in the world,—Lake Tahoe. Its surface, like a shield of lapis-lazuli, is 22 miles long and 10 in breadth, and entirely surrounded by imposing snow-clad mountains. Its altitude is very unusual, 6247 feet above the sea. Yet despite its elevation and its glacial environment, these waters never freeze! They are magnificently clear, and reach a depth of more than 1600 feet. As if this were a prize too precious for one State to hold, one third of this fair crystalline expanse lies in the area of Nevada; the rest is claimed by California. Beautiful summer homes can now be found in this enchanting portion of the Sierra Nevadas, and little steamers furrow this transparent lake, much as a diamond cuts a smooth expanse of glass. Life here is wonderfully exhilarating. The tonic of the mountain air is such that one deep inhalation of its aromatic crispness is like a draught of sparkling wine. Nothing seems wanting to impart to this extraordinary lake the element of the unique: Thus, in addition to its singular height, depth, clearness, absence of ice, and these magnificent surroundings, the water of Lake Tahoe is so cold that decomposition is checked below its surface. There is a certain mystery too in the sad fact, that although many persons have been drowned here, no bodies have ever been recovered from deep water. Once gone, they rise no more, but disappear as quietly and effectually as a coin dropped into the sea. One naturally recalls the myths of lovely sirens in their ocean caves, who lure infatuated mortals down to scenes of dazzling splendor, and keep them captives there forevermore.

≈≈≈

Around Lake Tahoe the timbered areas
have been entirely swept off.

Marsden Manson, "Observations on the Denudation of Vegetation—A
Suggested Remedy for California," *Sierra Club Bulletin*, June 1899

By the end of the nineteenth century Lake Tahoe logging continued, but major operations were winding down or being abandoned. After decades of intensive activity, the lumber industry deserted timber camps, uprooted railroad lines, dismantled flumes, and ignored road maintenance.

In a June 1899 article for the Sierra Club Bulletin, *Marsden Manson, a Sierra Club member, pondered the loss of Lake Tahoe's forestlands, the rapacious nature of humans, the consequences of unchecked avarice, and his recommended use for the denuded timberlands.*

Marsden Manson was born in Virginia in 1850 but spent most of his professional life in California. He received a civil engineering degree from the Virginia Military Institute and a doctorate in engineering from the University of California, Berkeley.

During his career, Manson served in various capacities for California state and local government agencies. He was chief engineer of the California State Board of Harbor Commissioners, president of the California State Highway Commission, a member of San Francisco's inaugural Board of Public Works, and San Francisco city engineer. Marsden Manson authored or coauthored many scientific monographs on a remarkably vast array of subjects. Some of his writings focused on meteorology, glaciers, and climate evolution. A few dealt with cosmic topics such as planetary rotation and solar climate. Most of his reports considered more down-to-earth issues, such as road maintenance, garbage disposal, irrigation, sewer systems, and domestic water delivery.

In the following excerpt from Manson's "Observations on the Denudation of Vegetation—A Suggested Remedy for California," he lamented the devastation of Lake Tahoe's forests: "When one goes out over this fair land of ours and marks the rate at which its forests are being destroyed, its mountain forage areas devasted, he is tempted to regret that civilization should be permitted to spread its blight." But, in the next breath, Manson contended that the forest "destruction" could be utilized for the public good through "judicious use of this wealth of forest and of mountain pasture." After all, Marsden Manson argued, "man has it within his power to utilize to its fullest measure this wealth and to pass it down to future generations as a blessing, rather than as a blight and a curse,—and that he can even aid nature."

Less than ten years after this article appeared, Marsden Manson, city engineer of San Francisco and still a Sierra Club member, applied these principles to the question of a reliable water source for San Francisco. Manson was a leading participant in the city's campaign to dam the pristine Hetchy Hetchy Valley in Yosemite National Park to provide a reservoir and source of fresh water and hydroelectric power for San Francisco. John Muir, president of the Sierra Club, strongly disagreed with the proposal to commandeer national park land for use by a municipal utility. This would result in one of the great environmental controversies of the twentieth century.

When man, actuated by greed or ignorance, or a combination of the two, destroys the protection which nature spreads over rolling and mountain areas, he turns loose agencies which soon pass beyond his control. The protecting agent is vegetation, and whether in the form of forests, brush, or forage plants and grasses, the balance between it and denuding forces is easily tipped, when the inexorable law of gravity unchecked by myriad blades of grass, by leaves, roots, and vegetable mold, gullies the hillside, strips the mountain slope, converts the rivulet into the torrent, and causes the steady flow of the river to become alternately a devastating flood or a parched sand-bed. When once this balance has been destroyed, man cannot turn back the torrent and bid it flow once more a living and life-giving stream.

It would seem that this lesson had been learned so thoroughly by the human race that there would be little use to lay its precepts before a civilized community. But when one goes out over this fair land of ours and marks the rate at which its forests are being destroyed, its mountain forage areas devasted, he is tempted to regret that civilization should be permitted to spread its blight over the temples in which the savage worshiped.

But it must be remembered that this destruction ceases in the judicious use of this wealth of forest and of mountain pasture, and that it is only indifference and incivism which permits greed and ignorance to go unrestrained until they destroy the balance,—that man has it within his power to utilize to its fullest measure this wealth and to pass it down to future generations as a blessing, rather than as a blight and a curse,—and that he can even aid nature by extending vegetation over barren areas. But this requires that the reckless destruction of forest, and the wasteful and continuous devastation of pasture should be replaced by systematic utilization of these sources of wealth. . . .

The Sierra Nevada has fared even worse. Around Lake Tahoe the timbered areas have been entirely swept off, with the exception of a few thousand acres around Tallac, and some at the north end, reserved by the owners for later use. The mountain sides around the Hot Springs, and nearly all of the moraines and flats around the south and east sides of the lake, have been denuded. These areas, bereft of timber, are now ready to be abandoned to the State, large tracts being for sale at fifty cents per acre. The railroads, which were constructed to carry logs to the lake, have been torn up, and the region, shorn of its wealth and beauty, has been partly burned over to give a few sprouts to hungry hordes of sheep. . . .

There are, of course, interests now thriving on the free use of these areas which, for selfish reasons, will oppose any measure looking to staying the destruction by which they profit; yet, if our civilization is to stand—if this great commonwealth is to advance with the advancing ages, this devastation must cease; systematic and economic use of this wealth must take the place of the methods now in vogue. History and nature record no law more inflexible—no effect more certain—than that poverty and degradation follow upon the destruction of mountain forests.

Sources

The source materials related to Lake Tahoe in the nineteenth-century are remarkably varied and quite voluminous. Determining which selections and excerpts to include in *Gem of the Sierra: Schemes and Splendor in Nineteenth-Century Lake Tahoe* was daunting but also delightful, as it provided the opportunity to visit and enjoy many more wonderful pieces than could possibly be incorporated into the final anthology.

The bibliography that follows is divided by the time periods or decades presented in the anthology, corresponding to the chapters in *Gem of the Sierra*. Listed in each section are the primary sources that furnished most of the content of the anthology (such as newspaper and journal articles and books written during the decade or period indicated) and some secondary sources that were cited or referenced within that section. In a few instances, a secondary source was selected as the excerpt presented. A case in point are the secondary materials found in Chapter One—Roots and Reconnaissance: Precontact to 1860.

In his 1872 travelogue *Six Months in California*, British journalist J. G. Player-Frowd concludes the description of his Lake Tahoe visit by noting, "One could spend a month there most delightfully." The same could be said of the literature of nineteenth-century Lake Tahoe.

Preface

"Lake Tahoe Case Study," addendum to *Sierra Nevada Ecosystem Project: Final Report to Congress*, 216–76. Davis: University of California, Centers for Water and Wildland Resources, 1996.

Lindström, Susan, Penny Rucks, and Peter Wigand. "A Contextual Overview of Human Land Use and Environmental Conditions." Chap. 2 in Murphy and Knopp, eds., *Lake Tahoe Watershed Assessment*, vol. 1, 3–127.

Murphy, Dennis D., and Christopher M. Knopp, eds. *Lake Tahoe Watershed Assessment*, vol. 1. Gen. Tech. Rep. PSW-GTR-175. Albany CA: Pacific

Southwest Research Station, Forest Service, U.S. Department of Agriculture, 2000.

Player-Frowd, J. G. *Six Months in California*. London: Longmans, Green, and Co., 1872.

1. Roots and Reconnaissance

Downs, James F. *The Two Worlds of the Washo: An Indian Tribe of California and Nevada*. New York: Holt, Rinehart and Winston, 1966.

Frémont, John C. *The Exploring Expedition to the Rocky Mountains, Oregon and California, to Which Is Added a Description of the Physical Geography of California, with Recent Notices of the Gold Region from the Latest and Most Authentic Sources*. Washington DC: Gales and Seaton, 1845. Microfilm, March of America Facsimile Series, no. 79.

Goddard, George H. [GHG, pseud.]. "Lake Bigler." *Hutchings' California Magazine*, September 1857. 107–9.

Goddard, George H. *Report of a Survey of a Portion of the Eastern Boundary of California and of a Reconnaissance of the Old Carson and Johnson Immigrant Roads over the Sierra Nevada*. Appendix A to *Annual Report of the Surveyor General of the State of California*, 89–122. Sacramento CA: B. B. Redding, 1855.

Hittman, Michael. *Great Basin Indians: An Encyclopedic History*. Reno: University of Nevada Press, 2013.

Johnston, Verna R. *Sierra Nevada: The Naturalist's Companion*. Berkeley: University of California Press, 1998.

Lindström, Susan, Penny Rucks, and Peter Wigand. "A Contextual Overview of Human Land Use and Environmental Conditions." Chap. 2 in Murphy and Knopp, eds., *Lake Tahoe Watershed Assessment*, vol. 1, 3–127.

Lowie, Robert H. "Ethnographic Notes on the Washo." *University of California Publications in American Archaeology and Ethnology* 36, no. 5 (1939): 3–47.

McGlashan, Nonette. "The Legend of Tahoe." *Sunset*, August 1905, 375–78.

Murphy, Dennis D., and Christopher M. Knopp, eds. *Lake Tahoe Watershed Assessment*, vol. 1. Gen. Tech. Rep. PSW-GTR-175. Albany CA: Pacific Southwest Research Station, Forest Service, U.S. Department of Agriculture, 2000.

Nevers, Jo Ann. *Wa She Shu: A Washo Tribal History*. Reno: Inter-Tribal Council of Nevada, 1976.

Tulare County Record. "Description of Lake Bigler," July 23, 1859.

2. Development and Disquiet

Browne, J. Ross, "A Peep at Washoe." Pts. 1, 2, and 3. *Harper's New Monthly Magazine*, December 1860, 1–17; January 1861, 145–62; February 1861, 289–305.

Daily Alta California (San Francisco). "A Few Notes about Lake Tahoe," July 1, 1865.

———. "Lake Tahoe," November 18, 1867.

———. "Water from Lake Tahoe," October 17, 1866.

Knight, William Henry, "An Emigrant's Trip across the Plains in 1859." Pt. 3. *Publications of the Historical Society of Southern California* 12 (1923): 32–41.

Noy, Gary. "Lake Bigler, Lake Tahoe, Etc." Written especially for this anthology.

Pisani, Donald J. "'Why Shouldn't California Have the Grandest Aqueduct in the World?': Alexis Von Schmidt's Lake Tahoe Scheme," *California Historical Quarterly* 53, no. 4 (Winter 1974): 347–60.

Sacramento Daily Union. "A Cruise on a Mountain Sea, Number Three," August 1, 1866.

———. "A Day on Lake Bigler," September 9, 1862.

———. "Foreign Gossip," August 13, 1863.

———. "Sierra Lake," May 28, 1863.

———. "The Water of Lake Tahoe," October 9, 1866.

Sunset. "Naming Lake Tahoe," January 1908, 306.

Twain, Mark. "Samuel Clemens Letter to Sister Pamela Clemens Moffett, October 25, 1861." In *Mark Twain's Letters*, vol. 1, *1853–1866*, edited by Edgar Marquess Branch, Michael Barry Frank, Kenneth M. Sanderson, Harriet E. Smith, Lin Salamo, and Richard Bucci, 132. Berkeley: University of California Press, 1988.

———. *The Innocents Abroad.* Hartford, Connecticut: American Publishing, 1869.

"William Henry Knight: A Biographical Sketch," *Publications of the Historical Society of Southern California* 14 (1928–30): 84–86.

3. Delights and Damages

Avery, Benjamin Parke. *Californian Pictures in Prose and Verse.* New York: Hurd and Houghton, 1878.

Boddam-Whetham, J. W. *Western Wanderings; A Record of Travel in the Evening Land.* London: R. Bentley, 1874.

Crofutt, George. *Crofutt's Trans-Continental Tourist's Guide: Over the Union Pacific Railroad, Central Pacific Railroad of Cal., Their Branches and Connections by Stage and Water.* New York: G. A. Crofutt, 1871.

De Quille, Dan [William Wright]. *History of the Big Bonanza.* Hartford CT: American Publishing, 1877.

Forbes, A. B., Stuart Menzies, and A. Badlam. *Report of the Special Committee of the Board of Supervisors, Together with Communications of Gen. B. S.*

Alexander, USA, and Prof. George Davidson, USCS, on the Water Supplies for the City of San Francisco. San Francisco: A. L. Bancroft & Company, 1872.

Jackson, Helen Hunt. *Bits of Travel at Home.* Boston: Roberts Brothers, 1878.

King, Thomas Starr. "Living Water from Lake Tahoe." Sermon 19 in *Christianity and Humanity: A Series of Sermons*, 304–24. Boston, James R. Osgood, 1877.

LeConte, Joseph. *A Journal of Ramblings through the High Sierra of California.* San Francisco: Sierra Club, 1930. First published 1875 by Francis and Valentine (San Francisco).

McGlashan, Charles F., "Resources and Wonders of Tahoe," *Sacramento Daily Union*, May 29, 1875.

Mendell, George H. *Report on the Various Projects for the Water Supply of San Francisco, Cal.: Made to the Mayor, the Auditor, and the District Attorney, Constituting the Board of Water Commissioners.* San Francisco: Spaulding & Barto, 1877.

Muir, John. "Lake Tahoe in Winter," *San Francisco Bulletin*, April 3, 1878. Reprinted in *Sierra Club Bulletin*, May 1900, 119–26.

Price, Rose Lambart. *The Two Americas; An Account of Sport and Travel. With Notes on Men and Manners in North and South America.* London: S. Low, Marston, Searle, and Rivington, 1877.

Rice, Harvey. *Letters from the Pacific Slope; or First Impressions.* New York: D. Appleton, 1870.

Sacramento Daily Union. "San Francisco Markets, Etc.," July 20, 1870.

Tevis, A. H. *Beyond the Sierras, or, Observations on the Pacific Coast.* Philadelphia: J. B. Lippincott, 1877.

Twain, Mark. *Roughing It.* Hartford CT: American Publishing, 1872.

4. Visitors and Vexations

Brewer, William. *Up and Down California in 1860–1864.* New Haven CT: Yale University Press, 1930.

Burton, Margaret Davis, "The Fairy's Isle in Emerald Bay." *Pacific Rural Press*, September 21, 1889.

Cheney, John Vance. "A Day at Lake Tahoe," *Lippincott's*, August 1883, 214–19.

Churchill, Caroline Nichols. *Over the Purple Hills, or Sketches from Travel in California.* Denver CO: Mrs. C. M. Churchill, 1881.

Daily Alta California (San Francisco). "Trout Mining at Lake Tahoe," January 10, 1878.

General Allotment Act, "An Act to Provide for the Allotment of Lands in Severalty to Indians on the Various Reservations." *Statutes at Large* 24, 388–91, NADP Document A1887.

Jordan, David S., and H. W. Henshaw. *Report upon the Fishes Collected during the Years 1875, 1876, and 1877, in California and Nevada.* Appendix K to *Report upon United States Geographical Surveys West of the One Hundredth Meridian,* vol. 1, by George M. Wheeler, 187–200. Washington DC: Government Printing Office, 1889.

Lake Bigler Forestry Commission. *Report of the Lake Bigler Forestry Commission to Governor George Stoneman, Made in Accordance with Assembly Concurrent Resolution No. 31, Passed by the 25th Session of the Legislature of the State of California.* Sacramento CA: State Printing, 1884.

LeConte, John. "Physical Studies of Lake Tahoe—I." Pt. 1. *Overland Monthly,* November 1883, 506–19.

McGlashan, Charles F., "Resources and Wonders of Tahoe," *Sacramento Daily Union,* May 29, 1875.

Newlands, Francis. "Annual Address." *Reno Evening Gazette,* October 7, 1889. Speech to the Nevada State Agricultural Society.

Pacific Rural Press. "The Baldwin," June 3, 1882.

———. "Lake Tahoe," May 17, 1884.

Powell, John Wesley. *Eleventh Annual Report of the Director of the United States Geological Survey, Part 2—Irrigation: 1889–1890.* Washington DC: Government Printing Office, 1891.

Ramsdell, H. J., "The Great Nevada Flume: A Perilous Ride." In *Pacific Tourist: Adams and Bishop's Illustrated Trans-Continental Guide,* 233–38. New York: Adams and Bishop, 1881.

Sacramento Daily Union. "A Legend of Emerald Bay and the Origin of Tahoe Trout," November 19, 1881.

———. "Mountain Vandalism," July 27, 1889.

———. "The Quiet Hour," August 21, 1880.

San Jose Mercury-News. "Field and Wood," March 12, 1882.

Santa Barbara Morning Press. "A Lake Tahoe Romance," September 12, 1882.

Truckee Republican. "The Result of Energy: Operations and Works of the Truckee Lumber Company," December 15, 1883.

Wadsworth (NV) Dispatch. "Fish Commissioners," December 3, 1892.

Wheeler, George M. *Report upon United States Geographical Surveys West of the One Hundredth Meridian,* vol. 1. Washington DC: Government Printing Office, 1889.

Williams, George. *Report of the California Assembly Committee on Fish and Game.* In *California Assembly Journal of 1887.* Sacramento CA: State Printing Office, 1887.

5. Pleasures and Protection

Anderson, Winslow. *Mineral Springs and Health Resorts of California.* San Francisco: Bancroft, 1890.

Cohodas, Marvin. "Louisa Keyser and the Cohns: Mythmaking and Basket Making in the American West." Chap. 4 in *The Early Years of Native American Art History: The Politics of Scholarship and Collecting*, edited by Janet Catherine Berlo, 88–133. Seattle: University of Washington Press, 1992.

Cohn, C. Amy, "Arts and Crafts of the Nevada Indians," *Biennial Report of the Nevada Historical Society*, no. 1: 1907–8. Carson City: Nevada State Printing Office, 1909.

Finck, Henry Theophilus. *The Pacific Coast Scenic Tour*. New York: C. Scribner's Sons, 1890.

James, George Wharton. *California: Romantic & Beautiful*. Boston: Page Company, 1914.

Lambourne, Alfred. *Bits of Descriptive Prose*. Chicago: Belford-Clarke, 1891.

Manson, Marsden, "Observations on the Denudation of Vegetation—A Suggested Remedy for California." *Sierra Club Bulletin*, June 1899, 295–311.

McKinley, William. "Proclamation 437—Establishing the Lake Tahoe Forest Reserve in the State of California," April 13, 1899. William McKinley Presidential Papers, Series 5: Messages, 1897–1900. Washington DC, Library of Congress.

Mullen, Frank X. "Kill the Indian; Save the Man." *Reno News and Review*, August 15, 2021.

Office of Indian Affairs, Department of the Interior. *Annual Report of the Commissioner of Indian Affairs, for the Year 1897*. Washington DC: Government Printing Office, 1897.

Russell, Israel C. *Lakes of North America: A Reading Lesson for Students of Geography and Geology*. Boston: Ginn, 1895.

Sacramento Daily Union. "Lake Tahoe Wagon Road." June 25, 1897.

Sacramento Morning Union. "Brief Local Items." December 2, 1893.

———. "Swept by a Huge Wave—Commotion on Lake Tahoe Due to Fall of Cave Rock," November 28, 1893.

San Francisco Call. "The Unpleasant Serpent Coggins Declares He Saw at Lake Tahoe," November 21, 1897.

Sears, John F. *Sacred Places: American Tourist Attractions in the Nineteenth Century*. New York: Oxford University Press, 1989.

Shaw, David Augustus. *Eldorado; or, California as Seen by a Pioneer*. Los Angeles: B. R. Baumgardt, 1900.

Simpson, James Hervey. Appendix O to *Report of Explorations across the Great Basin of the Territory of Utah for a Direct Wagon-Route from Camp Floyd to Genoa, in Carson Valley, in 1859, by Captain J. H. Simpson, Corps of Topographical Engineers [Now Colonel of Engineers, Bvt. Brig. Gen., U.S.A.] Made by Authority of the Secretary of War and under Instructions*

from *Bvt. Brig. Gen. A. S. Johnston*, 459–64. Washington DC: Government
Printing Office, 1876.

Stoddard, John L. *Scenic America: The Beauties of the Western Hemisphere.*
Chicago: Werner, 1899.

Sudworth, George Bishop, "Stanislaus and Lake Tahoe Forest Reserves,
California, and Adjacent Territory." In *Annual Reports of the Department
of Interior: 21st Annual Report of the U. S. Geological Survey*, 499–561.
Washington DC: Government Printing Office, 1900.

Williams, Samantha M. *Assimilation, Resilience, and Survival: A History of
the Stewart Indian School, 1890–2020.* Lincoln: University of Nebraska
Press, 2022.

Printed in the USA
CPSIA information can be obtained
at www.ICGtesting.com
CBHW032138180524
8776CB00001B/138

9 781496 237828